CW00470832

*Words of Love*

BY THE SAME AUTHOR

Novels

*Slip On A Fat Lady*
*Plumridge*
*The Skaters' Waltz*
*Wild Thing (short stories)*

Biography and journalism

*Shout: The True Story of the Beatles*
*The Stones*
*The Road Goes On For Ever*
*Tilt the Hourglass and Begin Again*
*Your Walrus Hurt the One You Love*
*Awful Moments*
*Pieces of Hate*

Plays

*The Man That Got Away*
*Words of Love*

# Words of Love

## A Novella and Stories

By

Philip Norman

## HAMISH HAMILTON

London

*To Brian Eastman*

HAMISH HAMILTON LTD

Published by the Penguin Group
27 Wrights Lane, London W8 5TZ, England
Viking Penguin Inc, 40 West 23rd Street, New York, New York 10010, USA
Penguin Books Australia Ltd, Ringwood, Victoria, Australia
Penguin Books Canada Ltd, 2801 John Street, Markham, Ontario, Canada L3R 1B4
Penguin Books (NZ) Ltd, 182–190 Wairau Road, Auckland 10, New Zealand

Penguin Books Ltd, Registered Offices: Harmondsworth, Middlesex, England

First published in Great Britain 1989 by
Hamish Hamilton Ltd

Copyright © 1989 by Philip Norman
'Words of Love' by Buddy Holly © 1957 MPL Communications Inc.
Reproduced by permission of Southern Music Publishing Co Ltd, London.

1  3  5  7  9  10  8  6  4  2

All rights reserved.
Without limiting the rights under copyright
reserved above, no part of this publication may be
reproduced, stored in or introduced into a retrieval system
or transmitted, in any form or by any means (electronic, mechanical,
photocopying, recording or otherwise), without the prior
written permission of both the copyright owner and
the above publisher of this book.

Cataloguing in Publication Data
is available from the British Library

ISBN 0–241–12586–3

Printed in Great Britain by
Richard Clay Ltd, Bungay, Suffolk

# Contents

# Spring Sonata

Swavesey is the smallest and loneliest village along the coast of north Suffolk. You can easily miss it, as many do travelling the tree-lined road to Orford, that popular yachting and leisure resort. You must watch on your right for a stone gateway and keeper's cottage, and a double line of poplar trees to what must be some grand old manor house. A hundred or so yards beyond is the small white signpost left, its single arm pointed, with almost palpable lack of encouragement, to "Swavesey Only".

The visitor will already have noticed the strong presence of the Forestry Commission and its effort to make as much as possible of coastal Suffolk resemble the Black Forest in Roman times. From Woodbridge onward, the road is shut in by almost continuous plantations of the conifers which, these past 30 years, have covered heath and farm land with equal remorse-lessness. The trees are all alike, tall and thin with chewed-pencil trunks and foliage oddly caught aloft like panic-stricken skirts. Their rows stretch inward to infinity, lit by the occasional shaft of eerily-filtered sun. When no wind blows, their silence is profound and vaguely sinister, as if hordes of teutonic barbarians lurk within. Here and there, lay-bys equipped with national park-style picnic-tables, attempt to show a kindlier, more con-vivial face to the indifferent through traffic.

The side road to Swavesey passes through a further large tract of this official forest. It is a second class road, without white lines, winding downhill for about two miles. On your right, nothing is visible but dark foliage and pine-needly twilight. To your left, hill-planted groves slope to the sunken plain of coastal marshland. In summer the marshes can melt to faint yellow with broom and gorse; in winter they congeal to a bleak cold-tea brown. Summer and winter there is no movement but the curve of curlew on air, no sound but that wind-borne cry of heart-shivering solitude.

Swavesey's is a story familiar enough along this most hazily impermanent margin of East Anglia. First settled in the 5th century BC, it originally stood on a broad North Sea inlet, at the mouth of a river, the Swave. For almost a thousand years it was a busy small port, trafficking the manifold products of Norwich – then England's second city – to Holland and the Continent. Some time in the late 17th century, everything changed. First the river silted up, then the estuary and finally the sea itself. The bustling port was transformed into a purposeless hamlet, four miles inland.

Its maritime past explains Swavesey's single topographical oddity: why its Norman church, St Peter's, is three-quarters of a mile outside the village, up the winding road to the Wood-bridge turn. You catch a glimpse of it far away to the right, down the broad creek formed by two lines of banked-up forest. The church and a few pre-Jacobean houses are all that survive of the village's Elizabethan quay. On still summer days it's easy to picture the barques and feluccas drifting out past the green headland on flood tides of cow pasture and silver-green wheat.

Present-day Swavesey is a single street of cottages, mostly thatched and in traditional Suffolk pink wash, interspersed among tumbledown farm buildings and vegetable gardens, abacus-strung with ribbons of bird-scaring tin foil. In no time, the thatched eaves fall back from a triangular green whose amenities are a War memorial, a wooden seat, an overturned wire litter-basket and a hedge-mounted G.R. postbox. Nothing lies beyond but the warren of lanes down to the marshes or inland to cul-de-sacs of forest and uphill farmland.

You would call it a pretty enough place, especially on summer afternoons with front gardens in bloom and badger-headed blue tits spinning to and from their cosy family homes under snugged-down thatch. The city dweller finds it marvellous that silence and stillness can still be so absolute; that a road can be as safe to walk on as the path; that, for hours on end along the length and breadth of Swavesey, you can easily not see another living soul.

Though the sea vanished so long ago, its influence can still be felt in the vaguely marine look several cottages have, as if inhabited by vainly-hoping fishermen. Outsize gannets and black-headed gulls haunt the surrounding fields, swooping on the wakes of tractors like sluggish tramp steamers, screaming off all rivals from the pickings of the hard brown waves.

In winter, thick salt fogs roll up over the marshes, filled with the mournful bleat of sirens in distant shipping lanes. The gales that blow over the vanished estuary burrow the forest's green peaks and take heavy toll on trunks that have only the shallowest purchase in the earth. Dozens a night can be uprooted, to lie in tangles in the endless dark corridors or across the village's only access road.

Local people say that when the wind is in the south-west, you can stand among the crosses in St Peter's churchyard and hear the tide turn over Halesey Flats, eight miles away. On clear nights, the beam from Halesey Ness Lighthouse comes switching across the waterless dark, to flick and rattle along the dark palings of the forest, as if trying to find something in peril here.

Swavesey's least impressive dwelling, unluckily, happens to be the first you encounter along the scattered, motionless village street. It is a plain-fronted bungalow, dating only from the late Thirties, with a bluish slate roof and walls of dull sandy pebbledash. Two undersized windows flank a front door with an opaque glass panel set near the top. The same bungalow is reproduced ten thousand times through Britain's suburbia and in the hinterland of down-at-heel seaside resorts. It's less common to find one set down by itself in the East Anglian wilds, beside a long, hummocky garden up to fir forest edge.

Entering through its front gate in a threadbare holly hedge, you might wonder if the bungalow is even occupied. The grass in its garden is long uncut, the earth in empty flower-beds long unforked. In the left-hand window, a broken pane is stopped up with shrivelled yellow newspaper. There is neither light nor sound, but for the sea ghost wind in nodding conifers.

The door stands ajar to a minuscule hallway, crowded with cardboard cartons of papers, overstuffed carrier-bags, shallow wooden seed-trays, piles of fossilised coats and shoes, a bulbless lamp-standard and an old black invalid chair. To the left is a glimpse of a cold-looking bedroom; to the right, the sitting-room door stands open wide. Though only one person is there, you get a sudden curious impression of voices, smoke and laughter.

It is an oblong sitting-room with a bay window on the right, overlooking the long side garden and the forest. Too much furniture, and inevitable dust, make it dark, even at midday. You have to search a moment to find Mr Hallett in his chair by the fireplace.

Mr Hallett is ninety-six years old. He lives in this bungalow completely alone, caring and fending entirely for himself.

One's first impression is just of the smallness and bentness to be expected in one so extremely elderly. A fragile bald head between elfishly protruding ears. A high-set, aquiline nose, and eyes the faded blue of something many times rinsed out. One notices straight away the hands that have somehow escaped time's harvest of wrinkles, freckles, sore places and liver spots, and are still almost girlishly smooth and white, their fingers slender and tapering.

Feeling the cold more as he does these days, he keeps his outdoor coat on all the time. It is what others would term a "car coat", of cheap brown suedette with shawl collar and cuffs of synthetic lambswool. To its wearer, in whom stylishness refuses to abate, it adds a whisper both of the formal and the bohemian. You would guess Mr Hallett's connection with music even before noticing the music-stand by the window, the sepia guitar on a broken chaise-longue, the antique black violin-case marked "Neuner & Hornstein", the flaking piles of sheet music everywhere underfoot and, in shadow behind him, the slopes of a dark tortoiseshell upright piano.

Loneliness is everyone's deepest dread but for most a bleak season that comes and goes. Mind shrinks from the immensity, the appalling perpetuity of Mr Hallett's loneliness.

At such a time of life, what else could be expected? His wife, to whom he was married fifty-three years, died almost twenty years ago. His only son, a schoolteacher living far away in England's accessible parts, is nearing retirement, in poor health and growing nervous about driving long distances. Every other close relative – his mother and father, his uncles and aunts – left him a lifetime ago, in any terms but his. He has outlived all his cousins, his nephews and nieces, his great-nephews and great-nieces. His one grandchild is a woman now almost forty and still unmarried. The line of which he is a breathing link back to people who remembered the Indian Mutiny – and themselves knew people who remembered Waterloo – stops at the end of the two generations he has sired. The loneliness stretches forward as well.

What is the inscrutable caprice that rubs out greatness at its apogee, scores through babies in the womb, hangs terminal sickness round the golden necks of toddlers, knocks away whole generations with one idle flick, yet has time again held back from, stepped round or passed over a conductor of small orchestras, player of light concert pieces and sometime teacher of piano and violin?

Simple eyes, for which staves and rests were the only concern, have been shown the whole stupefying score. They have seen the Old World change to the New, the sky and moon brought down, the ages revolve from light to dark and the Hun return from history. They have seen the Future approach in gleaming triumph, then suddenly falter and fall back, never to return. They have nearly seen – they may yet fully see – the century from its wonderstruck beginning to its pillaging and polluting, Godforsaken and terrified end.

Having such a lease on life is, at the last, but a ringside seat on death. Though the blade still ply unaccountably to the left or right, over or under, it has gouged and cleaned one's existence to the bare bones. Childhood playmates and schoolfellows, dead; friends of youth, adolescence and maturity, dead; enemies, competitors, well- and ill-wishers, former employers and employees, friends of friends, those remembered as younger than oneself, those remembered as children, even babies, all gone. Never mind the limitless, nameless dead heaped up in each second of the nine and a half decades. Never mind the dead of battle, blitz and concentration camp. Never mind the surging, mountainous dead of modern times, the dead of genocide made commonplace, of famine grown plenteous, of ever more frequent and forgettable technological disaster and murder democratised.

5

Against all the preposterous, incalculable odds, one living grain, christened Arthur Richard Hallett, survives. None of the wars has killed him. None of the peaces has killed him. None of the murderers has stumbled on him. None of the plagues has broken out in him. None of the cancers has chosen him as host.

The perfection of his health at age ninety-six verges on the abnormal. Save for some back trouble – borne since before the 1914–18 War – he is completely free from pain. Within the natural tentative frame of his great age, he is fully mobile. His heart and lungs disclose no blur or shadow to the X-Ray plate. His appetite, though tiny, is good, his digestion strong, his bladder unobstructed, his bowel-mechanism in order. The pixieish ears are innocent of plastic plug and wire. Most amazing are the faded blue eyes, in which unimaginable stores of sight have caused no ailment beyond a faint wateriness. At four years short of one hundred, Mr Hallett has yet to be prescribed his first spectacles.

Behind that frail, unextinguished blue is the same wondrous state of perfect working order. His mind is sharp, his speech distinct, his memory almost laceratingly clear. His right hand, when he holds it out from its lambswool cuff, is steady as a rock. His handwriting is exquisite, a tiny, delicate copperplate script originally learned in an Edwardian commercial office, refined in annotating countless sheets of music manuscript. Though no one remains to listen or applaud, he still makes music for himself every day and almost every night: on his tortoiseshell piano, his tired little sepia guitar, but principally on his "Neuner", as he calls the violin whose case never leaves the radius of his grasp.

His health and a mistake made in earlier life – that of accumulating savings – have sealed Mr Hallett's fate. Living by the outdated code that he does, he wishes to be a burden to no one. Beyond his weekly pension and yearly Income Tax demand, the state pays him no attention. His modest capital places him among what Government terms the "affluent" elderly who can be safely left to their enviable leisure and freewill. The fact that he must arrange his survival five miles from the nearest food shop and post office, three miles from the nearest bus stop, ten miles from the nearest doctor, twelve miles from the nearest police station and fifty miles from the nearest hospital with emergency service, elicits the usual answer from late 20th century Britain's rugged pragmatism. If people opt for the self-indulgence of country life, they cannot also expect cossetted convenience.

In the village he is routinely known as a "wonderful old man" whom certain inhabitants have to thank for long-past inexpensive piano-lessons. He is appreciated as mildly eccentric for his musical past, his fur-collared coat and the fact that, when he sets out on the longish walk from his house to the postbox, he pushes before him the ancient black invalid chair which stands in his front hall. Wonderful old man or not, there is a reserve which can never be pierced. Though he has lived in Swavesey almost forty years, Mr Hallett remains a "foreigner".

His world is his unheated bedroom, his kitchenette-cum-scullery and this dusty, crowded little lifeboat of a sitting-room. He is here hour after hour, as the hours roll into yet another day to add to his vast existing store. As each new night falls he's still here, marked in the universe by dim light through threadbare holly, under the lines of firs that can roar like a dark, rolling reef.

In the corner diagonal from his chair stands a mahogany long-case clock of "North Country" type. Stout town hall columns flank its flowered face and the signature "J. R. Sizer, Warrington". Above is a painted seashore with sailing-boats drawn up which, as the day revolves, is slowly replaced by a peacefully-sleeping moon. Its sonorous tick amplifies the enormity of still more minutes, gathering to what seems a small gasp of inward jogs and whirrs as it prepares to strike yet another recklessly-accumulated hour. On a wooden tea-trolley nearby, a modern travel clock, held in an open oyster of sham leather, registers the same in amazed silence but for a tiny scrape of quartz.

The fireplace is of dingy red brick. In the empty grate, a khaki-coloured oil heater shaped like an old-fashioned rocket ship breathes out its faintly church-smelling warmth. Along the rough wooden mantelpiece above are propped half a dozen foreign picture postcards, each one boasting of a different creamy town and bright turquoise sea. At one end stands a short brass candlestick, at the other a grey china torso of Marie-Antoinette with a ruched tea-cosy for a skirt, covering a defunct cigarette-lighter on a lighthouse-shaped wooden stand. Scattered between are a pink ceramic pig, a carved wooden mug of fire spills, an outsize plastic Babycham with a blue bow, a chip of violinist's rosin, a scarlet tin ash-tray full of safety-pins and buttons, a ribbonless bronze medal, a pair of Jacobean candle-snuffers and an electricity bill.

Pushed into the oval mirror-frame there are also various old photographs: of a ferocious, foreign-looking man in pince-nez, of a trio of young men with piano, cello and violin, of a group of young men and girls on some long-lost sea front, of a lone woman, large and formally-dressed, standing in a sepia field near what looks like a caravan. Mr Hallett glances up at this last picture often, smiling and sometimes murmuring under his breath.

The chair in which he sits is of neutral green fabric, not outstandingly comfortable, with two meagre arms of plain wood. The outer end of each arm has a small hole drilled into it. His fingers touch these holes constantly through the day and, nearly every time, he will look up at the tiny snapshot of that rather large woman whose face is a shy half-moon under her Twenties cloche hat.

Beside him on a curved stem is an invalid's tray-table, covered by a sheet of clean newspaper. On it are today's *Daily Express*, a letter put back the wrong way into its envelope, a pre-war black Bluebird fountain pen and a Basildon Bond "Queen of Spades" writing pad. In summer, there also will be a jam jar of wild flowers from the hedgerow, daisies, campion and wild scabious that, once picked, seldom live longer than a day.

His view on the other side is his music-stand and the long, tussocky garden, bare but for a single pocket-handkerchief tree. At the end, with his 20–20 sight, he can see a compost heap, in aspect now ancient as some Pictish burial-mound. Beyond, until twenty years ago, there was a five-mile view up to the brow of a hill, silver with spring and gold with summer wheat. Now there is just a wire perimeter-fence and a red-printed notice, warning him not to light fires in the forest, leave litter or maliciously damage any of the trees.

The view he prefers is into the room, over things that have kept him company longer than people and are his only remaining contemporaries. Old tin trunks, lacquered chests, leather hat- and collar-boxes, collapsed suitcases with rust-crumbed clasps, their handles bearing string-tied remnants of railways and left-luggage offices ages extinct, directed to theatres and lodgings generations demolished, in boroughs and counties decades ago renamed. Cardboard confectionery cartons marked "6d per qr.", prewar mottled-grey box files and grimy manila envelopes. Dark khaki photograph albums; boxes, folders, wallets and packets stuffed with their overflow of miniature snaps or stiff portraits in embossed vermilion. Bundles of letters written in blue-black ink, ringed with frank old postmarks, stamped honest green or brown with the profiles of sad, conscientious kings. And, piled up everywhere, sheet music in antique pink or olive-green covers, titled in stern Germanic or airy copperplate . . . "Allegro: Fiocco" . . . "Petite Suite Moderne" . . . "Le Fiacre" . . . "Evensong". By East Hope Martin . . . "Shaminard's Autumn" . . . "Britannicus" . . . "The Mikado" . . . "A Blind Girl's Love" . . . "Chu Chin Chow" . . . "The Dream of Olwen" . . . "To A Wild Rose" . . . "I Hear You Calling Me" . . . "Where Are The Lads of the Village Tonight?" . . . "The Merry Widow" . . . "Maid of the Mountains" . . . Open on the music-stand – pages crumbling to brown as if the journey through time has gradually scorched them – is Beethoven's "Spring Sonata".

He sits in an old man's chair in an old man's room, amid an old man's random jumble. But he does not sit any way like an old man should. His back is straight, even though seated, his posture forward from his cushion and the lambswool collar of his coat. His face is alert, as if attending to more than silence broken only by the swish of firs. The cheeks that should be sunken are flushed; the eyes that should be closed, bright wide awake. His wrists slip from the fur cuffs ready for action, and he rubs his long, young fingers briskly over the cheerless oil stove. If it were not so implausible, you would think the strangest thing of Mr Hallett in his chair. You would think he almost liked still being alive.

Beside him, next to the fire-tongs, is a telephone of the solid black sculpted type now generally withdrawn from service. At long intervals this will give its archaic double ring.

When Mr Hallett lifts the receiver, he does not answer "Hello". He answers "Good morning", "Good afternoon" or "Good evening".

His voice has a faint tang of the Yorkshire where he was born and brought up, all that inconceivable time and travelling ago. He articulates with a rotundity and resonance that give a further clue to his past. After all these years, his accent still carries a whiff of pomade, astrakhan and boiled shirt-front. His most commonplace words retain some of the poised dignity of an announcement from the conductor.

Each receives its due value, colour and passion, like a note played from a score. And no note is forgotten, and no beat missed as the sonata turns a page . . .

. . . remember seeing one in Bradford, going along Clarence Street, puffing away: a lovely dark green it was, I can visualise it now. And that was a steam tram! We'd gone in for the Jubilee festivities, which would have been Queen Victoria's Diamond, in Eighteen Ninety-Six. They'd a big parade of troops and police and pit silver bands, and even the fire engines with their horses done up in bunting, and folk in fancy dress, all through the middle of Bradford. I remember how frightened I was of a man dressed up as a sea-serpent in a suit of red scales. I couldn't go to sleep for nights after, thinking about that red scaly man and his tail.

That isn't my very first memory, though. I can remember right back to being two. They found a cyst or goitre or some kind of little growth in my throat, and I'd to go into Keighley Royal Infirmary to have it removed. I remember, I lay in this little iron cot, and there was a fire burning in the grate and a bell-pull hanging above my head, and I was parched with thirst but they couldn't give me anything because it was too soon after the operation. I can tell you what the nurses said when I kept crying for some drink. "Oh, Baby – we can't catch the cow to milk it."

Mother being an invalid and Dad so busy in the shop, I had to have Middy Miff to come in and look after me. Mrs Smith, her real name was, I couldn't say that, so I called her Middy Miff. She'd put me on her lap and teach me songs, like "Nelly Bly caught a fly . . . " and "Where have you been all the day, down the alley, courting Sally, pickin' up cinders, breakin' winders . . . " We'd clap our hands in time to that one, and clap them a different way for "My mother *said*, I never *should* . . . play with the gypsies in the *wood* . . . "

Dad was an only child, but Mother had five sisters, all living at Ivy House, out on North Road, with their father, my Granda Antrobus. I used to sit with Granda Antrobus in the garden at Ivy House, where he had a little seat – or an arbour, as we used to say – built in an old holly tree. He called it, and I don't know why, The Caley Ole. I'd sit there with him in The Caley Ole and he'd sing me a song about being "hungry with eating and footsore with riding . . ." He always wore the same clothes, an old tail coat and waistcoat and an old-fashioned shirt front, and his trousers were so old, they'd got green mould on them.

When we'd left off singing, he'd take me into Ivy House and up to his room and show me a drawer he kept full of toffee pigs and liquorice whips and pink fondant mice with little bits of string for tails. And he always said the same thing. "Them as asks don't get. And them as don't ask, don't want."

"How do I get something, then Granda?" I'd say.

"That's for thee to find out, lad."

Then he'd shut the drawer on all those lovely toffee pigs and fondant mice and turn me round and we'd start to walk away. We'd almost get to the door, then Granda Antrobus would take hold of me and turn me round again. "Go on, love," he'd say. "Help theeself."

Ivy House was a fine place, though they'd no electric light; only gas. No running water either in those days, just a big old zinc bath you had to fill up from jugs and brass cans. And down the garden was what we called The Petty. Well, you know what that was: the Necessary House. It had a lot of gardening stuff inside it, and a big old varnished wooden seat with two holes. People then were a bit more companionable than now. Underneath there was just a long drop, and two pails. Every week, a local farmer named Mr Salter used to come and remove the pails, or rather the contents of them, and the land benefited as a result.

Five aunts in one house, can you imagine it? My Aunt Bertha ruled the roost, you'd say. She'd been a nurse, and had assisted at the operation when Edward VII had his appendix out. She was the one who, they said, saved his life by sitting him up on the operating table when she noticed him starting to turn blue. She just took hold of his beard and pulled; she was like that. Then there was Aunt Alice, Aunt Louie, Aunt Bea and – my special favourite – Aunt Nan. When they all got talking at once, which they sometimes did, it used to get a bit too much for Granda Antrobus, and so he'd go down the garden to The Petty and sit there and smoke his pipe in the dark.

Well, one day, what do you think! He's sat there in the dark, and suddenly sees a pair of eyes glittering at him. Granda Antrobus lets out a shriek they can hear all the way up in the front parlour. "Help – it's The Devil. He's come for me! Help!" Everyone rushes down, wrenches open the door and what do they find? There's Granda Antrobus with his kecks round his ankles, shrieking and hollering "Help, it's the Devil!" and there's Mr Salter's goat, that's got shut in The Petty and forgotten about.

Mine was a happy childhood, not like some of those you hear about. I had a happy home, a good mother, though she was an invalid and in pain, and a really fine dad. Mind, he could be strict. If he said do a thing, you knew you had to do it. But he'd never beat or strap you – not like my pal Sidney Sanford's dad when Sidney misbehaved. His dad got so angry once, he wrenched a piece out of the banisters and run upstairs to tan Sidney with that.

My dad was what they called a good provision hand. He'd learned the provision trade inside-out at Templeton's in Leeds. He could slice bacon to any thickness, he could grade eggs, he knew how to test cheeses for ripeness – whole cheeses I'm talking about, not processed stuff. Whole Cheddars and Stiltons and Double Gloucesters and Wensleydales. You tested them with a thing called a cheese iron that fetched a tiny sliver out from the middle. He was an artist in his way, my dad was, when he dealt with provisions. I used to think that when I'd stand and watch him whacking the butter into shape. He'd get it between these two wooden bats, and he'd whack it this way and that way until he'd make it a big pile on its marble base – like a castle, I thought it looked, with its lovely buttery towers and battlements. Then, if he was feeling pleased with me, quite often he'd break a tower off and say "Here, lad," and I'd pop it in my mouth.

My dad was a worker, that's the word for him. He was old-fashioned in this way, he believed the best way to get anything done was to do it yourself. Even with all the people he employed, I've seen him come up from the storeroom, thirteen stone steps, with a hundredweight bag of sugar on his back. Everything came in bulk, you see – the sugar, the butter, the currants, the Irish hams. We had to steep the hams ourselves to get the salt off, and break up the sugar and clean the currants and take the butter out of its cask and whack it into shape.

We sold everything in the provision line, but we were tea and coffee specialists. "Hallett's for Coffee", it used to say on our paper bags. We did our own blend, "Hallet's One-and-Eight". It cost one-and-eight a pound, you see. Not even twenty pence. My dad had made up a little rhyme that appeared every week in our advert in the *Keighley News*:

Hallett's Coffees lessen strife
Making peace twixt Man and Wife

I wish you'd seen our shop in Cavendish Street, Keighley: I can picture it now with its black and white floor, the coloured tiles around the hall, all the ladies in their big hats sitting on chairs beside the counter, and my dad and Mr Moodie, his chief provision hand, and little Lawrence, slicing the bacon, weighing out currants and sultanas, packing sugar in those little blue bags and totting everything up on the greaseproof with their beautiful sharp Royal Sovereign pencils. My dad was such a stickler, no one was even allowed to use a pencil with a blunt point or a chewed rubber on its end. A nice sharp Royal Sovereign behind your ear showed *you* were sharp, a good provision hand.

The counter was marble, all veined like Stilton cheese, and so were the two plinths where we piled the butter and lard. Going along, you had provisions first, then cooked meats and delicacies – brawns and hams and rounds of beef and cooked chickens and turkey and duck and goose, and ham-and-mushroom and beef-and-potato and game and Melton Mowbray pork pies. Then you came to the coffee-grinder, and the jars of Colombian and Blue Mountain and Kenyan and Javanese, and our own blend, Hallett's One-and-Eight, and the tea-scales and a great big line of dark old Chinese tea-caddies with all the varieties in. Along the front of the counter you'd got sacks of sugar, and boxes of broken biscuits we sold at threepence a pound, and barrels of apples, and grapes packed in wood-shavings, and rice and tapioca and porridge oats. Up at the far end was the cash-desk, with Miss James in it – or Miss Lightoller on Fridays. When the counterhands took the money, they packed it into a little overhead copper quoit and shied it off along a wire to the cash desk, and Miss James – or Miss Lightoller on Fridays – would take it out and put the change and the receipt in and shy it back.

We stayed open to eight every night – half past ten on Saturdays. And, of course, everything delivered. You'd go ten miles to deliver a pound of butter. I've done it myself, many a time.

Cavendish Street was the premier thoroughfare of Keighley – high-class establishments on both sides, the Town Hall and Covered Market and two theatres, the Medina and the Palace. Quite a show place it was, specially on Market Day. Of course there was a lot of poverty about as well. People that worked in the cotton and silk mills did so for very little recompense; I saw that myself later, when I worked in a cotton mill. They'd to start before dawn, the mill folk did. The mill owners paid a man called the Knocker-Up to go round at five in the morning with a long pole, tapping the bedroom windows along street after street. And from seven o'clock on, all day and into the night, you could hear those cotton and silk mills working. I

14

heard them when I woke in the morning and when I was turning in at night. "Ssh-ti-bom bom," they used to go. "Ssh-ti-bom bom. Ssh-ti-bom bom."

Mother couldn't do much about the house, having been an invalid since my birth, but where business was concerned she was sharp as paint. She did all the books and wages for Dad, and all the ordering and invoicing; she knew what was in that place down to every last tin of pilchards. She'd sit up above the shop in our living-room, in a little needlepoint armchair, totting up all the accounts – "Bought of Geo. Hallett so much and such and such" – and our cat Alexander would sit on the arm and watch her. Every few pages in the ledger, you'd come to a place where the ink was smudged, and you knew that was when Alexander had sneezed.

She couldn't really manage cooking either, though she'd toast a bap or muffin or sometimes a bloater in front of the fire. Dad used to cook high tea for me when I got in from school. Bacon and egg, he'd do me, or a Welsh rarebit, and for afters I'd have a handful of raspberry jam biscuits out of the shop.

I'll tell you, right from when I was a young youth, as we used to say, those two theatres in Cavendish Street, Keighley, the Palace and the Medina, used to fascinate me. The Palace was the premier variety theatre in Keighley. The Medina was big but not quite as big as the Palace. It had a tower with a Moorish dome on top, and Eastern scenes all round the foyer, with camels and oases and figures of men in turbans and curly slippers holding out candelabra lights. But the Palace always had the edge, through being on the Number One Circuit, which means to say it got all the top Music Hall shows and all the top names: Harry Lauder, or Vesta Tilley, or Little Tich, or Coram. They all did a week at Keighley Palace in between Leeds Alhambra and Bradford Theatre Royal.

As a little boy, I used to love to walk down Cavendish Street after dark, and see the Palace and the Medina all lit up, with the little blue light they had on top of the Medina's dome, and all the crowds streaming in. There was a certain bill on some hoardings for a play, that used to fascinate me. "While London Sleeps", the play was called, and the poster was of a lovely girl walking across a telegraph-wire away from a house in flames, and underneath her you saw the whole of London, Big Ben and St Paul's, under a full moon. In the play, a building really did burn and the heroine really did walk across the stage on a tightrope. They did the burning part with lights and red foil, but the tightrope was real. She was my first love, that girl on the poster who walked over the telegraph-wire. I'd lie in bed at night – with all the cotton and silk mills in the distance, going "ssh-ti-bom bom" – and imagine she was in my arms, on the telegraph-wire, with St Paul's and Big Ben and the whole of London fast asleep underneath us.

I attended two schools in Keighley. Until I was eight, I went to the Misses de Sautoys and when I'd passed eight, I went to Keighley Trade and Grammar School, which made my mother very proud. I'd to wear striped trousers and an Eton jacket, they called them – a little short black jacket, which you wore with a stiff turned-down collar like the pupils at Eton College.

Mind, the common boys made a show of you in the street if you'd on an Eton jacket. It was so short, you see, it didn't cover your rear end, and the back of it came down to form a point, so when you passed, the common boys used to shout out "This way to my arse!"

The first day there, I was a bit nervous, you can imagine, what with all these strange boys in their Eton jackets and the masters in their gowns and mortar-boards and the big, long corridors and the smell of cabbage and chalk. They took me in to this room and sat me down at one of the desks next to a certain boy, and said that Cowley would look after me. They were desks for eight boys, but each one opened individually and had its own inkwell, that the monitor would come round with an enamel jug and fill.

When this boy Cowley opened his desk, he'd got the inside of the lid all fitted up with rulers so that he could roll a marble from the top to the bottom. "Have you any alleys?" he said to me. "Glass alleys" were what we called marbles, the kind they used to seal pop bottles with. You'd break the bottle to get the glass alley out. "Have you got any alleys?" this boy Cowley said, and somehow or other after that we became best pals.

Oh yes, I liked school, I was a good scholar. French was always my best subject, and Physics. Handwriting, Physics and Maths. I was good at all that . . . Algebra, Euclid . . . You could ask me any of the axioms now. "A point is that which has position without magnitude." "A line is that which lies evenly between two points." "Parallel lines cannot meet, however far they are produced." "Pons Asinorum – three-point-one-four." "Area of a circle – pi r-squared . . ." Shall I tell you what nickname they gave me at school? My dad made a practice of hanging bunches of bananas on hooks along the top of our shop-window in Cavendish Street, so that's what they called me, "Banana Hallett".

Twenty-nine of us there were in Old Natty's class. I can still recite their names from the Register . . . Andrassy, Barnetson, Binns, Bolwell, Calthorp, Clerk, Cowley . . . Andrassy was the tallest in the class, and the dullest. His people were German, they'd two pork shops in Keighley. And oh, he *was* a dunderhead! In French, when you were supposed to say "il y a", Andrassy would always say "il why-ai". I remember Goyer, our French master telling Andrassy to translate the phrase "un peu malade" and do you know what he said? "A pot of marmalade, Sir."

Old Goyer used to give him jip. "Stand on your hind feet," he'd shout at Andrassy. "Stand on your hind feet and put your ears back, you son of a rabbit-skin wearing ancestor . . ."

Keighley Trade and Grammar was unusual for those times in having no chastisement. Mind, they were strict. You'd get lines or Extra School, or you'd be brought out before the whole class and have to stand there with heavy books balanced on your arms. The masters all had their ways of maintaining discipline. Goyer, the French master – he'd throw chalk at you. He'd pepper Andrassy with bits of chalk sometimes, Goyer would. With Gwynne-Roberts, the Maths master, it was sarcasm. The only one who tanned us was Old Natty, our form master. Shearing, his name was, H. R. Shearing, B.A., Lon. We called him Old Natty. A great big strapping chap, with a thick black moustache like villains you saw in plays, and always sucking something, like a lozenge or a bit of cough candy.

He'd tan us with a steel ruler, Shearing would. He'd broke a few wood ones on us, so he brought in this long steel one, the sort printers use. "Toby", that ruler was named. If anyone misbehaved, or sometimes if you just couldn't answer a question Shearing asked, it was Toby for you, that steel ruler, swiping down on your knuckles. When Shearing felt maungy, he'd go round the whole twenty-nine of us, asking the same question. "What are the Antipodes?" "Don't know, Sir." "Hold out your hand, boy", and swipe would come Toby, that steel ruler. I think he enjoyed it, because he gave the steel ruler a name like a pet animal, and he even tied some pink ribbon to it.

Well, one day, Shearing swishes in in his gown, and you could tell right off he was feeling maungy. Off he started around the class. "What are the Antipodes?" "Don't know, Sir." Swipe! "What are the Antipodes?" No answer. Swipe! Same question, same answer, don't know, swipe from Toby that steel ruler, boy after boy sucking his poor hand in flames or sitting on it, till at last Shearing comes to the end of our row where a boy named Pagett sat. His people were wholesale ironmongers in Garnet Street. He was naught but a little chap, Pagett, but nobody could top him for pluck.

So: "Pagett, what are the Antipodes?" No answer from Pagett. "Hold out your hand, boy." But when Old Natty brought Toby down on Pagett's hand, he must have turned it because the sharp end of it, not the flat of it, caught Pagett's fingers a cut that drew blood. Pagett went as pale as if he were going to faint, but he didn't: he jumped up and drew back his foot and he kicked Old Natty on the shin, again and again. Old Natty caught hold of him by the shoulder but Pagett still kept kicking and kicking his shin like billy-o, and Shearing let go and he limped back to his desk at the front of the class and he put Toby inside the desk, never said a word, and he limped out of the room.

A few minutes later, he came back with Mr Windsor, the head. Mr Windsor said, "Pagett – I want you. Come to my room." The next we see of Pagett, he's come to collect the things out of his desk. He's expelled. Now that was harsh, we felt, because he'd suffered a cruel cut from Toby that drew blood. But there it was. Pagett – expelled. And Shearing had to walk with a stick, and he limped for days after.

You might think that was the end of that, and so it was – excepting in the mind of one pupil.

The years roll on. I've begun in my profession, I've married my wife Delia, we're living with my parents out in Duxford, almost on Ilkley Moor. On Sunday afternoons, in the Jubilee Gardens, Keighley, they put on orchestral concerts in the band-stand. You could listen for nothing, of course, most people did, but if you paid tuppence, you could have a deck chair right in front of the band-stand.

Delia and I decided we'd have a chair. We'd paid our tuppences and we were sitting there on one side of the front row, listening to the band, a military one – Yorkshire Fusiliers, I think – playing Strauss waltzes, which they did quite well, and suddenly, in a deck chair right on the other side, who do you think I saw? It was Shearing. All those years on, of course, he'd aged a bit, his moustache had gone grey and he'd giglamps on. Still, I'd have known him anywhere. It was Old Natty.

I turned to Delia and I said, "Delia, that's our old form master in that deck chair over there. That's Shearing," I said. "And I'm going to go across and tell him off."

"Oh, no, no," Delia said, a bit horrified.

I said, "I am. I'm going to tell him what I think of him. 'Mr Shearing,' I'm going to say. 'I'm a professional musician. But if your steel ruler had injured one of my fingers like you injured Pagett's, I might never have picked up a violin.' "

I was ready to do it, honour bright. But Delia begged me not to. "Arthur," she said. "Sit down. You mustn't. You could end up in the police court, something like that." And so, for Delia's sake, I didn't. We just sat there in our deck chairs and listened to the music.

How I came to take up the violin's a funny tale, too. I'd never have tried to play music, I think, if it hadn't been for Madame Estelle and her beauty boxes, and going to London, and what she said about my hands. Have you got another moment to hear the story?

My Aunt Bertha, eldest of my five aunts who lived with their father at Ivy House, was a nurse as I've already mentioned – she'd nursed Edward VII. She'd been private nurse to various other notable people, too, and one of those was a woman named Madame Estelle who'd a business in London, selling beauty boxes by post. She made up all these powders and rouges and tonics and such-like and put them in pots, then she'd advertise in *The Lady* or *The Gentlewoman*: "To maintain the skin's bloom or the brightness of the eyes, send seven-and-six to Madame Estelle . . ." She lived and had her business in Newman Street, Soho.

Well, she'd been in the Royal Free Hospital for two major operations and, after that, had my Aunt Bertha in to nurse her privately. They took a fancy to one another and after Madame Estelle had recovered, they always kept in touch. Madame Estelle wasn't her real name, by the way; just a trade-mark. Her real name was Mrs Blanche Smart. Anyway, my Aunt Bertha quite often used to go down from Keighley to London to visit Madame Estelle and on one occasion during my school holidays she took me and we both stopped with Madame Estelle for a month.

Oh, I liked London, I thought it was wizard – all the lights and the crowds and traffic, and lovely theatres like the Theatre Royal, Haymarket; she took us there one night. Another night she took us to the Coliseum, and the water circus at the Hippodrome, and we walked round past the stage door after-wards and saw all the mashers in the cloaks and silk hats and eye-glasses, waiting for the ballet girls to come out. I'd never seen so much traffic – remember I'd hardly seen a motor car before. In London, they were ten-a-penny: motor cars, motor vans, motor taxis, motor buses as well as the horse-drawn ones, all so jammed with folk, you'd think they'd topple over, and every one with "Fry's Chocolate" written on the side. We saw Piccadilly, what they called The Dilly, and Delmonico's and the Empire and Eros, where at night they'd have all these green naphtha lamps going, and old grannies in topknots selling violets around the steps.

Another day, we walked all round what they called Seven

Dials, which was quite a dangerous place, really, but we had the manager from the factory with us, so it was all right. I remember, we came round a corner and suddenly saw all these women in aprons sitting out in the sunshine, shucking peas. One of them got hold of my cheek and pinched it and – in a real loud Cockney voice – shouted out to her mates, "This one's almost ready for market!" Well, I didn't know what to think!

Madame Estelle, Aunt Bertha's friend, was a character, I'll say that. She was a little tiny woman, quite attractive, but she smoked Russian cigarettes, black things with gold ends, and she'd a glass eye. Mind, you'd never have known it except on the days when she'd put in an odd colour. She'd got a whole case full of spare glass eyes, – brown and blue and violet, and one that she'd put in for a joke, which hadn't an ordinary pupil, but a pair of crossed Union Jacks.

We were sitting at Madame Estelle's, the first day we arrived – sitting having tea in Newman Street, Soho – when she suddenly reached out and took hold of one of my hands. "Why isn't this child a musician?" she said to my Aunt Bertha. "I've never seen such lovely hands."

The house where she lived – and where she made up these beauty boxes – had belonged to some Huguenots, I forget exactly who they were, but the room I slept in, right at the top, had a great big wooden mantelpiece all carved in dragons and gargoyles. It was fine to lie there at night and hear London going on all round you, the voices and motor horns, the mashers and ballet girls and violet sellers – no cotton and silk mills like at home. And, I remember, there was a farm. Right in the middle of Soho, a real farm where you could go for milk. So a cockerel woke you up in the morning and in Old Compton Street, in the midst of all that noise and traffic, you'd sometimes see cows going along to be milked.

Another time she took us out for supper to a restaurant named Leoni's where the theatrical people went; their pictures hung all round the walls. They had an ivory cat they'd sit down at table as an extra place to stop the company ever being thirteen, and there was a black waiter, the first black man I'd ever seen, barring make-believe ones in minstrel shows. I was a bit frightened of him, I remember, when he came and tied my napkin round my neck.

We had ravioli, and Angels on Horseback as a savoury, and to drink they gave me hock mixed up with seltzer. Whenever anyone came over to speak to Madame Estelle, she'd take hold of one of my hands and say to whoever it was, "Hasn't this child got lovely hands, don't you think? They're *musician's* hands."

So, came the day when we're going home to Keighley. Madame Estelle saw us off at St Pancras and she'd got one green eye in and one grey. She said, "I've got a present for you, Arthur, but you've got to promise not to open it until after the train goes." And what do you think it was? That's right, it was a violin. It was in a case marked "Scarth and Co, Charing Cross Road", and it had a lion's head on it, above the fingerboard. And she'd made Aunt Bertha promise to persuade my parents to send me for lessons.

Well, my mother needed no persuading, and she soon talked Dad into sending me to Rasch, in Leeds. "If he's going to learn," she said, "he'll learn with a tip-top man." Mind, I don't think she'd any idea how it would eventually come out with me and that violin with the lion's head. But, you see, she'd been so adamant in saying "Our Artie will never be a grocer." Not that Dad would have stood in my way or denied me anything he could give me. So it was all settled; I was to go to Rasch, in Leeds.

That was quite a thing, because Rasch was a virtuoso; he'd played with the Hallé, still did sometimes, and he took only a very few pupils. I'd go down to Leeds and see him for an interview – my Aunt Nan came with me – and Rasch took me into his music room and asked me all kinds of questions, smoking that china pipe of his, staring at me over his pince-nez and looking me up and down.

I found him rather frightening at first, with his ginger hair all sticking up on end as if he'd just read a ghost story, but, really, he was nice enough. He told me that if I wanted to become a musician, I must never look at books in bed. "It vill try your eyes Arthur" he said – he spoke like that. He said "vill" for "will" and "vork" for "work" and for "violin" he said "wiolin". "Vith me you vill vork," he said. And instead of saying "jam", he'd say "jom".

To look at him you'd know he was a Dutchman: he wore an embroidered waistcoat and sometimes a long silk dressing gown, and a little skull cap with a tassel. His trousers were what we called shepherd's plaid, and he'd a great heavy watch chain with a gold seal attached to it. But a fine teacher – and a first-rate player, of course. He'd hold that violin and that bow like two pieces of silk. As time went on and he got interested in me, it never really mattered when the two hours' tuition were up. "You played that very vell, Arthur," Rasch would say. "Now – ve'll have a cup of tea, and I'll ask my vife to come in and join us."

His wife played the piano, and also gave private lessons. An Englishwoman she was; they'd met in Manchester. So in his wife would come, and we'd have a cup of tea and a bit of cake – or a bit of bread and jam – and then the three of us would play something nice together.

As I progressed, I formed a little trio with two pals of mine, who were also studying music, named Mark Stillwell and Hector Leading. Hector's people were in soap, and he'd got what you'd call a natural ear. He could hear a classical concerto, then sit straight down at the piano and play it right off. His people made Leading's Patent Washing Soap, so naturally they'd a bob or two. They'd bought Hector a Bechstein baby grand, a really lovely instrument, and they'd given him his very own music-room. He went to the Bluecoat School in Keighley and Mark was with me at the Trade and Grammar, and was studying the 'cello. We'd meet and practise two or three times a week, usually at Hector's house in Spring Vale because he'd got that nice music-room all to himself. I started to pick up the piano, a bit, as well, off Hector. I always used to love it when he let me sit down and play his Bechstein baby grand.

Well, as time passed, our little trio became quite famous in the Keighley district. People would invite us to come and play for them at their Sunday musical evenings, though we were still just small boys, half the size of ninepence. You'd get an engraved card: "Mr and Mrs so-and-so request the pleasure of the company of Masters Hallett, Stillwell and Leading at so-and-so house on Sunday at 6 pm for songs, recitations and musical interludes. Dress: formal." The gentlemen would wear dinner-jackets, the ladies wore long dresses and carried fans and sometimes had ostrich feathers in their hair. We wore our Eton jackets. Someone would sing, someone would play a piano solo or a harp solo. We'd give them Bragha's "Prelude" or "The Allegro" by Fiocco or whatever else we'd been practising at Hector's.

It was a busy life, you see, what with going to Rasch – that journey into Leeds twice a week – and two hours' practice a day on Leo, which I named my violin, because of the lion's head; then I'd my school work to do, Caesar and Euclid and Algebra and, after school, the deliveries for our shop. I'd lots of other little jobs for Dad as well, like helping him unpack stock and display it on the shelves. I used to make these giant pyramids from tins of Marrowfat peas. And every Thursday, Market Day, I'd to run home quick at dinner-time and fetch a canvas bag with all Dad's week's takings in it, and go with that and pay it in to the Yorkshire Bank in Dale Street. It amazes me now, to think how, as quite a small boy I'd walk along with all that money – which it obviously was – and nobody thought anything about it. No one even *thought* it was other than perfectly safe for a kiddie to walk through the centre of Keighley on Market Day with a bank bag full of sovereigns and five-pound notes!

I'd a shilling a week pocket money from Dad, and people I delivered to regularly might give me a penny or a halfpenny tip, so I often used to finish up on a Saturday with a florin in my pocket which was a lot, really, for those days when you realise what the ordinary working man took home each week as wages. I'm speaking of before the First War now, Nineteen-Ten or -Eleven. A throwster on piece-work rates in the cotton and silk mills would earn about eighteen-and-six a week. I know that because when I worked at Taplow's in the office, I used to see the wage packets being made up.

But then, look at the price of things in those days: it was

tuppence for a loaf, eggs sixpence a dozen, milk sixpence a quart. You could get a penn'orth of pipe tobacco. You could get a *farthing's*-worth of sweets. And nothing ever seemed to go up from one year to another. All the time I was a boy in Keighley, aniseed balls or giant acid drops cost a penny for eight. My tram from Cavendish Street to school was a penny. If I took a letter down to post for my mother at Cavendish Street General, the stamp for it cost a halfpenny, same as always. They'd put it on a brass weighing-scales that had the rates for inland letters and parcels etched on it in brass. That's how sure you were it wouldn't go up. The price of it was etched in brass!

So you see, even though people were poor, they could manage somehow, they'd make ends meet. A man might bring home only eighteen-and-six a week, but his wife knew all the ways to eke it out, feed and clothe their kiddies, keep a clean, decent home and still have coppers to put by for Christmas or a few days by the sea. However poor and in want they might be, there were certain rules everyone lived by. You'd never try and hurt an elderly person. You'd never try and hurt a female or a child. When I think how I used to walk along, half the size of ninepence, with that bag full of Dad's takings . . . fear never entered my head, you see. I knew the world I lived in was safe.

There was no TV, of course; no radio and hardly any films. The main form of public amusement was the theatre, which I think had a lot to do with the way people were. You are what you see, aren't you? And what folk saw in the theatre wasn't ugliness and violence. It was glamour, it was excitement, beauty, melody. That was what took them out of their hard lives and the dreary work they'd to do. Saturday nights at the Palace theatre or the Medina, you'd be lucky to find a spare seat in the house. The prices they charged were so reasonable, almost anyone could afford to come and see a lovely show, even at a plush place like Keighley Palace. Orchestra stalls were one and six, fauteuils a shilling, dress circle half a crown. You could have a box for seven and six. The Amphitheatre was sixpence and the gallery – what we called the Gods – was tuppence.

I'd go with Hector and Mark, or with Henrietta, who was sort of my girl or young lady friend. We'd do the Palace if there was a really big turn, like Harry Champion, we wanted to see, but really I always preferred the Medina, because they had more plays. They'd a fine orchestra, nine-piece, led by a man named Claude Jepson. Plays then usually had incidental music, you see. There'd be a signature tune, and a theme for each character – taken from the Classics – and when things got exciting or comic or tragic, Claude Jepson and his orchestra would do the piece appropriate to the mood.

Oh, I did see some wizard plays there. "Marie of the Red Cross", by Lingford Cousins. "Defending His Honour", by H. Spencer-White. "A Blind Girl's Love", by Somers Trafford de Vere. That was a really heart-breaking one! And every time the poor little blind girl came on the stage, Jepson's orchestra played the same piece – Shaminard's "Autumn", muted.

I haven't told you about Henrietta yet, have I? I wasn't sure if I should, because of my wife, Delia. Because I feel that, even though Delia passed on nearly twenty years ago, she's still here, still keeping me company in a kind of way. I'd not want to talk about anything, even between us in confidence, that might run the risk of hurting my Delia's feelings, wherever she is, perhaps listening to us talk. But I'd like you to hear about Henrietta – some things about her anyway, if you've got time.

I'll tell you about Henrietta first off when she was seven years old and I was eight, which was when we first met. Before I went to Keighley Trade and Grammar, I was at this little dames school run by two ladies named the Misses de Sautoy, who'd lived in Brazil and in Argentina. The school was for girls, really, but they took boys up to the age of eight. At that time, I happened to be the only boy in the place. I'd sit on a form among all these girls, copying the alphabet out on my slate, or drawing peat pots or clothes pegs, which was all that kind of place taught you, really – and, of course, plenty of Bible study.

Oh no, I wasn't a bit embarrassed. I liked the girls and they all made quite a fuss of me. They'd pass me little notes, or chocolate toffees, and if it was needlework, they'd help me with that. At the back there was a little garden with swings in it where we'd go out for our mid-morning break. Well, one day I noticed this particular girl in a white smock, with a big straw hat on, following me round everywhere I went. She didn't say anything, didn't pass me a note, just followed me round and round that cinder path.

So this went on for a while and then one day, finally, she came up and said she wanted a swing and would I push her? I said "All right I don't mind," but I was pleased, secretly, because she was lovely-looking: she'd dark red hair and these bright green eyes and a lovely complexion, and near her mouth, a little beauty spot.

So we went across to the swing, she sat on it and swung her legs, and I'll tell you what her exact words were. "Push me nice and high, I like my toes to touch the sun." And that was Henrietta Haythornthwaite.

It was a beautiful, hot sunny day, what we used to call in Keighley "Royal weather". I'm pushing this girl on the swing as hard as I can, and up she's going and back she's swinging, and her sun bonnet's fallen off, it's rolling on the grass, and all her long red hair is streaming out behind her, and she's laughing and shouting out. "Higher, come on! Higher!"

I must have been daydreaming a bit, because, after giving one big final push, I was sure would take her over the bar, I didn't step aside quick enough; the swing flew back and caught me a great wallop on the forehead. The next thing I know, I'm lying on the grass, the younger Miss de Sautoy and Henrietta are kneeling beside me and I'm literally seeing red because I've blood in my eyes and all down my front as well.

I'd a nasty cut and a bit of concussion, but I was perfectly all right once it had been dabbed with iodine and bandaged. The Misses de Sautoy knew all about first aid, of course, having been in Argentina. I didn't want a bandage on my head, for fear folk would laugh, but the younger Miss de Sautoy insisted. "You can't go home with a bloody head," she said, which made me smile, really, because, being so ladylike, she'd *never* normally have used an expression like that.

I don't suppose you'd remember Haythornthwaite's Winter Warmers, would you? They were a kind of capsule people used to take in the depth of winter to ward off colds and catarrh.

Well, Henrietta's father invented those. He started as a chemist at one of the mills, and in his spare time he invented this capsule, which was a cold remedy, really, but it had a little bit of quinine in it, or something, that picked you up at the same time. Fiery things, they were, too: they made your eyes really water when you sucked one. Sir Ernest Shackleton took a tin with him on one of his Arctic expeditions, and wrote a really fine letter about them for a testimonial.

My dad had got to know Jack Haythornthwaite through business and the Rotary, and they were both on the committee at the Lib and Rad – Keighley Liberal and Radical Club. On Thursdays, which were early closing for us, Dad used to put on what he called his easy suit and he'd spend the afternoon at the Lib and Rad, playing billiards with Jack Haythornthwaite. I used to see Henrietta there and, in summer, at the Sunday League cricket matches, which our dads would frequent together.

She was beautiful-looking even then, with all that red hair, but a real tomboy, no doubt about it. I remember once, while we were meant to be watching cricket we came across this length of drainpipe some builders had left, and Henrietta dared me to crawl into one end of it and out the other. "I will if you will", she said. Well, of course, the inside was all filthy, covered with this wet oily stuff, and we both came out as black as a pair of Hottentots, our Sunday clothes quite ruined. She'd got a white lace pinafore on, and white kid pumps, but she just laughed in that way she had, and I started to laugh as well, even though I knew my mother'd play pop with me for spoiling my new sailor-suit. We sat there on the grass together, both as black as the Drop o'York, and we laughed and laughed and laughed.

She had this lovely singing voice even as quite a tiny thing: she'd sing to anyone, anywhere, and think nothing of it. When she was only about three, they put her in a play that ran at Keighley Medina ... *Margaret of the Red Cross*, I think was the name of it. Henrietta sang a song in that, *and* did a scene all on her own, kneeling and praying for her daddy to come home safe from the War. The management thought so much of her, they wanted to take her off on tour with them, but her father wouldn't allow it. She often used to say how very much she wished he had.

If you've another minute, I'll tell you a story about Henrietta to show you what kind of a person she was. I'd have been about eight – that means it's Nineteen-Oh-Two, the year after Queen Victoria's death. I'd got this front tooth that was loose, but it wouldn't come out, though I tried everything to make it. I'd wiggle it about, I'd even tied it to the doorknob and slammed the door, which was the old-fashioned way to pull out a tooth, but this one just wouldn't budge. So in the end, my dad told me I'd to go to have it extracted by Mr Eames the barber.

Now, that was a thing people still did at the time I'm talking about. Dentists, you see, were quite a new-fangled thing in Nineteen-Oh-Two. Most folk, if they'd a toothache, knew only one cure – the tooth had to go. If they couldn't hoik it out themselves, they'd get the barber to see to it because in olden times barbers used to be surgeons as well. That's how you got the striped barber's pole; the red stood for blood and the white for bandages.

Normally, my dad would have taken me, but on the day I'd to go, he was busy in the shop and all my five aunts were tied up as well, so Dad says to me, "Will you be a good boy, Arthur, and go to Mr Eames on your own? It's only a baby tooth," he said, "and if you bring it back home and put it under your pillow tonight, I daresay the Tooth Fairy will leave you a silver threepenny-bit."

So I'm walking down Cavendish, feeling a bit glum, and who do I meet but Henrietta Haythornthwaite.

"What's the matter?" she says to me. "You look proper maungy."

"I've to get a tooth pulled at Eames's," I said, "and I'm not looking forward to it."

"Hey-up," she says: she said it just like that. "Hey-up, don't be maungy. I'll come." So Henrietta came with me.

Eames's saloon was in Hothley Road, next door to the carriage-works. You went through a big tobacconist's first, with all these canes and walking-sticks in tubs; then you came into this big room under a skylight that was the hairdressing saloon.

Well, it's busy, and Mr Eames and his three assistants are snipping away, and there's men getting shaved, or with hot towels on, and you can smell all the sprays and lotions and the bay rum. As soon as Mr Eames catches sight of me, he knows why I've come. He was quite a nice man, really, though he hadn't a hair on his own head. If he'd to cut a child's hair, he used to fetch out this special little seat that was the shape of a cockerel. He'd set that on the big chair and say "Next young man, up on the cock's back."

No cock's back for me today, though: I've to sit in the grown-up chair so that Mr Eames can get a proper grip on my tooth with his pliers. That's all they were, just pliers, no different from the ones in our shed at home. "Open wide," he says, and this pair of pliers goes into my mouth. He catches hold of the tooth and starts yanking at it, but it *still* won't come! I've got my eyes shut so tight, I can see all these zig-zaggy patterns and the pain's really dreadful.

Well, Mr Eames goes on tugging and I'm crying, and after a time I can hear a lot of other shouting going on as well. So I open my eyes and look in the mirror. Mr Eames is bending over me, but he's got these two feet round his middle, and there's a couple of fists drubbing away at his bald head. It's Henrietta. She's jumped on his back, and she's pummelling him like anything and shouting, "Leave him alone you big bully! You leave Arthur alone!"

That was Henrietta all over: I don't think she was ever afraid of anything. And she'd always plenty to say for herself. She used to be looked after by this nanny named Miss Oakes who was in the Salvation Army; you'd sometimes see Henrietta marching with Miss Oakes and the rest of them, banging a tambourine, which she really disliked. Miss Oakes believed, like a lot of people, that children should be seen and not heard. If Henrietta opened her mouth to say anything, Miss Oakes used to push a ruler into it.

After I'd left the Miss de Sautoys and gone to Keighley Trade and Grammar School, like I told you, I stopped seeing Henrietta every day and walking home with her, and as we got older we stopped going to the Lib and Rad with our dads and she left off

30

going to Sunday League cricket. So we gradually got out of touch and went with other friends – as you do when you're growing up – and we didn't see each other again, really, to speak to until I was almost leaving school and I met up with her that day in Market Row.

Now *this'll* tell you something about how innocent I was in my early teens, though we never called them that. Up till I was nearly fifteen, I knew nothing about girls at all. Oh, I *liked* them well enough – and they seemed to like me. But I looked on them as just good pals, that's all. People in my form at school used to talk about doing this and that to girls, or they'd pass pictures round under the desks, but I thought it was all so crude and ugly, I didn't believe those things really happened. My dad never mentioned the subject to me, and Mother certainly didn't. I knew quite a good few girls in Keighley; I was on good terms with them *and* with their mothers, but it was for friendship, nothing else. We'd write in one another's autograph books: "By hook or by crook I'll be last in this book" sort of thing.

Some of my school pals had got properly smitten by this time like Cowley, who sat next to me in Old Natty's class. He'd left school by now, and gone on to the Technical Institute, so he was that bit more grown up. Every Sunday, he'd get himself all togged out in a cutaway coat and straw boater – lemon spats, even – and go waltzing off down beside the canal, hoping to meet some girl or another on the towpath, which was what we called "sparking". And if he met one and got her to sit down on a park bench with him, and perhaps put his arms around her and managed to give her a little peck on the cheek, that was what we called "spooning".

You could buy these special sweets called Conversation Lozenges to help you get off with a girl if you – or she – were a bit shy. Like hearts shaped of pink sugar they were, each one engraved with a motto: "You are my true love" or "Can you polka?" You'd hand one to a girl, and she might hand you one back: "Blue eyes are my favourite" or "You are somewhat too forward".

But I didn't get involved in all that. For one thing, I was too busy in my studies with Rasch in Leeds and practising on Leo, and my Euclid and Algebra, and all the bike deliveries after school for our shop. Any spare moment I'd got, I'd be going round with Mark and Hector, playing in our little trio.

Another thing I forgot to say was that when I was fourteen, my parents and I moved out of Keighley to a place called Duxford, six or seven miles away. Mother decided she wanted to leave that flat over the shop, so Dad took a house in Duxford named Havelock Villa, which had a big garden attached to it, and three big greenhouses. He'd always liked growing things, and he thought with these greenhouses he could go into tomatoes as a sideline for the shop. That made another job for me, helping look after all the tomato plants, so you can see I'd no time left over for going out spooning and sparking like Cowley.

Now then: it's a few weeks before my fifteenth birthday, in Nineteen-Oh-Seven. I'm going along Manor Row in Keighley, pushing our delivery bike – nothing in it, I've taken all the orders – and who do you think's standing there, outside the Library? That's right, it's Henrietta. She's almost fourteen, and she's turned into a wizard-looking girl. I remember the dress she'd got on – it was light grey velvet, sort of crushed, and she'd a mackintosh cloak on over it. She looked as if she'd stepped right out of a bandbox. And there's me in my old brown shop jacket and my bicycle clips; I felt quite embarrassed bumping into her like that. What I didn't know was that she'd found out I always passed that way going back to the shop, and she'd been waiting for me.

I said "Hello, what are you up to these days?" and she said she was at the Nesta Meacher Academy of Elocution and Dance. I said "I see you've put your hair up" – which she had, though it was still the beautiful dark red it had been when she was little.

"Yes, I did that a month ago,' she said. "Do you like it?"

I said, "It's very nice, but I liked it better when it was long."

Then she looked at me and said, "I hear you've moved and you're living right out in the country."

"That's right," I said. "I am."

"And I hear you've glasshouses," she said. "And a really lovely garden."

"That's right," I said. Because we *did* have a nice garden at Duxford.

"Oh," she said, "I would *love* to see it."

"All right," I said, 'I'll take you home for tea. But first we'll have to go and ask your mother if it's all right."

So I went and saw her mother and made sure it was all right, and we caught the tram together out to Duxford. Now, when I went home, I always used to get off at Duxford Cottage Hospital because you could take a short cut to our house from there, down a sort of little alleyway between the cottage hospital and the Recreation Ground. Well: we've got off the tram, we're half way down this hospital walk, and suddenly Henrietta says, "Oh Arthur, I *am* tired. Do you think we could sit down and rest for a moment?"

"But there's nowhere *to* sit," I said.

"We could sit on the grass under this tree," she said. 'I'll put my cloak down for us in case it's damp." So down we sat on her cloak on the grass.

We're sat there, talking, and after a bit Henrietta says, "I am *cold*, Arthur. Would you put your arm around me?"

"All right, I don't mind," I said. So I put my arm around her. She rested her head on my shoulder.

Then she looked up at me and she said, "Arthur, do you think I'm pretty?"

"Yes," I said. "I do." Because she really was, with all that red hair and those green eyes, and the little beauty spot she had next to her mouth.

Then she started to tell me how, ever since she was a baby, people just couldn't help kissing her. "Everyone's always done it, Arthur," she said, "and they still do. Even the boy who comes to our house on a Wednesday to clean the knives, keeps trying to kiss me."

"Well," I said, "you must get properly fed up with that."

Then she looked at me in this funny way, and said, "That depends."

In a little while we got up, she put on her cloak and we

continued on our way to Havelock Villa, she had tea with us, and a look round the garden and the greenhouses, and then I walked back with her down the hospital walk – past that tree – and I saw her onto the tram back into Keighley.

I thought no more of any of it until about a week later. I heard she'd been talking about me to a friend of hers, and guess what she'd told this friend.

"Arthur Hallett," she said, "is the slowest boy I've *ever* been out with!"

Mother had her way, of course, though I knew Dad would have liked me to carry on in the business – and I knew I'd be quite good at it, too. By the time I was fifteen, I was already a fair provision hand. We were good pals when we worked together, which isn't always so between father and son, and I think in lots of ways I'd have helped him build that business up even better. At about the time I was leaving school, we acquired a second shop premises, a bit smaller, in Fairlight Road just off Cavendish Street. Dad's idea was to have it partly as a grocer's and coffee specialist's and partly an off-licence, selling wines, spirits and bottled beers. To apply for the licence, he had to go before Keighley Magistrates at a thing called Brewster Sessions, and for some reason – I don't know why – they turned his application down. He was really quite upset, and I never liked to say anything about it at the time, but I've always had a funny feeling that if *I'd* gone before the magistrates and asked for that off-sales licence, I'd have got it.

Anyway, Mother was adamant. "Our Artie," she used to say, "will *never* be a grocer." Dad didn't argue. He was disappointed, but he only wanted the best for me, same as Mother.

It was Henrietta's father, Jack Haythornthwaite, who got me my first job, because he was a good pal of Rowntree, the head of the Counting House at Taplow's, and he knew in advance they were looking for a junior in the Foreign Invoice Department. Haythornthwaite recommended me to Rowntree, and that's where I went at eighteen shillings a week.

Taplow's was one of the biggest cotton and silk mills in Keighley, a really huge place, because, you see, most of our mills only used to turn out cotton and silk that was undyed, or what we called "in the griege", but Taplow's was different: it had its own dyeing works and it also manufactured high-class ladies' and gents' hosiery for home and export. So, you can imagine, it was quite a size. And, of course, employed hundreds of people – men, women *and* children. They were called "doffers", the child employees, because of something they'd do with the bobbins on the machines they minded. Every morning, a great crowd of these doffers used to collect outside the gate, all pushing and shoving and shouting out to the overseer, "Me, governor, wilt tha' have me?" Only little mites they could be, seven and eight years old, but desperate for that day's work in the mill because they might be the only breadwinners for their families. I remember, doffers' clothes never had any colour, they were just grey. And they wore wooden clogs that were green with mould.

The Counting House was where all the financial business of the firm got transacted. It was really just one big room partitioned off into various departments, Bought Ledger, Home Sales, Foreign – which was us – and at the end, under a big brass clock, the Comptroller's office, and Cashiers. It was quite an old-fashioned place even for those days. You sat on stools at high wooden desks, and everything had to be written by hand with a J-nib in great old-fashioned red ledgers. When I first went there, they hadn't a typewriter in the place. All down one side were high windows down into a yard where you could see great bales and bundles coming in, that they'd brought by ship into Liverpool then on to Keighley by canal. And, of course, that noise was going on, though you hardly heard it after a time. It was like your own heartbeat: "Ssh-ti-bom-bom."

I was naught but a skivvy at first – just an office boy. I'd to fetch and carry and keep the fire in – which we had in winter: always a coal fire – and run messages for Staples the invoice manager and Peyrôt the foreign correspondent. The firm sent me to night school at Keighley Institute to learn book-keeping and shorthand: I still know all that, dot and dash vowels, hook-n's, and the commercial language, "We are in receipt of yours of the fourteenth inst." I'd to do all the fiddly little jobs like filling inkwells – always Swan's banker's blue-black or fancy writing violet – and keep up the letter copy-book. No typewriters you see, no carbon paper. What you did, when a letter was written you had this big leather book with sheets that were very thin, almost like rice paper. You'd sprinkle some water onto one of these sheets, just enough to damp it, and then lay the letter on top, face down. Then you'd put both into an iron press that tightened with a handle you wound down on a screw thing from the top. You'd screw that down really tight and then unscrew it, and there would be your letter impressed on the rice paper page. But you'd to be careful not to dampen it too much or the ink ran everywhere in little rivulets.

We clericals were quite apart from the mill employees. We came in by a separate entrance and had our own staircase. Most of the Counting House staff hardly had any idea what went on down in the mill. You were supposed to be a cut above "manuals", like the doffers and throwsters. And, of course, our conditions were far superior to theirs. Those doffers worked under terrible hardship, really, and so did the women on the silk side, which was almost entirely female labour. Hundreds of these women you'd see, in great long workrooms lit by green lamps, spitting water from bottles on the silk to keep it moist – young girls, too, though as like as not they'd have babies at home they'd had to leave to come to work. In the morning, some of these girls used to give their babies a lump of sugar soaked in gin, and that would keep the baby quiet until its mother could get home to see to it at dinner-time.

Taplow's had a lot of overseas business. They exported to Belgium, Denmark, Germany – they even exported to Russia. Dyed cotton, baled silk, ladies' and gents' hosiery. When I was made up to foreign clerk, I used to have to write off to all these places like Hamburg, Bremen and Elberfeld. I had to memorise all the commercial terms in German, like "unversichert" – that was "not insured". "Brutto, kiste and hülsen" – with the two little dots – meant "net, gross and tare".

I started off out in the main clerical office, then when I was made foreign invoice clerk they put me in a cubicle with

Peyrôt, the foreign correspondent. He was a Belgian, Henri Peyrôt, spelt P.E.Y.R.Ô.T. with a little cap on the top of the "o". He used to travel all over, seeing clients, getting orders. One week he might be in Brussels – where, I think, his people lived – the next week he might be in Berlin or Malmo or Stockholm. About twice a year, he'd go off to Russia and spend about a month travelling round, seeing clients there. When I was a junior, I used to have to book his rail ticket for him. Liverpool Street to St Petersburg, you could go direct, first class, fifteen pounds, seventeen and six.

He was a typical Belgian was Peyrôt: he wore his hair smarmed down flat and parted in the middle, and he'd got this heavy black moustache with waxed ends, the kind that men used to wrap in a special bandage when they went to bed to stop it getting out of shape during the night. And he had this thick, guttural speaking voice, and a rather rude way with him, though everyone said he was tip-top at getting on with clients. He never went anywhere without a tin of Abdullah in his pocket and his whiff-case full of cigars to offer people he was doing business with. He drew his expenses from Cashiers in *gold*, and he'd a special pass to come in by train every day from Bradford, where he lived.

I never liked him, you may know why presently. At first, I thought it was just because he was so foreign. Everything he said in that thick accent seemed to have a funny edge to it, and he'd stare at you with those great bulging eyes. Being Belgian, he ate a lot of onions and that wasn't nice either when he'd lean across my desk to tell me something, though he tried to hide it by sucking violet cachous. I remember the whites of his eyes, how grubby they were, and the bits of dinner that used to cling to his moustache. He'd go out every day at twelve sharp and wouldn't come back till past three and when he did, nine times out of ten, he'd be as tight as a tick. He'd just sit there for the rest of the afternoon, smelling of violet cachous and wiping his moustache and his ears.

Mind, I never said anything. He was the foreign correspondent and I was only a junior. But I made up a little poem about him, and I'd say it under my breath:

His legs are bowed and that may be
From holding up the beer, you see.

Nineteen Hundred and Ten, I'm talking about now, that was when they made me up from office boy. Then there was Nineteen-Eleven, when the King died: we all went into deep mourning for that. And no entertainment or music, other than devotional, anywhere until about a month after his funeral. Everyone felt genuinely cut up because he'd been a popular chap, our old King Teddy, though, of course, nothing at all like his mother. I expect you've heard what a devil he used to be for the ladies. While he was Prince of Wales and when he was King too, he'd be off philandering with all these Society women, whether they were married or not didn't make any difference. But everybody liked him because he seemed such a good sport, and he lived so well. And he'd not have been there to be crowned if my Aunt Bertha hadn't got hold of his beard and sat him up on the operating-table.

Then in Nineteen-Twelve we had the Coronation of King George, who seemed a nice enough chap, too; mark you, he'd been in the Navy for years. And his son was our future Edward the Eighth, who abdicated. I'll tell you a story my mother used to tell me about him, when he was a little boy and having lunch with his father and King Teddy one day at Buckingham Palace. If the King was talking, as you can expect, everyone else was supposed to be quiet, but this little boy would keep piping up, "Grandpa, Grandpa . . ." So King Teddy looked at him and he said – firmly, you know, but quite nicely – "You mustn't interrupt me while I'm talking. Wait a moment." So he finished what he was saying, then he turned to his little grandson and said, "Now, what was it you wanted to say?" And the little boy said, "I was going to tell you there was a caterpillar on your lettuce Grandpa, but it's all right, you've eaten it now."

Mr Rowntree thought a lot of me, so did Mr Steggles, the Comptroller, but if I'm honest my mind was never really on those foreign invoices, fee notes and bills of lading. All I really wanted to be doing was playing Leo, my violin. When I used to put him back into his case in the morning, after my hour's practice, I used to think to myself "Only another eight hours before I can fetch Leo out again." I used to take bits of music in the Counting House with me and hum or la-la them over to myself while I was running up and down columns of figures or writing off to clients in Bremen and Elberfeld – it used to drive Peyrôt, our foreign correspondent, mad. I'd sometimes even mix up my music score with my shorthand exercises. Honour bright, I wouldn't remember if a curve on a bit of paper was a bass clef or a "th" short form.

After I left school, I kept up that little trio with my two pals Hector Leading and Mark Stillwell. Then Hector's father told him he'd to forget music for a bit and study for his surveyor's exams, so Mark and I joined an amateur orchestra called Lord and Fletcher's, which had quite a good reputation in and around Keighley. This one man named Lord was the conductor, and did all the arrangements. He could take a new piece, go home, write out all the parts and have them ready for us to practise the next day. "Lord will provide," we younger ones, who were a bit cheeky, used to say. Fletcher was the first violin. When I first joined, I was his "repet", which meant Leo and I just played thirds – all the bottom line – and I'd turn the page over for him, or if he broke a string I'd change it for him and lend him Leo to carry on with meantime.

When we joined Lord and Fletcher's, of course, it was no more Eton jackets. I'd to get myself a suit of evening clothes made at Bateson's Bespoke Tailors in High Coniscliffe. Three guineas it cost me, made to measure, four fittings, a beautiful suit with satin-faced lapels and a silk lining to the coat. And I asked them to put in a special little inside pocket, where I could keep a bit of rosin for my bow.

We thought we were really moving up, did Mark and I, sitting in Lord and Fletcher's in our dinner suits and our boiled shirts and dickey-bows. We did a big subscription dance in Keighley Public Rooms every Wednesday and, every other Saturday, an Olde Tyme Dance at the Mechanics' Institute, so I'd to learn all the Olde Tyme things, the Velita, the Boston Twostep, the Gay Gordons, "Bladon Races". Another thing we did with Lord and Fletcher's was play selections at the Town

Hall for Groom's Crippled Girls. This troop of girls, who were all disabled, used to travel round the country giving displays of how to make artificial flowers. People would pay to go in and watch, have refreshments and listen to Lord and Fletcher's Orchestra playing "Orpheus" or "Tales from the Vienna Woods".

After that day I took Henrietta home to see our garden, we started walking out together. But . . . I wonder if I can explain this to you. It was never really quite like that with Henrietta and me. We'd very seldom make what you'd call a date with each other. It was more like, I'd meet her on a Saturday afternoon in Cavendish. I'd say "Are you going up or down?" She'd say "down" and I'd say "Well, I'm going up." And she'd most likely say, "All right then, I'll go up as well."

I'd sit for hours, puzzling over why I acted with her the way I did. I knew she was the prettiest girl round our way, and there were any number of boys who'd have given their eye teeth just to walk with her round the Jubilee Bandstand. But, for some reason, back when we were little at the Misses de Sautoy, she'd decided I was the one. She made no bones about it either, which was unusual for a girl in those times. I've told you how she'd follow me round that garden and how she waited for me that other day in Manor Row. I liked it and expected it, but there was something in me – I'll never know what – that always fought against it. I'd say I was going up Cavendish when I was going down, or pretend I'd got appointments with girls far less pretty than she was. For a long time I made this whole pretence about writing to a girl named Chocolate Alice, who worked in the sweets kiosk at the station and had a black tooth in the front on the left.

Everyone who'd seen her in our little local shows said she could easily have been another Vesta Tilley or Marie Lloyd. Her tutor at Nesta Meacher's wrote her people a note, *begging* them to let him use his influence to get her started in the profession. But Jack Haythornthwaite wouldn't have it. Stage people were thought low, you see. Her father said she could finish up at Nesta Meacher's but then she'd got to get a proper job of work. She'd found a job in a ladies' gown shop, run by a woman named Mignon who was a proper tartar, honestly! If one of the girls in the shop was fitting a gown and she did something this woman Mignon didn't like, "rip" would go the whole sleeve: she'd wrench it straight off, or rend the gown all open down the back. Ooh, she was an article!

Henrietta used to pour all this out to me because I sympathised: we had that love of the stage in common. If it was warm, we used to go into the Jubilee Gardens and sit in a shelter by the Canoe Lake, and she'd tell me all about Mignon's funny little ways and how much she hated selling ladies' gowns.

"They think they've beaten me, Arthur," she used to say. "But they've not. I'll show them all one day. I'll pay them all out."

Then, if we were all alone in this shelter, she'd turn and look at me and say, "I like you better than the knife-boy, Arthur," meaning she wanted me to kiss her, like the knife-cleaning boy had tried to. Which was when things used to get a bit difficult. Because I knew she wanted me to do things other than kiss her, and I never would. Call it the way I'd been brought up. I didn't want to encourage her into something she might regret. I was a romantic, you see – still am! A lot of the time, Henrietta'd not wait for me to make a move. *She'd* be the one to catch hold of my hand or put her arms round my neck. And, lovely as she was, that strange something in me always made me want to pull away.

Now then. We've come to the year Nineteen-Twelve – and a red-letter day in my life. If you've got another minute, I'll tell you what happened on that red-letter day, Wednesday, October the twenty-sixth, Nineteen Hundred and Twelve.

It's a nasty wet afternoon and I'm sitting in our cubicle at the mill: Peyrôt's out. I'm just dotting the i's on a long invoice to Berlin, written in three different coloured inks, when Miss Proudfoot, from Rowntree's office, puts her head round the door and says I'm wanted privately on the telephone. Well, that was quite unusual, and I thought it must be bad news, about my mother's health or Dad's business or something. So I go along to Mr Rowntree's office, the outer office where the telephone is, and I put the receiver to my ear a bit nervously.

"Hello – Mr Arthur Hallett?" this very nice, educated voice says. "I'm speaking from the Palace Theatre. This is Lambert Hartnell, the Musical Director."

"Oh yes," I said – because, of course, I knew Lambert Hartnell. "What can I do for you Mr Hartnell?"

"I'm in a bit of a scrape," Lambert Hartnell says, "and I'm hoping you can help me out of it."

Then he tells me the third violin in the Palace orchestra has gone down with double pneumonia and pleurisy, and they're urgently needing a sub for the next fortnight's bill with George Lashwood.

"I've heard about you from Fletcher of Lord and Fletcher's," Mr Hartnell says, "and I'm wondering if you could come in and sub for me as third violin and repet?"

Can you imagine what went through my mind? Me, Arthur Hallett, playing in the pit at Keighley Palace! *Me*, playing for George Lashwood on the Number One Circuit!

"I'd need you full time for a fortnight," Mr Hartnell says. "I'll pay you the rate. And I'll esteem it a personal kindness, Mr Hallett."

"Well . . . I'd like to," I said, and honestly, I could hear my voice trembling. "But do you think I'd be all right?"

"Fletcher says you're first rate," Mr Hartnell says. "And that's good enough for me. Just be here first thing Monday morning for band-call, when we run through everything."

"All right, Mr Hartnell," I said. "I'll do it."

So that's what happened. I saw Mr Steggles and arranged to take my next summer's holiday in advance, and I went and subbed for a fortnight as third violin and repet in the orchestra at Keighley Palace: two houses a night and a matinée Wednesday and Saturday.

You can guess, my heart was in my mouth a bit, that next Monday, when I'd to take Leo along and meet Lambert Hartnell and be put through our paces in front of the whole orchestra *and* company. But Mr Hartnell was very nice: he saw me in the Manager's office first and we agreed terms, then he took me through to the pit to meet his leader, a man called Childers, and Bull, the second violin, and all the rest of them.

My stars! that *was* an orchestra: he'd three violins, viola, 'cello, double bass, oboe, bassoon, clarinet, flute, French horn, trombone, tuba, two trumpets, cornet, full percussion with timpani – but no piano. Mr Hartnell could play – very well – but he'd got it all balanced up so that he could do without. And there was a lady harpist, from Edinburgh, named Miss Flora Patiniot.

Well, all the orchestra were as nice as could be when Mr Hartnell introduced me, and then he sat me at the desk between Childers, the leader, and this other man, Bull, and we ran through the overture, which was a really lovely thing called "Petite Suite Moderne". It had a slow movement that was a flute solo, with the violins pizzicato. Leo and I seemed to keep our end up there all right, and I turned the pages over for Childers. Our second set piece, after the intermission, was "The Dream of Olwen", which I knew well from doing it with Lord and Fletcher's: in fact, Mr Hartnell used Lord's own arrangement. So that went very well; then we had a break for ten minutes and Mr Hartnell took me out into the gangway and he said, "You'll more than suit us, old man. Welcome to our abode."

Then at eleven sharp, the company start to come in, and my eyes are popping now, because these are big people to me. They'd arrived on the Sunday and spent the night in their various digs, which every town had a lot of, especially on the Number One Circuit. Lashwood and the other top turns stayed at the Royal, of course. The rest stayed in various private hotels and boarding houses that specialised in putting up stage people. But, whoever they were, at eleven sharp, they'd to be at the theatre for band-call.

First off, it was the Corps de Ballet, all these really lovely girls up on the stage in their everyday clothes, and holding little muffs because the theatre was quite cold. The leading girl comes down and hands their book to Mr Hartnell and she says, 'We'll be doing number two, six and eight." You see, every turn carried a book of all the musical pieces they all wanted played, and wrote in special notes and reminders for cues. So for the Ballet piece, you'd make a note like "Dance, four in the bar, watch coryphee" – that's leading girl – "for change". The drummer always got a lot of special cues, like "long roll when Chinese slide down wire by pigtail" or "snap snare when four balls go up at once".

So that was what Music Hall people called their books. And it was a strict rule of the profession that every turn had to provide a part for every member of the orchestra. On that first morning I remember quite a famous soprano – it might have been Miss Ada Colley – came out on the stage and said to Mr Hartnell, "I've only the piano part for this, Maestro, but it's a well-known song – I'm sure your gentleman and lady will know it." Mr Hartnell looked up at her and he said, "Madam, if there isn't a part for everyone, the thing doesn't get played." That was the rule you see, and besides, Hartnell could be a bit of a terror with artistes. Bull, the second violin, told me he'd got so disgusted with an eccentric dancer once, Hartnell had, that he'd just stopped the orchestra and thrown this man's book up on the stage.

I only wish I could describe to you how it felt, that opening Monday night, to be sitting in the pit at the Keighley Palace, tuning up Leo with that wizard fourteen-piece orchestra, looking all around at the stalls, the dress circle, the boxes, hearing that lovely hubbubby noise of the first house coming in. I could see Mother – Mr Hartnell had arranged a special fauteuil for her, where she could get in and out easily. And Dad was there, so were Henrietta and her parents, so were Mark and Sidney and quite a few from the mill: Mr and Mrs Steggles, the Rowntrees, Miss Proudfoot. All to see me in my professional debut. I could hear them calling "Overture and beginners" behind the curtain, and all the ballet girls laughing and chattering, and there was a gap along the bottom where you could see these feet in little coloured pumps running to and fro. And all the gold tassels on the red velvet were shining and shivering, and the folds of it were sort of billowing out as if there were a great strong wind behind, that could hardly wait to get free.

Then our red light goes on for the start of the overture. The house lights go to half. Up comes Lambert Hartnell – great applause – he bows to the audience, then to us. His baton's up;

we're off with a great roll on the timps, then Leo's against my cheek, my eyes go down, I've forgotten everything but that bottom line, those thirds and fifths, and turning over the page for Childers. Next thing I know, we're through the pizzicato movement and not one slip-up: everyone's clapping like mad. Then the house goes pitch-dark. The footlights go on through the curtain. A bell rings to warn us; up shoot the tabs – there's the Corps de Ballet on their village green. What I'll never forget is the great gust of cool air I felt billow against my face, all scented with greasepaint and perfume and rouge and feathered dresses and pomade.

It was a tip-top show, I'll tell you. They started with that lovely chorale – "Poet and Peasant" – then they'd a troupe of French midgets, Les Frères Robert, all in blue and gold tights, doing somersaults over a camel's back. I mean a real live camel, not stuffed! They'd got it stabled in the motor garage behind the Royal Hotel. These Frenchmen led it on, put springboards either side of it, then one of them would jump on his springboard and send his mate somersaulting over this camel's back to land on *his* mate's shoulders. Just like little blue and gold balls they were, bouncing to and fro. The camel just stood there, perfectly docile, though they couldn't stop it doing quite a lot of its business on the stage. Before the next turn, a stagehand had to come out with a big shovel and pick it all up.

Then, let me see, Fong and His Flags came after Les Frères Robert; then it was Tillotson, Eccentric Dancer, then the Musical Siddells, who were father, mother and two daughters. Between them they'd mastered about twenty different musical instruments: tuba, cornet, trumpet, trombone . . . I forget them all. Flute, recorder, clarinet. The father finished up in a Scottish kilt, playing the bagpipes and blowing up a balloon at the same time from one of the pipes. And he'd these miniature bagpipes he put on his fingers and played like penny whistles. Then it was Miss Ada Colley – I told you about her, didn't I, and what a wigging Mr Hartnell gave her at band-call? But I must say, her voice was thoroughly exquisite.

All this was wonderful to me, because in the orchestra-pit, I'd the best seat in the house. I could see those little French chaps'

faces, and their eyes shut tight as they went flying to and fro . . .
it made you quite giddy looking up at them.

Then there was Bryn, who was a strong man, sort of a
Eugene Sandow type. Really, an enormous chap, with a great
broad chest and huge muscular arms. He'd got his head shaved,
with a black topknot like the young men wear it nowadays, and
he'd a little black moustache he used to wax into two sharp
points. He came on in a tiger – or it may have been a leopard –
skin, and a collar with metal studs in it round his neck and
thongs round his legs. Some of the women used to scream, he
looked that ferocious. "Bryn the Terrible", his billing was.
He'd lift up these heavy barbells, or bend railway spikes or
break a chain against his chest just by puffing it out. He'd got
this real cannon, a field piece, like they fetch out for the
Queen's birthday, and he'd stoop down and hoist the whole
thing up on his back as if it were just a featherweight. Down-
stage, he'd got a pile of about six cannon-balls – great lumps
of lead shot – and for a finale, he'd throw each one of these
cannon-balls up in the air and then catch it on his neck at the
back. I remember what a smack each one of these great lumps
of shot made against his flesh when it came down.

The second intermission was quite long, because they'd a
special bit of scenery to put up for Lashwood. Then came our
second set piece, "The Dream of Olwen", Lord and Fletcher's
arrangement, so I was quite all right. Then a few bits and
bobs of dancers and a mandolinist: nothing too good in case it
spoiled Lashwood's entrance, which was what we called "front
of curtain". They lowered the Intermission curtain that was
covered with adverts for the big town shops like Battersby's,
and for Haig whisky and Epps's Cocoa and Apollinaris table
waters. The lights went up to half, and out came Lashwood in
his silk hat and cloak, with gloves and silver-topped cane, just
ambling along as if he'd happened to stroll in off the street. In
our running-order it said "Loquitur, 8 mins", which meant no
cues for us for eight minutes. We could settle back and enjoy it
like everyone else.

I don't suppose you've even heard of George Lashwood, have
you? You'll have to take my word for it that in those days –

Nineteen Hundred and Twelve – he was as big a draw as you could get on the Number One Circuit. It's hard for me to describe to you what he did because when you thought about it, it didn't seem much. He talked a bit and sang a bit, and screwed this monocle he had into his eye, or sometimes let it drop out. He'd just got a sort of way with him that people in those times really loved. He'd stand there and . . . well, sort of chat to you about the way the world was, or sometimes chat about it to the Musical Director – who he called "Maestro", of course – or to somebody you couldn't see in the wings. Whatever he said, even if he was just pulling his gloves on and whistling a little tune, which he sometimes did, you could have heard a pin drop in that house. After a little while, he'd make a signal to someone in the wings, and one of the ballet girls would come out with a cup of tea and hand it to Lashwood, and he'd just go on chatting and sipping his tea. It was all so natural, people thought it was just champion.

Our next cue was when Lashwood said, "Now my friends, I must return to the scenes of my boyhood." Up went all the adverts for Haig whisky and Polly, and there was Lashwood's own special bit of scenery, painted like an Elizabethan manor house, beautifully done with towers and battlements and hedges cut in the shape of birds and animals, and a maze. Then he'd sing a song he'd made quite famous, entitled "Where Are the Lads of the Village Tonight?" I could play it for you now, *and* sing it. It's about a traveller who returns to the scenes of his boyhood and finds that all the young men have gone off to fight in the wars. Of course, in those days most people never imagined there really *could* be a war, and young men really *would* have to go off to fight, and never come back. It was just a song you heard on the Halls.

Well, those two weeks just flew! Every time I walked in through that stage-door in Tarrant Place, I felt I was walking on air! Two houses a night, and a matinée on Wednesday and Saturday. Between houses I hadn't time to get all the way home to Duxford and back, so I used to put Leo in the safe in Mr Hopper the manager's office and go for a cup of cocoa round at Henrietta's.

They used to say on the Halls that if the limelight ever once fell on you, you were lost. That's what must have happened to me, because when Lashwood came to the front of the stage for the last verse of "Where Are the Lads", a bit of his limelight always fell into the orchestra-pit. I'd expected it to be green, but it was a sort of bluey colour. Do you know what I'm talking about when I say "limelight"? *Real* limelight that they used to shed from the wings, out of a brass cylinder. Terribly dangerous, too, it was because the lime had to be kept under intense pressure. There was a man killed by it once at Keighley station. This porter was carrying a cylinder across the line and he dropped it, and blew his head off.

And, of course, I got to know quite a few of the company, like Tillotson, who was a Lancastrian, and Fong and the Miss Siddells. I even spoke a word or two of French to the Frères Robert, which tickled them. Lashwood was a bit standoffish, being so big. He'd sit in the bar of the Royal every morning in lavender spats and drink a bottle of Pol Roger champagne on his own. And he ate nothing but game. They said at the Royal he'd send down to the kitchens at all hours for partridges on toast or a bit of guinea fowl.

He was a bit standoffish, as I say, but Bryn the strong man was a really lovely chap. You'd have thought he was ferocious to look at him, in all those leather thongs and chains, and those huge muscles, but really you couldn't have found a nicer, gentler person. He travelled round everywhere with his mother. He used to say she was the only one he could trust to shave his head without cutting him. Little tiny thing she was, next to that great hulking man. He'd kneel down in front of her and change her shoes for her, or rub her feet if they were cold.

"I think the world of her," Bryn used to say, "and I know she's only ever going to do me harm once in my life. That's when she goes away and leaves me."

So you can guess what a letdown it was at the end of those two weeks, when Mr Hartnell's regular repet was fit again, and I'd to go back to work in Taplow's Counting House, making out invoices and seeing to the foreign ledgers. Up to then, I'd enjoyed my job and got on well with the people I worked with, but, oh dear . . . that first Monday morning back, seeing the mill and the doffers, and going in with everyone climbing up those stairs. It was a letdown: that's the only word for it.

I found I'd become a bit of a celebrity, because nearly everyone had been in to see Lashwood and have a look at me in the orchestra pit. I'd quite a crowd round me, asking all about what Lashwood was like and what Miss Ada Colley was like, and when Mr Steggles came in he shouted out "Where's our young Maestro?" They all gave me such a welcome and were so interested, I felt quite guilty not being glad I was back. But I wasn't. I felt lost. That limelight had got into my blood, you see.

Still, I'd no idea of leaving – and I wouldn't have, I think, but for a rather nasty thing. I'll tell you if you've got another minute, though I've not spoken about it to anyone since it happened. I didn't tell my parents at the time. I never even told Delia.

You remember I mentioned Eugene Peyrôt the foreign correspondent, who was Belgian, and the trips he used to take to Russia and all over? The one I shared the little cubicle with? Well: when I first got back, Peyrôt had gone away to Malmo or somewhere, and I didn't clap eyes on him for about another fortnight. I came in from my dinner one day and there he was, feet up on his desk, with that big moustache and those two little waxy curls on his forehead. He didn't once ask me how I'd got on; it was just "Oh, you're bloody back, are you?" I took no notice because that was the way he'd always been with everybody.

What with me having been off for two weeks, a lot of work had piled up, which meant I'd to stay late almost every night, until nine or ten o'clock sometimes, to get it all done. Oh, it was murder! Sitting in that cubicle, adding columns of figures, reckoning gross and tare, and all the time thinking what they'd be doing down at the Palace, Mr Hartnell coming up and bowing, and the bell for the Overture! I'd sit there nearly grinding my teeth, I was so frustrated.

On this particular evening, I'm still there at about half past nine . . . thinking "Time for the second intermission". I suddenly hear footsteps on the stairs and in walks Peyrôt. He'd been off all day with some Liverpool buyers, so I knew straight off what to expect: he'd be the worse for drink. And I was right. You could smell the ale as soon as he opened the door.

"Oh, hello," I said. "Forgotten something?" And I just went on with my figures, thinking he'd be straight in and out because, as I told you, he lived nine miles away, in Bradford. The firm gave him a special pass on the railway to come back and forth.

I'm holding my breath until he's gone, so as not to smell the ale, but he doesn't go. He sits down at his desk, still in his hat and coat, and puts his feet up, among the papers, same as always. Doesn't say anything; just sits there, staring across at me and breathing in this funny sort of asthmatic way, and I'm looking down at my ledger and thinking "What on earth's the fellow up to?"

After a moment or two of that, he slams his feet down and gets up and comes over and stands next to me. He makes out as if he's looking down my column of figures but, really, he's so much in drink, he seems scarcely able to stand upright. He sort of staggers, and puts one hand on my shoulder to steady himself. But when he *is* steady, he doesn't take his hand away again. It's still there, resting on my shoulder.

Then he starts talking to me about how much the firm values him, which I knew they did, and how he was the only one allowed to draw his expenses from Cashiers in gold. He stood there, leaning over me, talking about all the sovereigns he's got in his money belt, and now his hand's moved off my shoulder and it's fiddling and twiddling with my neck at the back, and I don't know what to say, because he *is* my senior, and I think to myself, "He might be just being friendly in a Continental way." But then he says, if I like, he'll show me his money-belt. "*Do* you like?" he said . . . *Do* you like? and starts to unbutton his trousers.

Then, of course, I understood what was happening: I jumped up and said, "Now Mr Peyrôt, there's no need for this."

That put him in a rage, and he came up to me, grabbed my

coat lapels and forced me back across the room, right up against the table where all the foreign ledgers were, and the letter-copying book. And he's shouting things in Belgian *and* English and saying he'll bloody well show me, and all this foul breath is fanning in my face, till I think I'm going to faint. He's got me against the table and then he reaches behind me – and I find I can't move, I'm trapped. What he'd done, he'd gathered up my coat tail and put it in the press we used for impressing letters in the letter-copy book, and then he'd screwed down the vice on it so it'd pinion me there.

I'm trying to fend him off, but he's a big, powerful man . . . and he's started to interfere with my trousers as I'm caught there, and he's mumbling all kinds of obscenities, "Let's see what you've got" sort of thing . . .

Luckily for me, there was somebody else in the Counting House, a man named Norton, on the Home Sales side, who I'd not realised was there as well, working late. I must have cried out, though I can't remember doing so: anyway, this man Norton came running in to investigate and saw what was happening. Peyrôt tried to make light of it, but this man Norton wasn't a fool . . . he'd sized the situation up. He gave Peyrôt a look as if he was ready to knock him down, and pushed him away and freed my coat-tail from the letter-copy press. Then he looked at Peyrôt. "The first thing tomorrow morning," he said, "I'm going straight to Mr Rowntree the Comptroller, and I'm going to lay this whole matter before him."

Peyrôt wasn't dismissed. No, they kept him on and the whole business was hushed up. He made the excuse to Mr Rowntree that he'd been in drink, and he promised, on his mother's grave – those were his words – that such a thing would never, ever happen again. He was so tip-top at his job they were frightened some other mill would snap him up, so he got let off with a severe reprimand. I could have brought charges, but it'd have meant bringing scandal on the firm and on my dad and our shop. So when Mr Rowntree asked if I'd forget the matter, I agreed. The worst thing about it was, Peyrôt and I had to go on working together in that tiny cubicle. He never made any reference afterward to what had happened. But as long as we worked together after, he'd never speak direct to me or look at me in the eye.

So that wasn't very nice, having to go on sharing a room under those circumstances, and feeling as restless and discontent as I did after that wonderful time at Keighley Palace. One moment I felt I'd ascended to the heights; another, I'd fallen down in a pit of serpents and slime. And to make it worse, three or four times a day, I had to get up in front of Peyrôt and go across and use that same letter-copying press.

Well, the months wear away. I'm still a foreign invoice clerk and walking out with Henrietta. Folk are even starting to ask when we're going to *do* something, which meant get engaged. But I'd always quickly change the subject. You can believe this or not, but it's God's honest truth. I'd a sort of premonition that a very important event was going to happen soon, and I mustn't be tied down to anything or anyone.

And I was right. Something did happen ... have you got another moment to listen?

One Saturday afternoon – this is Nineteen-Thirteen – I'm on my way up Cavendish to meet Henrietta, and I bump into Lord, of Lord and Fletcher's Orchestra.

"Hallett, I've been looking all over for you," he said. "I've had an urgent wire from an agent pal of mine who books for Codlin's Amusements in Llandudno, North Wales. They're wanting a light orchestral trio to play in their Chinese Café, a twelve-week season starting Whit weekend, and my pal's wired me to see if I can recommend anyone. I thought of you straight away, because I know you don't feel that suited in your present work."

Well! It was like an answer to a prayer!

"Mr Lord," I said. "I'll go if I have to sleep in a deck-chair on the promenade." And that's how I turned professional.

I forgot about my appointment with Henrietta, and went straight off and found my two friends, Mark Stillwell the 'cellist and Hector Leading the pianist, to see if they'd make up that same little trio we'd had before.

Mark said right away he'd come – he didn't care for his job

overmuch either. But Hector couldn't. He'd got a good situation at Banks, the surveyors, and he said his father'd never stand for his giving it up.

For a bit I thought, "I'm snookered." I'd got to have a pianist if I was to take on the engagement. Then Mark said he'd heard there was a very good pianist at Keighley Picture House in Salter Street, which at that time hadn't long opened. I ran straight over there and sent in word I'd like to speak to this man when he'd got a moment. I waited at the side door and, in between performances, this tall, sandy-haired chap, quite young, came out, smoking a cigarette.

I'd got no time to shilly-shally around. I went straight up to him and I said, "How would you like to spend the summer in Llandudno?"

This chap took the cigarette out of his mouth and thought for a moment. Then he said, "I *would* like a change." So this was it: my trio formed.

Ooh, but my dad played pop with me when I told him and Mother I'd handed in my notice at Taplow's, and what I was going to be doing. He looked at me – I can see him now, across the tea table at our house in Duxford, his moustache-cup in his hand, his expression quite thunderstruck. It was hurtful to him you see, having worked so hard to give me a first-rate education and a decent start in life: he thought I was plain daft to be chucking in my position and prospects just for a hobby, which was how he saw it.

"But how are you going to *live*?" he kept saying.

"I'm to get a guinea a week," I said. And I showed him the letter I'd got from Codlin's, confirming it.

Poor Dad: I don't think he believed it, even then. But he shook his head, and took a swallow of tea, and then he said, "It's your life, Arthur my boy. You're old enough to do what you want. And whatever happens, you know you can always come back here and be sure of a good business and a good name."

And Mother gave my hand a squeeze under the table, and I could tell what *she* was thinking. She'd said it in front of Dad so often, "Artie will *never* be a grocer."

It was almost panic stations, because they wanted the three of us for Whit, in less than a month's time, and we'd not even had a rehearsal yet *and* I didn't know whether this new chap would fit in, having taken him sight unseen. Dudley Ramage, his name was. Luckily, he was a nice player and a very nice chap, and highly educated. He'd been to Oxford University, and he'd travelled the world to all these exotic places like Japan and Siam. He could have entered politics, he'd such a keen mind. But music was all he cared about. So he'd taken this job at Keighley Picture Palace and, luckily for me, was just starting to feel like a change.

So we rehearsed with Mark, and that went well – we rehearsed in the Committee Room at the Lib and Rad – and I got together all the pieces I'd collected and that Rasch my teacher had given me, because we'd to play two hours each evening in this Chinese Café, and I was worried we'd not have enough things. Dudley Ramage gave me the tip that there was a firm called Goldman's Music Lending Library, up in South Shields, that you could write off to and hire pieces at one-and-six each. So I wrote off to them: Goldman's Music Lending Library, 42 Maritime Parade, South Shields. And on top of everything, I'd to work out my notice at Taplow's, which I tried to do conscientiously.

What with the excitement, and then having to get straight on and rehearse with Hector and this new man, Dudley Ramage, I'd not had a chance to tell Henrietta about it, or even explain why I hadn't kept my appointment with her, that Saturday when I bumped into Lord. She heard of it from her father first, which made her quite upset, though I didn't expect her to be, because up to then she'd been so keen for me to get on with my music. Did I tell you that she came into the Palace every night, both houses, while Lashwood was on, to watch me play and tell me what she thought about it? *And* she'd wait for me between houses, to walk round to her house for my cocoa and arrowroot biscuit.

"So I shan't see you for over two months," she said. I remember, we were on the number 7 tram and I was just getting off to go and rehearse at the Lib and Rad with Mark and Dudley Ramage.

"Well," I said, "you could always come up to Llandudno. I've heard it's very nice."

"Will you write while you're away?" she said.

"Oh yes," I said. "I'll send you plenty of postcards," and I got off then at the corner by Battersby's because I was so eager, I couldn't wait for the stop at the Guildhall. I didn't realise how upset she was. She was just a part of Keighley to me, and home and routine and all that. I thought, "Whenever I come back, Henrietta will always be here."

We went up on a Sunday afternoon. We'd to go by train to Preston first, then change there on to the Connaught Flier, along with a whole great gang of Music Hall people who were going to engagements that week in Llandudno. We saw Nellie Wallace *and* George Robey both get on at Preston – and I believe we saw Little Tich. Llandudno was Number One Circuit, you see, being a tip-top holiday place. The Connaught Flier wasn't meant to stop at Llandudno Junction, but on a Sunday, as it went through, it used to slow right down so that all these artistes could hop off with their cases and hampers and whatnot.

So . . . who do you think hops off the Connaught Flier alongside George Robey and Little Tich and all of them, on the Sunday before Whit week, Nineteen Hundred and Thirteen? That's right. The Arthur Hallett Trio, with our valises, and Leo, don't forget him, two umbrellas, a walking-stick and Mark's 'cello case.

At Llandudno Junction, we'd to get on a little train that ran round the coast about six or seven miles to Llandudno proper. Oh, and it was a lovely hot sunny day . . . Royal weather. And such excitement to see the sea and smell that air. We'd pulled our window right down to the first notch on the strap, and we could hear all the artistes talking and the ballet girls laughing in the other carriages, and smell the cigars and Turkish cigarettes . . . and the water truly did look glorious. Then we came round a bit of a curve, and there was Llandudno . . . the Great Orme, and the Grand Hotel . . . the pier! Mark and this man Dudley Ramage and I looked at each other and we said "Well! This is really A1."

Then we came into the station and that was quite a pande-monium because, on Sundays when this particular train arrived with the Music Hall artistes, all the theatrical landladies in the town used to be at the ticket-barrier, waiting on people who'd booked in with them – or, if they'd still got vacancies, hoping to snap up a few who weren't suited yet. A chap I met later on at Barnsley Hippodrome gave me a good tip to remember if ever I was stuck for digs and a gang of these theatrical landladies were at the station. "Look for the one in the cleanest apron," this chap said. "If she's got a clean apron, chances are she'll keep a clean kitchen and a clean house."

Codlin's Amusements, who'd booked us, ran a big place at Scarborough, one at Morecambe, and they were just starting up in North Wales, in Prestatyn and Llandudno. The place they'd engaged us for, The Arcadia, was brand-new – in fact when we arrived, just before Whit Week, they'd not even quite finished building it. There were still workmen on the forecourt with stone things in long wooden rods, smoothing the marble down.

Mind, it was a handsome place, sort of like a conservatory . . . great big tall windows . . . long blue and white sun-blinds . . . lawns all round it, with palm trees and exotic shrubs. And they'd a roof garden. When Codlin's did anything like that, they spared no expense. But what we couldn't understand was why they'd put it so far along the seafront, right away from the pier and the Great Orme and all the other theatres and halls. We found out why, later. Codlin's had been told by someone on the Town Council that there was to be a second pier built right here, around the bay, and they'd built The Arcadia slap-bang where this second pier was meant to go up – which, unfortunately, it never did. So the poor Arcadia finished up high and dry.

I'd said I'd sleep in a deck chair on the prom – well, I wasn't obliged to do that. Codlin's had booked the three of us in with a Mrs Lewis in Hillcrest Road, a very nice place just near the bottom of the Great Orme, two minutes from the sea. We had a big room at the top with a view over the pier and right round the bay. Separate beds, we had; breakfast and evening meal and our washing done, all for eight shillings a week.

Have you been to Llandudno ever? It's a champion place . . . leastwise, it used to be. Remember, I've not laid eyes on it since before the Fourteen War. Oh, but it was wizard then. Beautiful sands, and that magnificent promenade . . . and the Great Orme. Let me see, how can I describe that? It's a rock, sort of a big headland, with paths and stairways cut into it, and botanical gardens, and a funicular railway you could catch from the top. There's the Great Orme at one end of the shore, and right round the bay near Prestatyn, there's the Little Orme. And the funny thing is, the Little Orme always looks the bigger of the two.

They'd a fine pier as well, which had this famous hotel, The Grand, standing right on it at the shore end, under the Orme. It was a castle – honour bright! – standing on its own crags, with towers and turrets and battlements and flags flying. Then you'd got this pretty little pier, we could see from our bedroom window, with blue and white pagodas on either side of it. At the end, you could take a steamer and go a day-trip to Liverpool. I'll always remember the name of the steamer that used to put in there. It was called "La Marguerite".

Mrs Lewis wasn't really a theatrical landlady, but a lot of people who were with Codlin's for the season stayed with her, like Charles Eady, the under-manager, and Mr Raoul, the mâitre-d'hotel. But she took other boarders as well. There was a man named Warren, who took stickybacks on the promenade. Sort of quick photographs they were, we called them stickybacks. There was a man named Drew, who did lightning sketches, funnily enough, and a real character named Carstairs Copping, who ran a troupe of minstrels on the sands. He stopped with Mrs Lewis every year. I remember, he always said the same thing to her in the evening when he came in to high tea. His troupe were called The Magnets, you see, and their great rivals were The Golliwogs. They were always at war with another, these Magnets and Golliwogs, trying to snaffle the best pitch and take the crowds away from one another. And every evening, when Carstairs Copping came in he'd take off his straw hat and shy it onto the hallstand, and he'd shout in this great booming voice, "Mrs Lewis, Ma'am! The Magnets have beaten The Golliwogs into a cocked hat!"

The Chinese Café, where we'd to play, was on the top floor of The Arcadia. A tea-room was what it was, really, though you could have morning coffee there, or little savouries on toast or oysters and brown bread and butter. But the big thing was the one-and-threepenny set teas. They'd done it all up to look Chinese, with pink silk hangings and paper lanterns, and all the crockery Willow Pattern. The dais we'd to play on had two Chinese screens on it, telling the story of the Emperor and the Nightingale, which I remembered hearing when we were little ones, sitting on the floor at the Misses de Sautoy. I remember the part where the Emperor woke up and found Death sitting on his chest. And the part where someone said, "How can I tempt your appetite, Highness? A peacock's egg rolled in honey?"

We were on every morning from half past eleven to a quarter past twelve, and in the afternoon from three to half past four, while they served teas. There was a lady pianist as well, who used to come out in a big picture hat and play Strauss waltzes while we were off on our break. We called her Flossie, I don't know why. I think Ramage started it.

We'd been engaged just for that one place, the Chinese Café. But straight after Whitsun, the under-manager, Eady, came to me and he said, "Mr Hallett, could your trio play for dancing?"

"Play for dancing!" I said. "I should think we could! Two of us have been playing our heads off for dancing at Keighley Mechanics Institute!" So three nights a week, if it was fine, we played for dancing up on the roof garden. We got thirteen-and-six a week extra for that.

It all went wonderfully well, because, like I told you, I'd had to go out and find this pianist, Ramage, after my pal Hector let me down, and we'd had so very little time to run through things. The first time we got up on that dais, with the Emperor and the nightingale, I was quite nervous. I looked out at all these folk having their tea, and thought to myself, "I wonder if they'll notice us. Perhaps they'll not even stop talking to listen . . ."

Any road, no time for that. I lifted up my bow, and off! We started with "The Vision of Salome", a lovely one I still play here sometimes: lots of nice double stops. And shall I tell you what happened when we finished? They clapped us! Really clapped us hard. I remember bowing and looking round all those faces, and hearing that wonderful noise . . . and blushing to the roots. My first applause! I wish I could describe it to you. It was like being rubbed all over with golden guineas.

Ramage was a nice pianist, though I'd noticed he was a bit inclined to drag back on a note. The good thing about him was, he'd been playing for the films in these bioscopes – he knew how to fit in with anything, which was why he fitted in so well with Mark and me. We carried on "The Druid's Prayer" . . . then "Evensong" . . . "The Raymond Overture" . . . "Britannicus" . . . a little 'cello piece for Mark to do as a solo, named "Rendezvous". And selections from *Gondoliers* and *Mikado*: "A Wand'ring Minstrel I" . . . "Take a Pair of Sparkling Eyes". People away on holiday just loved all of those.

The thing I'd been most nervous about wasn't the playing: it was having to get up there and *talk* to them. Being leader, I'd got to introduce each piece and make announcements, and I'd not done any public speaking before. That man Lord, of Lord and Fletcher's, gave me a piece of advice before I left Keighley: "When you've to say something," he said, "just talk to that one friendly face, and you'll find you're not nervous at all."

So that's just what I did. I looked around the people having tea in the Chinese Café, and over there I can see a really lovely girl, sitting with some friends. I remember the dress she wore, a sort of a pale sea blue. I looked straight at her and I said, "Good afternoon, ladies and gentlemen. The Hallett Trio welcomes you to the Chinese Café . . .' This lovely girl seemed to catch my eye, and smiled, and I smiled. And that was the finish of my stage fright. For ever!

Mark you, I'd been brought up to speak the King's English. And another thing, I remembered how beautifully Lambert Hartnell used to speak at Keighley Palace, when he'd say "Ladies and gentlemen may I crave your indulgence for a moment . . ." I tried to speak as much like Lambert Hartnell as I could. But not too formal. Being a holiday place, you had to be a bit friendly. So I'd put in the odd little joke. For example, when we finished the midday session on Fridays, and all the folk were going back to their hotels and guest houses for lunch, I used to end up by saying "It's always fish on Fridays."

Shall I tell you what I remember most about that season in Llandudno? It was light. I mean, electric light. In those days, you see, it was still a novelty. Most people had gas, the old mantles, that you'd to light with a match. And you were brought up not to waste it. You'd to go to bed with a candle, I often did at home, and in the morning, if it was winter time, you'd get up and have to move around in the dark.

But at the sea there was electric light everywhere, blazing: on the promenade and all over the theatres, in the gardens, all up around the Great Orme and along the pier. People found that exciting. They'd stop up really late – far later than they would at home – just to walk about and see all the electric light. The prom at Llandudno and the municipal gardens used to be crowded till well past midnight every night, bar Sunday. You got a wonderful view of it all from The Arcadia's roof garden . . . lights all round the bay in one direction, like strings and strings of gems between the lamp posts, and in the other direction, all the lights in the towers of the Grand Hotel, and the big globe lights they'd got along the pier, you'd see reflected in the water like long, shivery golden legs.

And all day long, and every night until late, you could hear music. Orchestras in the theatres . . . bands in the parks . . . quartets and trios like ours in the hotels and supper rooms. You couldn't hear the sound of waves but it was mixed up with the sound of violins.

We finished at The Arcadia at half past eleven. Then we'd walk back to Mrs Lewis's, and she'd have a nice supper waiting for us. I remember, she often did us very nice fried skate. We'd have a pot of tea, and Ramage would smoke . . . perhaps have a word with the other boarders, like Eady or Carstairs Copping. When we'd gone up to bed, we'd as like as not lie awake jawing . . . because there'd still be plenty going on outside, and music coming from the Pier Pavilion, if they were playing a midnight house.

We'd get Dudley Ramage to tell us about his travels in

Japan. He'd told us all about those lovely girls who'd serve you tea, even give you a bath if you wanted one. "Oh, they're little belters . . ." he'd say, then give a yawn and start to drop off.

"Cough up another story, old man," Mark would say, from the bed next to mine.

You always dressed up rather for the prom . . . blazers and straws. Reminds me of that song Florrie Forde used to sing. "He's a Duke by the briny, he's a swell by the sea . . ." Folk togged themselves to the nines to drive up and down in their landaus or tricycle chairs. Even the kiddies, in the goat-carts, always had on their best sailor-suits.

We'd plenty of time to go about, seeing everything. We might stop and look at Punch and Judy, which had a funny name at Llandudno: Codman's Wooden-Headed Follies. Or look at a minstrel show. Mind, we'd to take care it was The Magnets, not The Golliwogs. Carstairs Copping used to write on this blackboard in coloured chalk and set it up next to the charabanc office: "Performance, three o'clock this day. Weather and tides permitting."

Such a lot of things went on on the sands. One man made pictures out of sea shells. I remember, one day he'd done a jungle scene with lions, tigers and elephants. And there were jugglers. Fiddlers, barrel-organists, donkey and pony rides. On Prestatyn beach, just round the headland, they'd camels! Llandudno didn't have camels. Only donkeys and ponies. Or you could go lovely walks . . . up into the Great Orme, to the botanic gardens there, or see a show in the Happy Valley, or have a walk out along the pier, which cost a penny. On the pier, they'd slot machines, mutoscopes, What The Butler Saw. In those blue and white kiosks you could get your fortune told or have your skull read by a phrenologist. And they'd music, too, in a little tea pavilion at the end. A haunted house. An American shooting-gallery.

If you only paid tuppence for a deck chair and sat there, you'd not be bored. There'd always be something going on out at sea. A beautiful yacht or steam launch might be coming into the bay, or "La Marguerite" from Liverpool. I remember being up there with Mark and Dudley one afternoon, and seeing a chap called Professor Sparshatt ride a push bike off a board on the roof of the tea pavilion, straight down into the drink. All those high-diving chaps you got at the seaside used to call themselves "Professor" . . . I never knew why. Down he went on this bike, straight in like a stone! You'd not have thought the human body could survive it. But a moment later there he was, bobbing about in the sea and waving, quite all right!

That fortnight by the sea used to be a big thing in people's lives. Two weeks of sunshine and fresh air, after spending all year in a place like Keighley or Preston, with the fogs and rain waiting for trams on dark mornings . . . well, they were two weeks of redemption. I expect you've heard of Wakes in the old days, when all the factories used to shut down together, and everyone went off on special trains to Blackpool and More-cambe. They'd saved all year, and if they didn't spend every farthing, they'd think they'd not had a good enough time. Any cash that was left over, they'd give away in tips on the last night. Rather than take it home, they'd chuck it out of the train window.

Llandudno didn't have Wakes, of course. The big thing there was boarding-house parties. All the boarding houses used to have their regular visitors, year after year – the same people stopping in the same month, like more of a club really. Each lot would get themselves photographed each summer, grown ups and kiddies all together, sitting round Mrs so-and-so and the people who worked for her, out in front of the place or on the sands, if it was one of the ones with a private beach, which many of them had. That photographer named Warren, who lodged with us at Mrs Lewis's, used to take any number: "The Happy Boarders at Sea-View, or Sea-Spray" or whatever it might be.

Did you know that Llandudno was the very first place in Britain to permit mixed bathing? Before that, there'd be one bit of beach for gentlemen and another for ladies, and to undress you'd go into what they called a bathing machine. In the *real* old days, my mother remembered it at Scarborough, the females' bathing machines used to be harnessed to horses and pulled right down into the water, and each one had a big awning on it so that no one could see the occupant until she'd got right in. Honour bright! They couldn't even show an ankle.

All that was well past, though, in the year I'm telling you about, Nineteen-Thirteen. Everyone just frolicked about in the sea together, and got undressed and dressed out in the open, with just a towel or something round them. If you'd no costume, you could hire a Council one ... in fact, now I remember, the place you hired out costumes from was one of these old bathing machines. And another one had its wheels taken off and was used as a ticket office for the pleasure cruises.

Everyone felt so much freer and easier, you see, with all the fresh air, and that blazing electric light. When people got by the sea, they'd do things they'd never think of doing at home. The men would take off their coats and collars and boots, and their wives would hitch their skirts to paddle with the kiddies. People sang and played games and put on novelty hats. It was freedom. Especially for the girls! Groups of five or six would go off on holiday together. Their mothers didn't mind that: the idea was, they'd chaperone one another! You'd meet a great line of them, swinging along, arm in arm and if you were a young man, they'd all look you well up and down. A chap would go up to a girl on the sea wall and say "Hello, what's doing?" and she'd most likely say "Anything you like, kiddo."

Mark, my school pal – who played the 'cello with me – was a right one for the girls. And they liked him, too. He was rather tall, and a swell dresser, but the thing was, he knew how to make them laugh. He'd got this ebony stick with a silver top in the shape of a duck's head. The beak of it was mounted on a hinge. If he saw a young lady he wanted to spark, he'd make a little quacking noise, and he'd push this duck's beak up and down with his thumb. I've seen him get off that way any number of times.

Dudley Ramage, our pianist, was a couple of years older than Mark and me and, like I told you, he'd travelled the world, to Japan and Siam and I don't know where else besides. His father, I believe, worked in one of those foreign banks. He was a graduate of Oxford *and* Leyden universities. He knew Latin and

Greek, and he could quote from the great poets – whole passages of Shakespeare and Milton he'd rattle off without drawing breath, hardly. "Plato" was what Mark and I called him.

Now there *was* a swell dresser. He'd got this whole cupboardful of cream linen suits – do you know, without a word of a lie, he'd go back to Mrs Lewis's three times in one day to change. His shirts were all tailored for him down in London, and he was that fussy about how they'd to be laundered, and how his collars and cuffs had to be starched, he nearly drove poor Mrs Lewis, our landlady, to drink! And that 'tache of his, he treated like a brother.

Ramage liked the girls, too, and he and Mark were always wanting to be off along the prom, looking to see what they could find. I'd go with them sometimes, but other times I'd not bother. Oh, I liked the girls, and they liked me! But I'd quite often be busy, doing a special arrangement of some new piece that had arrived from Goldman's. Mrs Lewis was very good: she set up a table for me in her best parlour, where the piano was, so that I'd have a bit of peace.

For another thing, I was always more interested in the wonderful shows that were put on, at places like the Theatre Royal, the Pier Pavilion and the Winter Gardens. *Beautiful* shows, with people like Vesta Tilley . . . Harry Champion . . . Arthur Prince, who I saw at the Royal, with his little sailor doll. You'd hardly credit a little seaside place like that had *three* houses on the Number One Circuit. On my free afternoon, I often used to go to the Grand Hotel, right on the pier, that wonderful fairy castle of a place I told you about. I'd go into the Grand Palm Lounge and sit and listen to a wizard orchestra that was led by a man named Bertini. Oh, he was a splendid chap! He wore full white tie and tails, and he never smiled. If ever he sat down at the piano and played four bars, you felt honoured!

One lovely sunny Sunday evening, I remember, we three were up in our room at Mrs Lewis's in Hillcrest Road, and Mark and this Dudley Ramage – "Plato" – said to me "Do you fancy a mooch along to the Little Orme?" but I'd got a free pass to the orchestral concert at the Pier Pavilion, which they always did with a full Welsh choir, and I said "No". So off I went to the orchestral concert, and off Mark and Ramage went, towards the Little Orme.

When I got back, at about nine o'clock, there was no sign of either of them. I went in to Mrs Lewis and asked if they'd come in and gone out again, but she said she'd not seen them. So I sat and had a bit of late supper with Eady and Carstairs Copping, and the time got on to ten and then half past . . . still no sign. So I thought I'll not wait up.

At about half past eleven, Mrs Lewis came and knocked on my door.

"Mr Stillwell and Mr Ramage have sent a note," she said. "They've been invited to stop with a cousin over at Prestatyn, and won't be back until tomorrow.'

Well, that was the first I'd ever heard about either of them having a cousin in Prestatyn. Still, I thought, if they've sent a note, that must be all right. So I went to bed, and in the morning, just before we were due at the Arcadia, the two of them rolled in.

"Oh, hello," I said. "I didn't know either of you had relatives in Prestatyn."

Then my friend Mark turned a bit red and he took me to one side and told me what they'd really done.

What had happened was this. They'd been on the prom, right out by the Little Orme, and they'd got talking to two girls who were sitting in a seafront shelter with a little dog on a lead. These two girls came from Burnley and their names were Esther and . . . what was the other one called? I know! Gladys! Esther and Gladys from Burnley. Anyway, the four of them sat in this shelter for a bit, chatting . . . "How long you down for?" sort of thing . . . and then these two girls said to Mark and Dudley Ramage, "Perhaps you'd like to come back to where we're staying and have tea."

So that's what they did. They went back and had tea with these two girls, Esther and Gladys, where they were staying, which wasn't a boarding house but a sort of self-contained flat. They had a fine tea and a nice talk. Then, guess what one of these girls said to Mark and "Plato"!

"How would you like to stop here with us the night?"

Well, my friend Mark had never heard anything like it. He was just an ordinary Keighley lad, same as I was. While these girls were taking out the tea things, he whispered to Dudley Ramage, "What do you think we should do?"

And Ramage said, "Let's stop!"

"But we're booked in at Mrs Lewis's," Mark said. So then Ramage wrote that note to say they were visiting a cousin, and got it sent round to Mrs Lewis. And both of them stopped the night with these two girls.

In the morning when they got up, Esther and Gladys cooked them a breakfast and saw them off. And, for the two of them, the whole thing was ten shillings!

Dudley Ramage was the one who got me to ask Henrietta for a visit. I remember him coming in to breakfast one morning while I was reading a letter from her – she used to write to me once or twice a week, sometimes more. "Who's this correspondent of yours who's so ardent?" Plato Ramage said. So I told him about Henrietta. "Have you got her photograph?" he said. "No," I said, "I haven't, but she's a pretty girl. You can ask Mark there: he knows her." "Why don't you get her to come up for a week then?" Ramage said. So Henrietta came.

Well, when Dudley Ramage saw her, his jaw almost dropped onto his toe! I'd met her at the station – her and her friend Doris Mitchell – and brought them back for tea at Mrs Lewis's before I walked them round to the place where they'd booked in. Dudley Ramage and Mark had tea with us, and Ramage couldn't take his eyes off Henrietta. As we were going downstairs afterwards, I remember, he caught hold of my arm. "Are you going to get wed?" he asked me, and I said, well, I wasn't sure.

"Do it," he said, "or somebody else will ahead of you. She's a pippin."

But ... here's something I'll never understand. When I met her at the station with Doris, she looked as lovely as I'd ever seen her. She'd on a grey, fitted coat, that she'd got from Mignon's shop, and a grey velour hat with a big, wide brim. I was a bit late getting there, the train had already come in and the two of them were waiting on the platform. Henrietta turned round and saw me, and her face lit up with that same wonderful smile. And, do you know, I was already thinking about the time I'd bring her and Doris back to the station and put them on the train for Preston and Keighley.

My mother was convinced I wasn't getting enough to eat, and she'd packed a big hamper with things from the shop, and Henrietta and Doris brought it with them, or, rather, it came in the guard's van. Oh, there was bottled tongues . . . tins of red salmon . . . a Dundee cake. All sorts of things. Even Brand's Essence. Mother must have thought we were in danger of getting rickets.

We'd a very nice week going round all together, Henrietta, Doris, me, Plato Ramage and Mark. That man Warren, who took the stickybacks, would sometimes join us because, between you and me, he had a bit of a soft spot for Henrietta as well. I've still got a photo he took of the lot of us, standing on Llandudno front together. In the morning while our trio played, Henrietta and Doris would go out on their own, round the shops or something; then in the afternoon they'd come down to the Chinese Café and sit and watch us. And nights when we played for dancing up on the Roof Garden, the two of them came along to that. They didn't have to buy tickets, of course, being with us.

Do you know, in all that week, now I come to think about it, Henrietta and I only did one thing on our own that I can remember. We went a day-trip on "La Marguerite" to Liverpool and had a walk-round there and tea at the Royal Exchange Hotel. I can picture everything she wore that day as well . . . like her little pheasant-shaped brooch that fell off and almost got lost over the side. I can remember the little boy who picked it up and handed it back to us. And all the things we could hear them singing down below in the Saloon.

I'd known from her letters that she wasn't happy. She'd been writing me all summer how much she hated working for Mignon in that dress shop. "Oh, you are *lucky*," she kept saying. "You've got away, and you're doing the thing you like

67

. . ." She told me on the boat she'd had two or three offers of stage work from agents who'd seen her in amateur things in Keighley. But Jack Haythornthwaite still wouldn't hear of it.

"I'm that browned off," she said, "I'm thinking I might throw everything up and just go off . . ."

"Well, why don't you?" I said.

"There *is* a good reason," Henrietta said.

"Oh?" I said. "What's that?"

Then she looked at me with that look of hers, and I'll tell you exactly what she said. "You still need giglamps, Arthur, don't you?"

Another night, after we'd finished at the Arcadia, we had supper with Carstairs Copping, who ran that minstrel troupe, The Magnets. He insisted on treating the five of us because he said The Magnets had done three shows in the best place, right beside the pier, and The Golliwogs, their great rivals, hadn't had a look-in. So we went to a sort of wine lodge place, up in the main town, and had Welsh rarebits and tankards of stout on Carstairs Copping. And he did tell us some stories! He'd run away from home and gone on the Halls at twelve years old in a team of acrobats, and he was such a little chap, they'd put him right on top of the human pyramid.

"But weren't you frightened, right up there?" we asked him.

"Oh, no" he said. "If you're top man, you're in the best place, because everybody else has to look after you."

I suppose he'd have been in about his early sixties then, but he was full of ginger – he could still do cartwheels and back somersaults and walk on his hands. He did that on the prom, just to show he could, as we were walking back to Hillcrest Road. I remembered how amazed everyone was to see this little man going along on his hands with his hat still on his head and his pipe in his mouth, and all his keys and loose change and everything raining down onto the pavement.

After our talk on "La Marguerite", Henrietta said no more about wanting to get away from Keighley, and just seemed happy going round in the gang of us, or with Doris when Plato, Mark and I were playing or rehearsing. She didn't want to cast any blight on Doris's holiday, I suppose, or upset me

68

either, so she just kept her own counsel. Mind, if we were all at some show and there was a female singer or soubrette on the bill, I'd see Henrietta, next to me, clenching her fists. I knew what she was thinking. "*I* could do that as well, or better." She must have made her mind up what to do even before she came away on holiday. But – giving me a chance, you see – she held her peace right up until the night before she and Doris were due to go home.

It was a beautiful warm evening, hardly a breath of wind, and we'd got a really fine crowd for dancing up on the Roof Garden, being as it was Saturday and lots of people's last night away. Oh, and it looked a picture with all those potted palms and the Chinese lanterns overhead, and you could hear the lovely swishing noise of the girls' dresses as they went round, and all the dance-pumps sliding over the boards, and from down below came the sound of the waves, and the orchestras that were playing for other dances, and strings of lights were shining, on the pier and along the prom to the Little Orme. I can see that moon now, floating its reflection like a pink wineglass out in the sea.

While we were playing a nice little thing called "Reunion", a waltz, I turned round and saw Henrietta, standing there.

"Can I take you round once?" she said.

So I thought "Why not?" I handed over the solo to Dudley Ramage, put Leo, my violin, carefully on a chair, then I took Henrietta in my arms and round we went, just once.

I remember the exact words she said. "They'll *not* beat me, Arthur. I'm going to leave home and do what I want, same as you're doing what you want."

"I think you're right," I said. "And I think you'll do wonderful."

Then we came round to the dais again and – I don't know why, because it wasn't like me – I leaned forward and gave her a kiss.

And that was that. Next day, Henrietta and Doris caught the train home. A month later, I got a card from her with a Buxton postmark. She was in the Corps de Ballet at Buxton Alhambra.

★

I often thought it was a pity we only had that short time together at Llandudno. I'm sure if we'd gone on, we'd have done quite well, perhaps got a residency at one of the big hotels in Leeds or Manchester. But Ramage said he wanted to go back to Oxford and sit another exam in his ancient studies. And Mark, my school pal, was getting jip from his people over the situation he'd given up to come away with me. So when that twelve-week season for Codlin's ended, that was the end of us. Mark resumed his job with Battersby's in Keighley and "Plato" Ramage went off to Oxford. I never saw or heard from him again.

I went back to Keighley myself just for a week or two, to see Mother and Dad and all my friends. But I didn't stop long. "Otherwise," I thought to myself, "they'll think that season with Codlin's was just a flash in the pan, and I'm back for good" sort of thing. So what I did, I bought *The Era*, the paper all the musical profession read, and in *The Era* I saw an advert for a leader violinist at the Constitutional Hall picture house, in Ilford, right down almost in London.

"Oh, that'll suit us," I said to Leo, so I wrote off and applied, and they wired back "References satisfactory come for interview". They gave me the job straight off, and I spent two months as leader there: The Constitutional Hall, St Mary's Road, Ilford.

In those days, you see, there weren't so many picture palaces as such. They'd show pictures in all kinds of places . . . even in tents sometimes. The Constitutional Hall was sort of a Masonic place, with statues to the Arts and Virtues outside it, but they'd got it all done up with a screen and really good operating-room, and they put on all the big films, like *The Cossack Prince*, *Circle C's New Boss*, *Dido Queen of Carthage*, *Jean Lafitte*, *Privateer*. And there was a first-rate orchestra: sixteen-piece.

The films were silent, but that's not a good adjective, really, because you'd always got at least a piano, a string quartet or, in the best places, a full orchestra. With there being no speech, all the atmosphere had to come in the music. You'd be horses one minute, galloping over the prairie: then you'd be an express train. The big American pictures had special scores that came with them, and you might put in all kinds of extra sound effects on top of that. I remember when *Ben Hur* was showing, we did any number. There's a scene in *Ben Hur* of slaves rowing in a galley with this soldiery chap beating time on a drum – I believe he was called the hortator – and for that scene, the manager, Mr Hall, got a big lump of iron chain, and our percussionist hit it with an iron staple in time to the hortator's drum on the screen. I didn't much like the music that came with that, and I substituted a piece of my own, called "Britannicus".

It was hard work there. The place opened at two each day, and "The King" wasn't till gone eleven – and you were playing nearly all the time. There never had to be a moment on the screen when music wasn't heard. In *Dido of Carthage*, the only bit of quiet in the whole three reels was when the Queen came downstairs. And full evening dress we wore, even though the audience couldn't see us. We sat at the side, behind a sort of black curtain. I used to go to a haberdasher's in Ilford named John Stubbington, and buy paper collars and paper cuffs for a penny a dozen.

Our conductor was a man named Rawlings, who used to get very annoyed because, you see, the screen stood on a podium that was hollow and you could crawl under it from the back. Sometimes during the performance, a courting couple would get underneath the podium and heave about so much, they'd knock the screen right over, and Rawlings would have to run out from behind the curtain and stand it up again.

I'd been there playing for the films just on two months when, all of a sudden one night, fire broke out in the operating-room. No one was killed or injured, thank God, but it did so much damage, the whole place had to be shut down for extensive repairs, and all the staff, including the orchestra, were given notice. So there I am, reading *The Era* again, and what do I read? "Leader violinist required, Hippodrome Theatre, Barnsley. Apply with references to Laurence Edge, Musical Director." And here I am, off back up north again on the good old London-Midland.

★

I'm in the pit at Barnsley Hippo my first time, trying out for leader with this Laurence Edge, who's a great big bully-looking man with whiskers. And it turns out I know every single piece on the stand, the overtures, the marches, the Alder and Tovan arrangements, everything. So we go through a few things, then Laurence Edge closes the lid of his piano and he goes out into the Stalls and has a word with the General Manager, who had a double-barrelled name, E. J. Farrer-Jones. Then he comes back to me, and these are the very words he says: "How long can you stop?"

I was engaged as leader violinist at fifty-five shillings a week. And how long do you think I held that situation? I'll tell you! Two weeks! And now if you've got another moment, I'll tell you why.

I've been there just two weeks – two different bills, with Thursday changes – and I'm settling in and getting on nicely with the orchestra, and my repet, and on the third Monday everyone comes in for band-call with the new artistes, ten-thirty sharp, and we find that Laurence Edge, the musical director, isn't there. A message has come, he's got severe neuralgia and he's bilious, and his doctor's written a note to say he can't work. Mr Farrer-Jones, the General Manager, calls me into his office, and he says "Can you take the orchestra for band-call, while we find out how things stand with Edge's health?" So I take the orchestra and we run through everything with the artistes – getting their books, like I told you, rehearsing their special music, marking cues for the acrobats, the prestidigitators and all those.

At twelve-forty-five, everyone goes off for lunch. And it so happens on this particular day that Mr Farrer-Jones decides he'll have his lunch at the Old Hall Hotel. Any other day, he'd have gone to the Grapes Vaults over the road, but today he feels like a change. And as he walks into the saloon bar of the Old Hall Hotel, who's the first person he sees? It's Laurence Edge, and he's not ill with neuralgia at all. He's drinking Bass ale with Florrie Docherty, the town prostitute!

Mr Farrer-Jones goes straight back to his office at The Hippo, and he wires Mr Bowstead, secretary to the company, at 18

Bridge Street, Manchester, and by the end of that dinner-hour, Laurence Edge is out on his ear, sacked! The next thing I know, I'm called back into Mr Farrer-Jones's office, he tells me Edge is dismissed and he's prepared to offer me the post of Musical Director at four guineas a week.

And that's how I got to be Musical Director of Barnsley Hippodrome, a Number One Circuit House – 1,300 seats – at just turned twenty-one.

So I'm really thrown in at the deep end, aren't I? And on top of everything else I've got Laurence Edge sitting in my old place as leader, because, though he was sacked, Mr Farrer-Jones said he'd to work out his two weeks' notice as per contract. And didn't he give me beans! He'd spend every dinner-hour supping ale and come in to rehearsal tight as a tick. When I came to the rostrum, Edge would call out "This is the new Musical Director-ee!" One night, he just stopped playing and started talking to a lady in the front row. He even got out a photograph and showed it to her, telling her she looked like some cousin of his.

But I'd got the orchestra with me; that's what mattered. I'd wondered if there mightn't be a bit of bad feeling among the older men, me being so young and taking the baton over everyone's head. But all of them in the pit backed me right up to the hilt. Edge told me at first that he'd smash my violin, but he simmered down after a while, and even apologised. "It wasn't me talking," he said. "It was the ale."

"Mr Edge," I told him, "it's all right. Let's say no more about it."

"Mr Hallett – you're a white man," he said to me.

There was only one really bad slip-up after I took over, and that wasn't my fault: it was the artiste's. My first band-call as MD, I got this book down from The Great Amandus, who was quite a well-known turn on the Halls before the Fourteen War: a quick-change specialist. He'd bring on a little screen, and keep going behind it and appearing in all kinds of different costumes – a Red Indian, an Irish Washerwoman, a Hussar, an Organ Grinder with Monkey, or the Pope of Rome or General Baden-Powell.

At band-call, The Great Amandus hands his book to me with all the different pieces he wants played with each costume. We run through the cues, and it all seems straightforward. Monday night, first house: no trouble. Amandus comes out in a cap and apron and a pair of clogs . . . we play "The Irish Washerwoman". He runs behind his curtain and comes out as The Pope of Rome . . . that's our cue for a little devotional piece. Now he's a Red Indian, we do war drums. Every single piece on his book he gets bang on cue.

Now then: midweek, we did what we called a Thursday change, which meant two or three new turns, like acrobats and trampolinists, came in on the middle of the bill, and the big turns, at the top and bottom, swopped things round a little bit, so that anyone who's seeing them a second time – which a lot would – doesn't feel they've seen it all before. The Great Amandus comes to me and says he wants to alter the order of his quick changes, and he give me his book pinned, as we called it, which means to say he's pinned his musical pieces in a different order.

Well . . . either he'd pinned them wrong, or he accidentally took the pin out . . . I don't know. But on the Thursday night, first house, The Great Amandus comes on – big applause. He runs behind his little screen. I look at his book, and it says "Nautical costume. 'Hearts of Oak' ". We strike up "Hearts of Oak . . . jolly tars are our men . . ." and out comes The Great Amandus togged as a nigger minstrel! He looks murders down at me, but he's got no time . . . off he runs behind his screen again. I don't know what's going on. I look at the music: "The Irish Washerwoman". We start up with "The Irish Washer-woman", and out Amandus comes, dressed as The Pope of Rome!

Well, of course, after the first house, Amandus comes to me and he raises Cain. But when we look, the music has been played just as he'd pinned it. So Amandus holds out his hand and says, "Sorry old man. My mistake."

Oh, that *was* a theatre, the dear old Hippo . . . that was what you *call* a Palace of Varieties. If I shut my eyes, I can see it now. I'm shutting my eyes and seeing it just like I did as I'd cycle up Bolsover Street with Leo strapped on my back. There it is at the top with its beautiful golden dome, and all the bills in front along both sides. I can practically read what's on them. All this week . . . "Little Tich as The Gamekeeper – and his big boots" . . . "Cinquivalli, The Human Billiard-Table," "Monsieur Grais, His Dog and Baboon," "Frank Groom – Black Fun," "R. J. Knowles, The Very Peculiar American Comedian," "Arthur Prince and Jim in a Nautical Ventriloquial Sequence," "Chergwin, The White-Eyed Kaffir."

It was a size and all, The Hippo was: eighty-three feet from the stalls to the top of that dome. I know I could make myself quite dizzy looking up from my stand, specially if there was some sort of aerial ballet going on. Farrer-Jones used to be very keen on all that kind of thing – Palladino's Flying Ballet; Pipifax and Panlo, and the Chinese acrobats, who used to slide down on wires, from the top of the Gallery to the stage, just hanging on by the pigtail. There was a kind of wheel thing on the wire, and these Chinese would just loop their pigtails round the wheel and come whooshing down, one at a time.

I could tell you about a night when one of the wheels stuck, half way down the tightrope, and the Chinese chap just hung there by his pigtail, kicking his legs. Oh, it was dreadful! They'd to get in Barnsley Fire Brigade with a long ladder to fetch him down.

It was one of the North's biggest and oldest as well, The Hippo, because it *had* been what they called a "Chairman's Hall" in the real old days when a Chairman would call up all the turns from a table, with all his special pals round him, buying him cigars and wets. In those days, you'd be served drinks – and food as well, if you wanted – throughout the performance. There were still little tray things fixed to the seat-backs in the Orchestra Stalls, and the inside aisle seats were called "whisky stalls" because people sat there so that they could be quicker to the bar, which used to run all along the back. A lot used to come in on just a promenade ticket and stand there and just get drunk . . . or meet ladies who weren't if you know what I mean. Quite a place in the old days, The Hippo was. Outside, above the entrance, it had this big gilt clock with a sort of nymph on it, which the locals called a very rude name on account of what had used to go on in the promenade bar. I'll tell you what they named that nymph on that clock, though it's a bit saucy. They called her "Cunt on Tick".

All that had gone by Farrer-Jones's time, of course: by then it was a thoroughly respectable house. No refreshments in the auditorium; drinks served only in the bars; no coats or wraps to be hung over the Dress Circle balcony, which was all dark red plush, a pin in the brooch of some lady's cloak could easily have damaged it. Those were Farrer-Jones's rules. And woe betide anyone who didn't use the ash-trays provided! I saw a chap asked to leave at once for throwing a lighted cigar down on the carpet and treading it out with his foot. F-J was at his usual place at the back of the stalls, and he saw what this fellow did – a good customer, but that didn't matter. "Go to the box office," Farrer-Jones told him. "Get your money back and leave my theatre."

"But why, what have I done?" this man asks, sort of dumb-founded.

"You threw a burning cigar down on the carpet and trod it out with your foot. I saw you," Farrer-Jones says. "You would not do such a thing to your own home, and you'll not do it to mine. Please do as I tell you." And this fellow went like a lamb.

He was a stickler, F-J was. He'd not have any nonsense, especially not the sort Laurence Edge got up to with Florrie Docherty. He was no prude – and some of the comedians we'd on were quite broad, you know – but he insisted that the house, its management and staff must be like Caesar's wife. Value for money, that was F-J's creed. He was always in front – that's in the foyer – when the house went in, and he'd be there after "The King" as well, so that if anyone felt they'd not seen a good show, they could tell him about it personally. And always full evening dress, white tie and tails, with both hands behind his back, holding a programme. And nothing ever came on that stage in any house that Farrer-Jones didn't see. He'd got a little table set up at the back of the stalls, looking down the centre gangway, and there he'd sit and watch, and if anyone wasn't right on the ball, didn't matter who they were, they'd get a note about it straight away from Farrer-Jones's table. He didn't smoke and hardly drank, but, prompt at nine o'clock every night, he had a tray brought to him there with a pot of tea on it, and two Kiel finger biscuits. He used to bring his own little packet of tea with him into the theatre every week.

Bramwell Slater, my leader violinist, used to say "F-J doesn't like the twentieth century," because he'd not allow a typewriter in the place, and he'd not use a telephone, even though he had to deal with all those agents and managers. In an emergency, he'd wire. Otherwise, he did it all by letter. He wrote all his letters himself, addressed his own envelopes, even stuck on the stamps. As he finished each letter, he'd chuck it down on the floor beside his chair. And about two or three times a day, Miss Blount, his secretary, would come in, pick all the letters up off the carpet and take them to the post.

The thing about Farrer-Jones was, he lived, breathed, ate, drank and – I believe – slept and dreamed Music Hall. And he'd only settle for one thing: The Best. And folk knew it. Because they came to us from all over – Wakefield, Huddersfield, even Leeds and Manchester. When your Robeys or your Chevaliers were topping at the Hippo, you'd have a queue all the way down Bolsover Street and round the corner, and you'd turn away as many as you let in.

When Marie Lloyd came, it was more like a Royal visit. Everyone took a holiday, there were flags and bunting, and the Silver Town Prize Band; the Mayor and Corporation met her off the train, then she drove through town with the Mayor in an open landau. And she didn't have horses in between the shafts of that landau – she had men. Folk thought so much of her that *they* got in between the shafts and pulled her along. Another time, I remember, they brought her to the Grand Hotel sitting on a fire engine. *She* didn't care. However they got her there, she'd be joyful.

I MD'd for them all: Marie Lloyd, Robey, Eugene Stratton, Vesta Tilley, Harry Champion . . . all those wizard Number One tops. A lot of places, what they'd do if they'd a big name as top, they'd not bother getting a decent bottom and middle, but at The Hippo, Farrer-Jones insisted on first-rate bottoms and middles as well . . . like The Zancigs, head-balancers . . . Kain and Lorenzo, mandolinists . . . Datas, memory man . . .

Carlton, comedy card-manipulator . . . Selbrook's Bicyclists . . .
Tiffany's Dogs . . . And always a really first-rate magic act:
mesmerism, prestidigitation or illusion.

When I first arrived, Farrer-Jones was feeling very pleased
with himself because he'd got Chung Ling Soo as top of the
bill, three straight weeks. You've probably never heard of
Chung Ling Soo. He was a Chinese illusionist, one of the finest
on the Halls. And oh, he was magnificent. He'd come on in
these beautiful Oriental robes, to the sound of a gong; he'd got
a bald head and pigtail, and he only spoke the little tiniest bit of
pidgin English. And, here's a thing, he wasn't Chinese at all! His
name was Robinson. But what a turn! They said Houdini
himself hadn't been able to work out the illusion Chung Ling
Soo did right at the end. His assistant would fire a gun at him, a
real Smith and Wesson revolver, and Chung Ling Soo would
catch the bullet in his teeth.

But shall I tell you who the biggest draw were, after your
Robeys and your Marie Lloyds? It was the ventriloquists. You
could virtually guarantee a full house, two houses a night, seven
nights a week, if you'd a top vent' act – Fred Russell with
Coster Joe, Arthur Prince and Jim, or Coram and his little
bugler. Why they were so big, I couldn't say. I think it might
have been because their dolls got away with things a real person
couldn't. That little Coster Joe of Russell's used to get away
with murder. He'd sit there on Russell's knee in his coster cap,
with all his pearly buttons, and he'd pass the most dreadful
remarks, all about how dim-witted we were in the North, and
how he hated his digs and the food and the landlady, and, do
you know, the audience loved it! Oh, they loved it to death!
He'd even shout out to Farrer-Jones at his table at the back.
"Ay ay culley" . . . that sort of thing, and even Farrer-Jones
would smile and answer "Don't be cheeky." The character was
that strong, you see.

I remember how annoyed Fred Russell used to get if anyone
called Coster Joe a dummy. You'd to treat it like a real person.
For instance, if you went backstage between houses and you
didn't say "Good evening" to Coster Joe, he'd give you socks,
Russell would. And on Fridays, when the ghost walked, which

means when the company was paid, it wasn't Fred Russell F-J gave the money to. It was Coster Joe.

All those top vents' played what we called *in scena* – that's with their own special bit of scenery. Arthur Prince's was the deck of a battleship, with all the dreadnoughts at anchor round about. Prince was a Naval officer and Jim was the midshipman. Coram was a Guards officer outside Buckingham Palace and his dummy was a little soldier, sat on the back of a stuffed horse. Prince was always the bigger draw of the two, which, I think, made Coram try that bit harder. He'd got another soldier as well, even smaller, that used to stick out of a pocket in his tunic, holding a bugle. Coram used some sort of control thing in his trousers-pocket that could make this bugler talk and turn its head and move each eyebrow and lift the bugle up, just as if it had a life of its own.

The last thing in his act was the little soldier lifting up the bugle and playing "The Last Post". Pitch dark but for one pin spot on Coram's jacket . . . and total silence but for the bugle notes . . . it gave you goose-pimples, honestly.

There was another vent' I'll never forget, named Tattersall, who dressed as a woman and worked with life-sized dolls that could move about on their own. He used to build them himself out of papier mâché and dressmakers' forms, and machinery that was bits of clockwork engine, his wife's knicker elastic and I don't know what else. Tattersall used to stand onstage, dressed as a nurse – sort of a Queen Alexandra sister, with a cloak and a big headdress – and he'd be holding the figure of an old man that was life-size. This old man's coat-sleeve had Tattersall's real arm in it, so he could smoke his pipe, scratch his head, even pick his nose if he wanted to. My cue with the orchestra was "Hearts and Flowers". When we struck up with that, the figure of an old lady would come gliding out of the wings, turning her head from side to side and dabbing her eyes with a lace handkerchief.

The trouble was, being onstage with the old man, Tattersall had to leave the winding-up of the old lady to a stage hand, and he couldn't ever be sure the stage hand would do it properly. It was meant to be a serious moment – dramatic vent', they called it – but sometimes, as we began "Hearts and Flowers", the old lady would come gliding out from the wings with her head swivelled back to front. One time, she got half way to Tattersall, then turned round and fell into the orchestra-pit with us. Another time the stage hand wound her up too much. She came across the stage, I should think, at about fifteen miles an hour, went straight past Tattersall and off the other side. They didn't catch up with her until she was almost at the stage door.

I'll tell you, I've never seen anyone sweat the way that poor vent' Tattersall did before every house. The spray used to fly off him like it does off an orange when you stick your finger in it.

Talking about all this reminds me of the only time in my life I ever got the worse for drink. It happened not long after I'd taken over the baton at Barnsley Hippo. I went there end of September, was appointed MD first week in October and then, pretty soon, we'd got Christmas: a lovely panto, *Puss in Boots*, and a fresh bill coming in New Year's Eve, so it was a pretty busy time for us in the pit. The second house ran to midnight and the whole company came onstage for "Auld Lang Syne" as Nineteen-Fourteen came in.

Afterwards, Farrer-Jones gave us a big party backstage – and, of course, being F-J it was "Have whatever you want." I'll never know what possessed me but at that backstage party, I consumed the following: One pint of stout in a pewter tankard. One cobbler rum. One whisky Mac'. Two glasses of port – and I may have had another one for the road.

I'd got no head for drink at all. The most I'd ever gone in for would have been a glass of mild shandy. Bramwell Slater and Tommy Frost, my 'cellist, took me out the stage door, to the place where I left my bike. I'd got two and a half miles to cycle back to my rooms in Gilbert Terrace. "He'll never get there," Tommy Frost was saying. "Oh yes he will," Bramwell Slater said. "Put him on his bike."

So the two of them put me on it, and they strapped my violin-case over my shoulders, gave me a shove and off I went. And, without a word of a lie, I went the whole two and a half miles back to Gilbert Terrace without a wobble!

But when I woke next morning, first day of Nineteen-Fourteen, I wanted to die! I lay in that room and, honestly, I wouldn't have cared if the *whole* of the Kaiser's army had come marching past the end of my bed, with fixed bayonets. And I can put my hand on my heart and say in all truthfulness I've never been the worse for drink from that day to this.

I told you about Bryn the Terrible before, do you remember? About how he used to lift a twelve-pounder field piece onto his shoulders, then throw the cannon-balls up and catch them on the back of his neck. And how he used to travel everywhere with his mother, and be so devoted to her. This great big enormous chap, who could balance two grown men on each arm, really used to dote on this little old lady. I've seen him kneel in front of her, at their digs, taking her outdoor shoes off and putting her slippers on for her, as gentle as a woman. And buying special delicacies for her, like coltsfoot jelly, and cutlets, and fresh figs. He kept his head shaved, to look more ferocious, and his mother used to shave it for him. She was the only one he'd trust to do it, his Mam.

Well, mid January, Farrer-Jones brings in a bill from Leeds Empire: Bessie Belwood, serio-comedienne, top, Cinquivalli bottom, The Three Judges middle, and number five, just before first intermission, was Bryn the Terrible.

"Oh, hello," I said, because, of course, I'd met him the time I first subbed for Lambert Hartnell in the orchestra at Keighley Palace. So it was nice seeing him again, and we got together to arrange his music and effects; "Entry of the Gladiators" when he came on, and various drum-rolls to go with things like lifting this cannon on his back, and bending an iron railway spike and the finale, which was throwing the six cannon-balls up and catching them one by one on the back of his neck.

After we'd finished, I asked him how his mother was, and he told me he was a bit worried about her. She'd contracted some sort of stomach upset, and couldn't keep anything down, not even milk. A doctor in Leeds had diagnosed gastric influenza and said that at her age she'd better not travel but, of course, they'd to come on to Barnsley by train for Bryn's engagement. He'd put her to bed at their digs with a nice fire and every comfort. He was buying hothouse grapes, peeling and stoning them and feeding them to her, but it was still no good. Nothing seemed to want to stay down.

Another doctor went to see her, and prescribed some medicine, but she went on getting steadily worse and worse. By mid week, she was so bad, they took her into Barnsley General. The specialist there diagnosed cancer of the stomach. She'd had it for months, apparently, but hadn't liked to say anything for fear of being thought a nuisance.

Poor Bryn was distraught. I remember looking up at him onstage as he was bending those iron spikes, and seeing the tears pour down his cheeks. Each night, he'd catch the last cannonball, then run straight off, throw an old coat over his costume and race to the hospital to be with her. They said he even slept there, on the floor next to her bed.

When we all came in for first house on Friday, we were told she'd passed away that afternoon, and Bryn was in his dressing-room, crying. Tommy Frost and a few others had heard him through the door, and they said it was pitiful.

F-J went in to him and told him he'd better cancel going on tonight, but Bryn pulled himself together and said no, he'd appear as per programme. And so, grief-stricken as he was, he made himself up and put on his costume and all these thongs and his leather collar, and he went out there and started lifting his gigantic weights and barbells and whatnot. And, do you know, from where I was, right underneath him, he seemed to do it as effortlessly as if every iron spike was just a straw and each great barbell was naught but a bag of feathers.

Then the lights go out, all except one pin-spot on Bryn. The long roll starts on the timps, and the house goes quiet. It's his final feat, with the six cannon-balls, these great lumps of lead shot weighing over a hundredweight apiece. He takes the first one, tosses it up: down it comes on the muscles he's trained at the back of his neck, with a great *smack* you can hear even through the cymbals as our percussionist bangs them together. Second one ... up, down, *smack*. Third ... up, down, *smack*. Fourth ... up it goes ...

Nobody ever knew quite what happened. I'm sure, as I live

and breathe, that in the whole of that house and in the orchestra, there wasn't a movement or a sound or anything which might have put him off as he threw up that fourth cannon-ball. It had to be his grief as made him misjudge it so it came down just a fraction of an inch out of true. This time, there wasn't a *smack* with the cymbals. No, it was a *snap*. It was bone. That cannon-ball broke Bryn's neck and killed him right there, centre stage, in front of 1,300 people, then it rumbled down and fell over the edge of the stage, straight through the skin of one of my percussionist's kettledrums.

Tragedy like that quite often happened on the Halls. The things people did were so dangerous – and very few safety precautions, they had. You'd get trapezists killed in falls, acrobats crippled. Chung Ling Soo, that Chinese illusionist, was killed round about the same time, trying to catch a bullet from a gun between his teeth. And I remember another man, who worked with rings, coming to a shocking end. The Safety Curtain fell and decapitated him.

So there it was next day in the Barnsley Chronicle: DEATH OF BRYN. A terrible shock to everyone. But . . . you've heard the saying and it's quite true. The show had to go on.

Monday morning it's band-call as usual, a whole new company onstage and yours truly down at the rostrum, collecting all their books, like I explained, with the pieces that wanted playing and the special cues. So we go through the whole bill, Albert Whelan top, R. G. Knowles bottom, Devine and Devine, the dude comics, middle, then the speciality turns, Tiffany's Dogs, Monsieur Grais and his monkey, the Brothers Krone-mann, Head Balancers, and last of all, Corps de Ballet. As I took their book, I'm half turned round, telling my boys some-thing – I don't even see who passes it down to me.

Then this voice says "How are you, Arthur?" And there she is!

"Bless me," I said. "Henrietta! It can't be!"

"It is, you know," she says.

Well, I can't say much there, not with everyone looking, but straight after band-call, I'm round at the stage door to meet her when they all come out to have their lunch.

"I thought you were in Buxton," I said. Because remember, that was the last I'd heard of her: Buxton Alhambra.

"Oh, I've been lots of places since Buxton," Henrietta says.

"But you knew I was here," I said to her. "Why didn't you write or wire that you were coming?"

"I didn't know myself," she said. "I was down to go to Nottingham this fortnight, but that fell through. The agency I'm with only gave me a half day's notice to come here."

Well, I looked at her as she stood there. It was as if the scales fell from my eyes.

"Oh, I'm that glad to see you, Henrietta," I said – and I took her hand – never mind who was looking! – right by The Hippo stage door in Bolsover Street. I remember, she'd on grey kid gloves. And her breath coming out on the cold air like champagne.

"Let's go and have our lunch together," I said. "I've got *so* much to catch up with." And I know what I meant by that, and so did she.

Of course, the first thing I'd to tell her wasn't very nice. It was about poor Bryn. She was most upset by it. I mentioned before how agreeable he was to both of us, that fortnight in Keighley when I was subbing with Lambert Hartnell. He'd have us both round in his dressing-room . . . do his muscle dance for us, offer us whisky . . . and coconut ice. Really, no one could have been nicer.

There'd to be an inquest, naturally. Farrer-Jones and the company manager, Rushby, had to go to the Coroner's Court and give evidence. Farrer-Jones told all about Bryn's having been bereaved, and the state he was in that night before he went on. The verdict was Death by Misadventure.

There were no relations bar a brother somewhere out in South Africa, who Farrer-Jones did his best to notify. I don't know whether he succeeded or not. They were buried side by side, Bryn and his mother. One great big coffin that took eight pall-bearers to carry and one little tiny one like a child's. So he *was* with his Mam in the end. Our padre from The Hippo performed the rites and Farrer-Jones gave the oration, finishing up with some lines from *Julius Caesar*. Let's see if I can remember them. "His life was gentle, and the elements so mixed in him that all Nature might stand up and say 'This was a man'."

But you know how it is when you're young. You can't keep up a long face for ever. And I was so excited, with her having turned up so sudden like that. All I could think of was what a wizard girl she was, and what a lot of time I'd wasted with all those silly carry-ons of mine, pretending I was going down Cavendish when I was going up.

Henrietta was that used to me, I don't think she believed it at first. "Are you really pleased to see me, Arthur?" she kept saying.

"Oh, I *am*," I said. "Did you think I'd not be?"

"I didn't know," she said. "All the way here on the train, I was wondering what kind of welcome I'd get."

"Hetty Haythornthwaite!" I said. "You've brought the sunshine! Now then: I want to hear about everywhere you'd been and everything you've done since I saw you and Doris off at Llandudno."

So she told me all about it. And my eye, *was* it a tale!

She said that right after she'd got back from Llandudno, there'd been this opening in the Corps de Ballet at Buxton, the Alhambra Theatre, and she'd decided she'd got to try for it, no matter what her father said. So on the Wednesday, instead of going to Mignon's, she'd taken a train to Buxton, auditioned for this place and got it. It was a show called *What's Doing?* I think. Anyway she got herself into it, did Henrietta, easy as kiss your hand.

Of course, when Jack Haythornthwaite found out, there were ructions! Girls just *didn't* defy their fathers, you see. She told me she'd left a note pinned to a door, saying "I can't help it. This is what I want to do with my life," sort of thing. "I'm going to it with your blessing or not." When she got home having got the job, there was a dreadful scene and in the end, her father ordered her out of the house.

They paid her next to nothing . . . I think it wasn't even a pound a week she got. That was full Corps de Ballet, dancing, singing and playing odd little walk-on parts. She'd to lodge in this terrible hostel in Buxton, where an old lady with a pigtail had all these chamberpots . . . For about eight weeks, I think she more or less lived on fish and chips. "And Arthur," she said, "do you think I liked it?"

"Yes," I said. "I think you did."

"You're right," Henrietta said. "I loved it no end. Oh, I loved it to death!"

Then she told me she'd joined a touring company, Riddings Rascals, and got stranded down in London and had very nearly starved. This man Ridding was supposed to have got the company booked with Moss Empires and The Canterbury and I don't know what else, but when they arrived at Euston, Henrietta said, there were about twenty policemen waiting for Ridding at the ticket-barrier. As soon as he saw them, he just threw down his cases and legged it, and that was the last they ever heard of him.

Henrietta had got quite friendly with another girl in the company and after Ridding took off, this other girl said why didn't the two of them team up sort of thing? So that's what they did. They worked out a little song and dance act together . . . and what was it they called themselves? Oh, I know! The Vesta Sisters. A "vesta" was what we used to call a match. That was it. Hetty and Lettie, The Vesta Sisters – Two Bright Sparks.

Anyway, after a lot of trying they got in to see a London agent, quite a good one, named Loibl, who seemed very nice and helpful. This Loibl said he thought he might be able to get them something, and in the meantime, would the two of them care to join his partner and him for supper at his house on Clapham Common. Well, I expect you can guess the rest. Over supper, it was made clear to these girls that if they wanted to get on well, they'd got to you know what . . . When they refused, Loibl turned nasty and ordered them out of his house, wouldn't even get a cab to take them home. And he put it round all the other agents and company managers they'd to have nothing to do with The Vesta Sisters because they were awkward and unreliable.

But Henrietta and – what was her name? Lettie – she and Lettie got their own back. Here's how. This man Loibl had the most magnificent house, full of exquisite carpets, sofas and I don't know what. So what they did, the two of them, they waited until they knew Loibl'd gone out of town on business, then they went to his house and got in through a downstairs window. They ran a basin of water and they went through all those beautiful rooms, damping the sofas and armchairs and the Axminster carpets; then they sprinkled mustard and cress seed everywhere. You know how quickly that grows, don't you? It'll come up overnight on any surface that's wet. And when Loibl, this agent, came home and opened his front door, what did he find? All over his lovely velvet sofas! Mustard and cress, growing like anything!

"By gum," I said when she'd finished telling me all this. "You *have* had some times."

"I have," she said. "But I'm on my feet now. I'm with a good firm of agents, Earnshaw's in Salford, and they're getting me into first-rate things."

"And what do your people think to it now?" I said.

"Mother's pleased," she said. "But Dad's still maungy about it."

And, you know, her Father never *did* forgive her for defying him like that. He never went to see her in anything she was in, or ever took the slightest interest.

I'll tell you something! My orchestra couldn't believe their eyes! "We always thought you were impervious," Bramwell Slater, my leader violinist, said to me. It was sort of a standing joke in The Hippo pit that Arthur Hallett *never* walked out with young ladies from the Chorus. I had this percussionist named Finch, who was extremely good, and had played with the Liverpool Phil. But he'd got the most terrible stutter. Now and again at band-call, one of these ballet girls'd give me a bit of a look. Next day, I'd get a smile. Next day, she'd speak. "And *your* name was?"

"It's n-n-no g-g-good," would come Finch's voice, from among the cymbals and timps. "You're w-w-wasting your t-t-time."

And now here's Arthur Hallett the Impervious rushing off to meet his young lady and walking arm-in-arm with her . . . not caring who saw! Mind you, we were discreet. We'd both got our jobs to do. If we spoke to each other at The Hippo, it was always as MD and artiste. It was "Mister Hallett" and "Miss Haythornthwaite".

We'd heavy snow all that fortnight, and it was cold as charity. But, snow or no snow, we were full every night, both houses, packed up to the Gods. Overture: "Le Cid". Chorale: "The Waking Dawn". "Entry of Gladiators" for those head–balancers, The Kronemanns. Interlude, "In a Monastery Garden", with animated sculpture by Felix King. "The Sabre Dance" in A for Tiffany's Dogs, and that little French thing, "Le Fiacre" – The Cab – to bring R. G. Knowles out, front-of-curtain. And a Grand Spectacular to finish, with the Corps de Ballet dressed as all the Dominions and Ada Colley in the middle as Britannia.

Henrietta played Gibraltar in the Grand Spectacular and she was in a sketch with R. G. Knowles, sitting on a motor car that had broken down. They thought so much of her, they'd hoiked her out of the Chorus and given her a song to herself, just before First Intermission. There she was, quite alone, with a lime on either side of her and one at the back. I remember, she wore this green dress that was all fluffy, and green velvet pumps that tied right up her leg. She came and stood right at the edge of the footlights, opened her arms and sang her heart out to that great big Hippo. I can see her face now, with the light shining up into it, and her book in front of me on the desk. "Property of Hetty Haythornthwaite. I Hear You Calling Me."

I'd got this other piece, too, I'd meant to use as an incidental while they were putting up the flats for the Grand Spectacular. I'd arranged it for French horn and strings, but when I looked at the words, they were wizard, really. This is how they went. "I'm telling the birds, I'm telling the bees, I'm telling the flowers, I'm telling the trees . . ." Then it went on, "The cosy old nook and the flowing old brook, and the shadows that fall, I'm telling them all . . . how much I do adore you."

I showed it to Bramwell Slater and I said, "I've arranged this for the Entr'acte. But these words want singing, don't they?"

"Well, why don't *you* then?" Bramwell Slater said.

"What me?" I said. And he said, "Yes, you sing it. Go on. I dare you."

So I did. I sang that song from my rostrum the whole week, both houses, while they shifted to the first tableau in the Grand Spectacular, I was that full of beans about everything. Every word was for Henrietta, you see. Just like every word was for me that *she* sang with those limes on her, standing up there in that green fluffy dress.

Mind you, the first time I did it, I thought "Should I have?" Because we'd some tip-top singers on that bill, like Miss Ada Colley for instance – a splendid mezzo-soprano – and Devine and Devine, who were what we called "dude comics". They'd a song, that was famous, about "Lord Percy Pimpleton". Well, one of these Devines came up to me just as I was going off to meet Henrietta, and I thought "Now I'm for it." But do you know what he said? "You're on the wrong side of the footlights, old man."

He and the other Devine told me that if I'd throw in with them, they'd teach me to sing properly, dance . . . everything. I'd got the aptitude, they said: I only wanted training.

But I said "No". I couldn't have stood all the travel on Sundays. You had that year-round as a turn on the Halls. Hence the saying: "Only fish and Music Hall artistes travel on a Sunday."

Henrietta and I spent every minute together that we could. I'd meet her in town in the morning and we'd have our lunch and be together in the afternoon, if there wasn't a matinée. After last house, I'd wait for her and we'd walk round to this little place all The Hippo people used, where you could get coffee and hot soup and pies and saveloys. And there we'd sit in the corner, under the Virol advert, talking till all hours, The digs her company were in were a bit out of town, and if she missed the last tram, she'd to walk back through all that snow and cold. So I arranged for her and another girl to get a room where I lodged, 26 Gilbert Terrace. That meant we could travel back on the same tram together.

"I can't believe this, you know," she said to me one night. In fact, she kept saying it. "Are we really all right now, Arthur?"

"Yes," I said to her. "Believe me. We really are."

If you've another moment I'll tell you what happened. I'll tell you because I know it'll go no further.

At the start of that second week Henrietta was there, I got ill. I didn't know what the matter was. I'd a temperature, I sweated, my arms and legs pained me, I could hear this ringing in my ears and when I looked in the mirror and felt my face around the jaw, it seemed to be all swollen and distended.

Everyone told me to go off sick, but I wouldn't. No: I couldn't bear to leave that theatre and that pit, even for one performance. But, honestly, I didn't think I'd weather through the week. My face felt like a football, I could hardly lift my arms to conduct. I was sweating that much, I'd to change my shirt two or three times in an evening.

Henrietta told me I was daft to keep on, but I would do it. Even Farrer-Jones couldn't sway me. "See a doctor," he kept saying. "If you've not got one in Barnsley, I can recommend you to someone. Let Slater take the orchestra," F-J said to me. "Take a sick-note and get yourself right."

"No," I said, "I'll carry on. As long as I've got that eight minutes loquitor with R. G. Knowles, so's I can slip down under the stage and put on a fresh shirt, I'll manage."

Well, I don't know how, but I carried on through to the Saturday, and bit by bit started to feel a little better. Whatever it was seemed to've gone straight through me. My face was still a bit swollen, but the pains and temperature had gone.

The only trouble was, my mother had found out I was bad, and she sent me a wire, "Please consult doctor immediately." I sent her one back saying "All well. No need to consult doctor", but would she have it? You know what mothers are. Back came another wire: "If you care for me indulge my wish", so, of course, I had to. I went to a doctor in East John Street that Farrer-Jones knew; he examined me and said it was mumps.

"Oh dear," I said. "I hope I've not passed it on to anyone at my place of work" sort of thing.

"You've not been working in this condition!" he said to me.

"Yes," I said, "I have."

"In that case, you're a young fool," this doctor said. "You might have done yourself more damage than you know."

"What do you mean, Doctor?" I said. Then he told me that mumps in an adult male, unless treated properly, can cause impotence.

Shall I tell you something? I didn't know what he meant. I knew it had something to do with the below regions, but I'd not the faintest idea what. I thought it must be some kind of disease or uncleanliness.

This doctor – Porter, his name was – sent me straight back to my lodgings to bed, and gave me a prescription for some medicine. And I'm lying in that room, worried to death, thinking I've contracted this terrible thing in the below regions, and what was I to do? And I couldn't tell anyone! Not even my closest male friend.

Then Henrietta comes in to visit me, and she's brought all kinds of things, like calves' foot jelly and lovely fruit, and I'm thinking "Oh my Lord. I've finally got it all right with Henrietta and I'm about to ask her to marry me . . . now I suddenly go and get this awful thing." Oh, I was that despondent, I could hardly bear to look at her.

I stopped in bed through the second week, and Bramwell Slater took the orchestra. And, of course, at the end of *that* week, the company she was in finished with us and went on to Huddersfield, the Empire there.

"It isn't very far," she said to me . . . still not realising anything's wrong. "What I'll do, I'll keep my room upstairs for an extra week, and next weekend, if you're better, I'll come back from Huddersfield, and we can spend it together."

So on the Sunday night, she goes off with her crowd to Huddersfield. And on the Monday, I'm much better, and there's a new company coming in. My temperature's normal and my face seems to be all right again. But all the time I'm going round thinking I may've got this uncleanliness, whatever it is, in the below regions, and what am I going to do about Henrietta, because it's out of the question asking her to marry me now.

On the next Saturday, after her last house in Huddersfield, she got the Theatregoers Special back to Barnsley, I met her and we had supper together, under the Virol sign. She soon noticed something was wrong, and asked me what the matter was. But,

91

of course, I couldn't tell her. I made some excuse or other about being tired and the company playing me up, something like that.

Then we took our tram back to Gilbert Terrace, where she'd kept her room for an extra week. We said goodnight on the first landing, and Henrietta took my face between her hands and asked me again if anything was troubling me. "If anything is, you can tell me, you know," she said.

"Yes, I know," I said. But I couldn't meet her eye.

"We *are* all right, aren't we?" she said.

"Yes, I said. We're all right. I'll see you in the morning."

So she went on up – my room was on the first floor, hers was on the third – and I went in and undressed and got into bed and lay there, not able to sleep, worrying myself to death. I can see that room now, and the way the yellow street-light came in, and the snow piled up on the windowsills.

"It's all spoiled," I kept thinking as I lay there. "Everything's ruined. But however am I going to break it to her?"

Then I hear a tap on the door.

"Who is it?"

"Henrietta."

I get out of bed, go across, open the door and there she is. And she's naked. It's true, as I'm talking to you. She'd come all the way down two floors, from her room to mine without a stitch on.

"Henrietta . . ." I said. Really, I didn't know what to say.

"Will you keep me warm, Arthur?" she said.

I've thought about it so many times, and wondered what I'd done if I'd been in my right senses, not frightened to death from sheer ignorance. You see, I didn't understand what it was she'd done for me, walking down all those stairs in the dark, cold house even though a door could've opened at any moment and somebody could have come out. It wasn't something lewd or shameful, do you see that? It was to show me what she'd do for me. To show me she'd do anything.

But I didn't understand. I was too full of my own troubles. When we were lying in bed together. I got despondent again. I thought "My body mustn't even touch hers." I saw she'd

92

another beauty-spot, just like the one near her mouth. Then I couldn't look at her any more, she was that lovely. I turned my face to the wall.

"Arthur," she said. "I'm cold. Will you put your arm round me?" Just like that day in the Hospital Walk, when we were on our way home to tea and see my dad's glasshouses.

I put my arm around her. She rested her head on my shoulder. But it wasn't any good.

Next day, I saw her off on the train to Rotherham, where her next engagement was. We'd almost an hour to wait at the station. She sat on a chair by the fire in the waiting room, and I walked up and down.

"I don't want to go," she said.

"I don't want you to," I said.

"Then why am I?" she said.

But I couldn't tell her; I almost came out with it, but I just couldn't. "I'm frightened of marrying you, because of a word I don't understand" that's what I should have said. But I just paced up and down, past the bench where she was sitting with her case. Every so often, she'd catch the front of my coat and try to hold me. I'd lean down and take her hands away.

"Arthur Hallett," she said to me. "If you let me go this afternoon, I'm gone for good. And you'll regret it for the rest of your life."

She was right, you know.

I have.

My mother was an invalid, you know that already. She'd been dropped as a baby, and her spine damaged, and I think I mentioned how giving birth to me left her more or less an invalid. She'd to take things very easy, never do any heavy work and often was in quite a lot of pain. But she never complained: not ever. If anyone asked "How are you today, Mrs Hallett?" she used to answer: "Well, if I was any worse, I'd be ailing."

My dad worshipped her and did everything he could to make her life comfortable, but of course he was busy in the shop, which wasn't so bad when we'd the flat above because he could always be slipping upstairs to look in on her, and I was there, too, to lend a hand, but after he'd bought the house at Duxford. and I'd left home to make a career for myself in music, he thought he'd better employ someone to look after her and keep her company in the daytime. And the person he found to do that was my future wife, Delia.

I first met her when I came home to spend a few days, which Farrer-Jones made me do, after all that disagreeable business I explained before ... So you can guess I wasn't much in the mood to think of courtship. But I *did* take a great liking to this young lady, Delia Farebrother, who was at home looking after my mother and being a companion to her.

Well ... it turned out she'd been having an awful time! Her mother'd died when she was a baby, and her father had married this wicked woman who hated Delia and wouldn't even give her enough to eat. When she was a little girl, she'd sometimes be so starving hungry, she'd have to creep out into their garden at night to grub up radishes or steal eggs from the hen-cote. Her father was a weak type of man, you see, and never crossed the stepmother in anything.

When she was about fifteen, she was found to be suffering from malnutrition that had caused a tubercular growth to form in the bowel. She'd to have one of those dreadful operations – what do you call it when you have to go to the toilet through a tube into a bag? Well, poor Delia had that done to her in about Nineteen Hundred and Nine, when it was in its infancy. *And* she'd one of the very earliest X-Rays, which were dangerous things then. In fact, one of the doctors got his hand badly burned through not putting on the right sort of protective glove before carrying out this X-Ray examination on Delia.

Somehow or other, she'd recovered from all these terrible things. They even took the tube out of her, so she could use the toilet normally. But her health was delicate for ever afterwards. When she was thirty and carrying our Warwick, she went to the doctor, and I'll tell you what he said to her. "Delia, you've done wonderful to live this long."

Not that she ever made any song and dance of it. She looked after my mother beautifully, did the housework, the garden;

nothing was too much trouble. But always *so* quiet and retiring. That came from her childhood, you see. At tea-time she'd go without something sooner than reach across for it or ask to have it passed. My mother used to get almost vexed with her not pitching in and having all that was there, like the rest of us. "Delia's one of the Royal Stand-backs", that was Mother's way of putting it.

When I'm home on visits, I get to know this young lady Delia Farebrother a little bit better, and I find out she's most highly cultivated, loves music and is well-read. Her father'd been a painter in oils and had known Monet – or was it Manet? I always get the two confused. One or the other, anyway. And so, we have long talks all about music and painting and the Brontës, which were her particular favourite. But what I always notice, above all, is her beautiful nature.

One day, I remember, it just popped into my head: "I'll ask Delia to marry me." We were sat out in the garden at Duxford, talking about a family friend who'd just got married.

"How about marrying *me*?" I said. And do you know what her answer was?

"I'll chance it."

We got married quite quickly, because I was expecting to be called up any moment, and I wanted her to have all the army benefits as my wife.

We got married in Chapel, out at a little place called Dursley, right on the edge of the Moors. We got married early in the morning, not long past eight o'clock, I don't remember why. I do remember my best man, Bramwell Slater, walked there all the way from Holywell, just outside Ilkley. Tommy Frost and Finch, my percussionist, who stammered, were witnesses, and after, we all went over the road for breakfast at the inn.

I was twenty-two years old, and . . . shall I tell you something? I was a male virgin. Delia was the first and the last woman I ever knew.

I was quite afraid, if you want the truth. Afraid for myself, because of it all having gone so wrong before, and afraid for Delia too, what with her being in such delicate health and so shy and sensitive. When the two of us were together the first time, I turned to her and said, "Delia, dear, it doesn't matter, really, about any of this, you know. I don't want to be just a breeding-machine."

And then . . . do you know what! It was as if a light had been switched on!

Then we had the War. That got going in the August. I remember when the news bills came out in Barnsley: ENGLAND DECLARES WAR ON GERMANY. The shop errand-boys all came out and cheered and threw their caps up in the air.

No one took it that seriously at first. It just seemed like another little upset in The Balkans like they were always having. "It'll be over by Christmas," everybody said. And no one really wanted to fight the Germans. We'd any amount of 'em round our way, like Andrassy, that pork butcher, whose son I went to Keighley Trade and Grammar with. Our Royal Family were all related to the German Emperor. I remember my mother telling me what a pet of old Queen Vic's he was – she even died in his arms. Oh, and hundreds of them in the musical and theatrical line. And on Bank Holidays in the public parks, you'd always see the German band in their little hats and leather knickerbockers, tooting away. You couldn't imagine wanting to do them any harm at all.

But then it got a bit serious, they conquered gallant little Belgium and started raping nuns – those dreadful Uhlans did – and killing poor little babies with their lances, and we started thinking "Really, these people ought to have a lesson."

I can show you my army paybook; it's still in that bureau: "Hallett A, Private, 14th South Yorks. Service number, 2227749." I joined The Colours at the start of Fifteen, but never carried a rifle or a pack. I'll tell you why that was, if you care to listen another minute or two.

When I was about twenty – still at Taplow's, a junior invoice clerk – I was found to be suffering from a curvature of the spine. *And* I know what the cause of it was. It was pushing those great heavy bike-loads of groceries uphill in Keighley as a boy, doing deliveries for our shop. Scoliosis, the condition is: you can look it up. It means acute lateral curvature of the spine.

Well, this is what happened. The Fourteen War was on and by the start of Fifteen, they were calling everyone up. I got this letter telling me I'd to report to the big military induction place they'd set up in Bingley. So our family doctor, Dr Sim, wrote a letter back, telling them I'd this condition of scoliosis and in his opinion was medically unfit for service. Back comes an answer: I'm to go to Keighley Public Rooms, February 21st, 10 am for assessment by an Army Medical Board.

Up I go before this Army Medical Board of various different local doctors, plus the Military Representative, who's an old Colonel with a red nose and, if you want my opinion, was a bit high tiddly-eye-tie. And what do you think happens! They take no notice of Doctor Sim's diagnosis or anything I say, and pass me A1 – General Service.

Back I go to Dr Sim, I tell him what the verdict is, and he says "No. Never!" He arranges for me to go up before the next Army Medical Board, a fortnight later in Preston, with a sketch of my spine that he's made. So off I go there, and what do I find? It's the same Military Representative, that old Colonel with the red nose, he's *still* three sheets in the wind and passing everyone, no matter what. And I'm classified same as before – A1, General Service.

So there's no help for it. I've got to go. I hand in my notice at Barnsley Hippo, take Delia to Duxford to be with my people, and off I go to the induction place, thinking "Oh my goodness, I wonder where I'll be in six months time! I wonder if I'll be pushing up the daisies."

Now: this is where the Arthur Hallett Luck comes in again. At the induction place, I'm stood in a line of seven recruits, number six in the line. We don't know what's to happen to us, we've just to stand there with a sergeant in charge of us, and wait. Well, time goes on, and the seventh man, next to me, says to the sergeant "May I go to the toilet?" and the sergeant says "All right. But be quick." When this chap comes back, *he's* number six in the line and I'm seven. Then an officer puts his head round the door and he says "Right! You six – Artillery. You, number seven, 14th South Yorks." I missed going in the Artillery by *that* much. I'm sure if I'd gone in there, it'd have been the finish.

So I'm in the 14th South Yorks, the infantry. And I'm thinking "Well, at least I'll be among friends" because nearly everyone I meet comes from round our way, and the company commander's Watson, whose people make Watson's Matchless Cleanser in Shipley. But mostly they're from Barnsley, where the regiment was raised; in fact, the 14th South Yorks always used to be known locally as The Barnsley Pals.

For training they sent us to a place called Wintringham Hall, near Hemsby in Norfolk. This old manor house, dating back to Elizabethan times, had been commandeered by the Army, and the grounds and parks and woods round about were where they instructed recruits.

I'm down there with The Barnsley Pals, my very first morning on parade. I remember, we'd to form up on a lawn next to an ivy-covered walk. Our company commander, Watson, comes along, he looks at me and can see right away I'm not standing straight. "What's the matter with that man's back?" he says to the sergeant. "Anyone can see it's not as it should be" sort of thing. "He's to report sick first thing in the morning."

So next morning I reported sick, which you'd to do at the Quartermaster's Stores, round by the old servant's yard. "Right, strip off," I'm told, "and wait in there for the MO." So I'm standing there in my birthday suit, and then this young MO comes in, he looks at me and says "Who the bloody hell let you in the Army?" So that's it; the Medical Board in Preston's overruled, I'm re-classified C3 – Home Service – and put on light duties pending discharge on medical grounds.

Till my discharge came through, they put me in the Orderly Room with another man waiting his ticket, an old boy we called Grandad, who'd lied about his age when he joined up. He wanted to go into the Army to get away from his wife.

We'd to go messages, make tea, light lamps, that kind of thing. A lot of the time we'd nothing to do but scull around this old manor house full of suits of armour, big old oak chests and I don't know what . . . and an enormous old underground kitchen with turtles' skulls, that had been made into soup, hung on the wall, and a magnificent sort of gallery place, where we used to wait to go messages, with portraits in oils all round it, and an oak table that Cromwell had used for one of his councils of war. Grandad scored the end of it into lines with his pocket-knife so we could play shove ha'penny on it.

So you see, I missed all that terrible stuff out in the trenches, because of the Arthur Hallett Luck. To the day I die I'll be grateful I never had to kill or maim anyone. I remember, one day, going up that great oak staircase at Wintringham Hall and looking down onto the lawn, where some of the ones I'd joined up with were having bayonet practice. This young lad, who couldn't have been more than about seventeen, was having to drive his bayonet into some kind of straw dummy that was meant to be a German while the instructor screamed and raved at him, horrible obscene things like "Go on! Kill! Go for the bloody heart!" Later on in our quarters, I saw that same young lad, sitting on his bed with his head in his hands, crying for his mother.

My ticket, and Grandad's, came through in the June, just a week or two before The Barnsley Pals went off to France. They gave me £15 and a railway pass back to Keighley. Delia sent me on my clothes, right down to kid gloves and a cane. Grandad and I went off to the station together. He wanted to walk it, but I said "No. This is a special day." So we paid sixpence apiece and did it in a governess-cart. And there at Keighley station was my Delia to meet me.

They said to me, "You'll do more good to the War effort playing your violin, Mr Hallett," and so that's what I did, more or less for the duration. I oughtn't to say this, because it was dreadful, really . . . but Delia and I had the time of our lives in the Fourteen War. Absolutely the time of our lives, for the following reason.

When I got home, my dad said "Right! You're to stay here with us, you and Delia, and you're to do nowt but take things easy for the rest of the year." So we stopped at home, Delia and I did, just seeing our friends and going about. That was the time I told you when we saw my former schoolmaster, Shearing – Old Natty – and I almost had it out with him about that steel ruler of his, till Delia restrained me. That was right after I'd come out of the Army in Fifteen.

One day, when I'd gone down into town to meet Delia, I bumped into this Dr Boak – B.O.A.K. – who was chief surgeon at the War Hospital in Bank Top, just near our shop, a great big War Hospital, and this Dr Boak said, "*I* know you, don't I? You're Hallett. You used to play in Lord and Fletcher's Orchestra." So I said, "Yes, that's right," and then he told me he'd formed an orchestra from among the wounded at the War Hospital, called The Fragments From France; nine-piece, a pukka affair with himself the conductor and pianist.

"But," Dr Boak said to me, "what we need is a really tip-top leader violinist, like you. Why don't *you* come in and play with The Fragments?"

And that's how I spent the Fourteen War; going all over with The Fragments From France, playing for the wounded – and having *the* most wizard time! What had happened, you see, the mill-owners were all coining a mint of money out of making khaki uniforms and feeling a bit guilty, so they'd got together and set up a fund for providing entertainment at all the big War hospitals, Bank Top in Keighley, and at Shipley, Buxton and the really big one for gas victims, down in Leeds. Dr Boak knew all these mill-owners – and truly, they looked after us as if we were Royalty! Sent big cars with chauffeurs to collect us and bring us home. Treated us to slap-up lunches, teas and suppers. Delia and I were just in clover. Because, of course, I said, "I'd very much like to bring my new wife along on some of these things." They said, "Mr Hallett, she's *more* than welcome."

I hadn't known quite what to expect, going into an amateur thing like that – and injured people, too – but I found they weren't half bad, some of them. When Dr Boak got a good player, he'd hang on to him, tell his unit he wasn't fit for duty, even if he was, just so's he could carry on with The Fragments. All ranks they were, jumbled up together. The oboist was Lieutenant Naylor, who'd been gassed twice – he came from Ruthin in North Wales. A private who'd had part of his jaw shot away was the 'cellist. And Sergeant Phillips of The Carbiniers, who'd been blown up by a fifty-pound shell, did the percussion and he could play the xylophone quite well, too.

He'd had his lung punctured, and he had to do these special deep breathing exercises to inflate it. Corporal Stacey was my second violin and repetiteur – a tiny little chap who everyone called Pip. Bless me – Pip Stacey! I hadn't thought about him for it, it must be, about sixty-five years.

And, of course, I gingered it all up a good bit – augmented them with a double bass-player, and a lady flautist whose name was Miss Violet Helmshaw, and got Dr Boak to persuade these mill-owners to buy them proper music-stands and get a new oboe for poor Lieutenant Naylor, and some other bits and bobs they were short. And they seemed to like me, The Fragments did, and liked having someone who could do good arrangements for them which brought the playing on even better.

The War hospitals we went to were sometimes houses that had belonged to millionaires, really wizard places with great sweeping front drives and baronial entrances, more like castles than houses, some of them. We'd play out in the garden, on a band-stand or a dais with flags, for hundreds of these wounded men, their doctors and nurses – a great sea of them all over the lawn in their blue suits. Wounded men in the Fourteen War always wore blue suits . . . and red ties. I don't know why that was. The ones who couldn't walk would be wheeled out in their chairs and put in the front row. Some even used to be wheeled out in their beds, so's not to miss us.

I've never played for audiences like those wounded men in those War hospital gardens. It must have seemed like Paradise to them, after all they'd been through at the Front. When you gave them "Dream of Olwen", or Shaminard's "Autumn", you could hear a pin drop, though it was open air. You'd think the birds had stopped singing, so's they wouldn't miss a bar. And *Faust* and *Rigoletto* – selections from – they just loved! And there was a show in the Fourteen War, you may have heard of, named *Chu Chin Chow*, that everyone adored. Oh, a wonderful, *wonderful* show! Even today, you sometimes still get an echo of it. When The Fragments played, we always finished up with the overture from *Chu Chin Chow*. My stars! When we got to that last bit – the trombones all together – I could feel the platform shake under my feet.

I've made it sound like nice times and I shouldn't, because it was dreadful, really ... the casualties you saw in the paper every week, lists and lists of their names right down the page. And not a family you knew that hadn't lost someone, a son or a brother. And nobody seeming to know why it was going on, or having an idea how to put a stop to it.

We saw the sorrow, too, up at Bank Top. A lot of the time when Dr Boak operated, he'd know there was nothing he could do. He'd get in touch with me and say "We've lost another one, Mr Hallett. Do you think you could be here when we bury the lad?" So I'd say "Yes, of course" and I'd be there with the 'cellist from The Fragments, Harding, and Pip Stacey when the dead boy's people came and we'd play at the service they had, hoping that helped a little bit.

I can still see some of the poor men in those gardens, listening to us, the dreadful yellow look of the ones who'd been gassed, and the amputees all along the front row with their empty pyjama-legs. And the blinded ones, listening to the music so desperately, as if they couldn't even bear to let the echo die away.

It was even worse what happened to some of their minds, you know. Young boys, who'd hardly ever been away from home, living in those trenches in mud you could drown in, if you stepped off the duckboards, and rats the size of cats ... seeing their friends gassed or disembowelled, or their heads shot off by a sniper if they just looked over without a periscope ... it was all just too much for some of them. There was a lad in my form, named Pagett, who'd gone out there with a bosom pal of his. Thought the world of each other, these two did. Well, there was some sort of night attack and afterwards, this other lad was posted missing. So Pagett went out looking for him, right into No Man's Land, searching in all the shell-craters and everywhere, to see if he could locate this pal of his.

Eventually, there his pal was, sitting up in a shell-hole, looking quite all right. So Pagett went up and said "Oh, hello" – whatever the name was – "I've been looking all over for you," and at that very moment, a spider ran out of this boy's mouth because, of course, he'd been killed hours before.

Pagett was discharged with what they called shell shock. When he came back to Keighley, he seemed quite normal, he was engaged to be married to a nice girl and had his full service gratuity. But a week after he came home, he hanged himself with his braces in his bedroom. And in the room were found hundreds of ties. He'd spent his entire gratuity buying ties, no one ever knew for what reason.

Then later on we had the Zeppelin raids. There was one came over when we were playing at Darwin in Lancashire. I remember a man came in and ordered us to put out all the lights. I believe they brought it down somewhere over near the railway station.

They attacked us from the sea as well, you know. People don't remember that. Two German cruisers, I forget their names, came and shelled Scarborough, that beautiful seaside place. Then they did the same at Bridlington and Hartlepool. About twenty people were killed – including, I'm sad to say, someone well-known to me. At Bridlington, they hit just one place, in Sea Street, a theatrical boarding house. The shell that struck that boarding house reduced it to rubble, killing three people. I don't suppose you can guess who one of those three people was. I'll tell you quickly, because it still upsets me to remember. It was Hetty Haythornthwaite.

It's funny what pictures come into your mind, looking back like this. I'll tell you what one just came into mine if you've got another minute – emus' eggs. Yes, I said "emus' eggs". They were in a house where Delia and I took furnished rooms towards the end of the Fourteen War: in a little village called Hoathewaite, right out on Ilkley Moor. Our landlady was a Mrs Tyson, a widow whose husband had been a sea captain and had brought all these things home from his travels, like sea horses and sea cows and the engraved teeth of whales. And a whole lot of emus' eggs, mounted in glass cases. There were two in the front hall, another couple in Mrs Tyson's sitting-room, another on the sideboard in ours and one on the mantelpiece in our bedroom. Delia used to say they gave her the creeps.

I remember looking at this one in our bedroom, and noticing

it had got a sort of indentation at the end of it, because the shell, funnily enough, was quite soft.

I called Delia and I said, "Look here, love. What do you suppose could have made that indentation in Mrs Tyson's emu's egg?"

"That was me," Delia said. "The only way I could bear to dust it was to shut my eyes, get hold of the end of it and give it a quick going-over with the cloth. When I opened my eyes, I saw I'd made that nip at the end of it. I've been worrying myself to death over it,' Delia said. "I'd offer to buy her another to replace it – but where am I going to find an emu's egg right out here on Ilkley Moor?"

I'd got to laugh, even though she was so upset about it. She could never bear to damage anything of anybody's. "Delia," I said to her, "let that be the *least* of your worries. She's got that many other emus' eggs, she'll probably never notice this one's got a nip at the end of it."

"Oh, do you think so?" Delia said.

"Yes – I think so," I said, and she never did. Leastwise, if she did, she never mentioned it.

We stayed at Hoathewaite through till just after the Armistice. It was where our son Warwick was born – December the third, Nineteen Hundred and Eighteen. I looked at those emus' eggs for hours, while I was pacing up and down, worrying about Delia.

You've heard of the Spanish Influenza epidemic, that killed so many thousands right at the end of the Fourteen War. Well, while Delia was carrying our Warwick, only a week or so before he was due, she suddenly went down with a raging fever. "I'll go for the doctor," I said, but she wouldn't have it. "I'll be all right," she said. "The doctor's got better things to do . . ." But the fever grew worse, and in the end I said, "I'm *going* to fetch him love, and that's all there is about it."

I went and got the village doctor, Dr Porteous, who lived up on the Dursley Road, and we came back to Ouse Villa – which was the name of the house where we lived – in Dr Porteous's pony and trap.

"Is it Spanish Influenza, Doctor?" I asked him when he'd examined her.

"No, I don't think it is," Dr Porteous said. Then he asked me if Delia had been to any army camps recently, or meeting soldiers in any sort of way.

"Well, yes she has," I said – because I remembered, just that previous week, she'd been with a party from our local War Comforts Committee, distributing woollen socks and mittens at the barracks just outside Shipley.

"That may be it," Dr Porteous said. Then he told me Delia had contracted a sort of Plague that the troops were bringing back from overseas, caused by the rats that infested the trenches out in France. "I've got a dozen cases like this," Dr Porteous said. "All over Shipley way, and all people who've recently had something to do with the barracks there."

"Plague?" I said – you can imagine how horror-struck. "I've seen nothing in any of the papers about it."

"No," Dr Porteous said. "It's been hushed up, because they're afraid of a national panic. A lot of it's being diagnosed as Spanish Flu. But you can take it from me, Mr Hallett – what your wife's suffering from is Plague."

Well, I looked at him. A great big old-fashioned doctor he was, with mutton-chop whiskers and this red face. And he still made his rounds in a pony and trap.

"Will she be all right, do you think Doctor?" I said.

"Mr Hallett," he said, "all I can tell you is this. Either she'll live or she'll die. It'll be decided in the next forty-eight hours."

Those forty-eight hours were dreadful. I'd to keep bathing her all over with damp towels, trying to make the fever go down. A lot of the time she was in a delirium. "No, don't let him get me," she kept crying out.

"Who, Delia love?" I'd say.

"The pharmacist," she'd say. "I'm frightened of him. Please don't let him come near me."

Then a really remarkable thing happened. I'd left Mrs Tyson with her and gone out for a breath of fresh air. I was walking down the main street of Hoathewaite, this little village, and I saw a sign that read "Champagne. Special offer – ten shillings a bottle." It was in the window of the wine and spirit shop belonging to the village pub, The Ash Tree. I'll never know why, but I suddenly thought to myself, "I'll buy a bottle of that and bring it home for Delia."

So I bought this bottle of champagne, took it home and said to Delia, "Come on love. Sit up and try a little bit of this." And she liked it! So I said, "Here you are, love, have some more," and she took another glassful. And from that moment on, she started to feel better. I don't know what the explanation was. Dr Porteous didn't either, when I told him about it. He just laughed and said, "It looks as if that champagne of yours worked the oracle."

But, do you know – when she went into labour with our Warwick, no doctor would come to her, for fear of catching Plague. I don't mean old Dr Porteous. He'd gone on holiday, leaving a locum in charge. This locum refused to attend Delia, so did the other doctor in Hoathewaite, Stiles. I stood and pleaded with each of them, but it was no good. Both of them shut the door in my face.

It was the village midwife brought our Warwick into the world . . . 2.15 am, December the third, Nineteen Hundred and Eighteen. I can see that clockface now, and the emu's egg next to it, when I first heard him cry out. Delia was narrow down there, and the midwife tore her during the delivery. "Now the doctor will *have* to come, Sir," this midwife said – meaning he'd not be able to refuse to come and stitch Delia where she was torn.

I'd heard of another doctor who lived in Dursley, about six miles away, so I ran over to him and banged on his door and said, "I don't expect you'll come either, because two others wouldn't, and she *did* have Plague, but we've cured that . . . and she's lying there, torn . . ." I could hardly get the words out, I was in that much of a state.

"Hold on," this doctor said. "I'll get my bag."

Well, I could hardly believe it. "You mean you'll come?" I said.

"Of course I'll come," he said. "If you'd asked me in the first place, I'd have come." Dr Beresford, his name was. Bless him.

So he came back with me to Hoathewaite, and he stitched Delia where she was torn and gave her a painkilling draught.

The baby was just fine. So was Delia . . . except that for ever after, she had these fears. She couldn't write letters. She was afraid of dogs and birds. And she could *never* go inside a chemist's shop.

This was how Dr Porteous explained it to me. "It's like a mental limp, Mr Hallett. She's perfectly all right, but she's always going to need the most tender loving care and attention."

"I'll give her that, Doctor," I said. "Don't fret on that score. Tender loving care and attention's what she'll *always* have from me."

You've got to understand how different things were when the world settled down after that Fourteen War. It's hard to explain to someone who doesn't remember what it was like before. I always think of Art class at school, when you'd dip your paint brush into a jar of clear water and see it turn all dark. That's what seemed to happen to our lives after the Fourteen War. Everything that had been clear seemed to go dark and sort of muddy.

There was no more Music Hall – hardly any. The pictures had come on so much, you see. All the lovely old theatres, like Keighley Palace and Barnsley Hippo, were turning themselves into bioscopes, doing what was called Pictures and Variety. You'd get three films, an interval, then three or four turns. But it was the pictures folk wanted, not the turns. It was a different thing altogether. You just sat still and watched. There was no more joining in, like they used to with Marie Lloyd. I remember, in the old days at Barnsley Hippo, how I used to *feel* the audience prickle in the back of my collar, almost like something living. Playing for the films was never like that. Even the darkness felt different. It may sound silly, but it's true. The darkness didn't seem as happy as before.

I'd one or two jobs at picture houses while I was still directing The Fragments – one over near Shipley, and at Darwin in Lancashire, where that Zeppelin was brought down. Then the vacancy in Cornwall came along, and it just happened to be at a time when Delia so badly needed rest and recuperation.

"Come on, love," I said to her, "we're off to green fields and pastures new. Pack the bags, now." Shall I tell you about us in Cornwall, too? Have you got time?

The position was Musical Director at the County Theatre, Truro. The Slack Circuit, my employers were. They'd got the County in Truro, The Picture House at Falmouth, a place at Newquay and one right the way down in Penzance. But the County was the only one to have an orchestra. It was just trios at the other places – I think, just a pianist, or piano-organist, down at Penzance.

I'll tell you, I used to have a pipe dream about going to Cornwall, right back when I was quite a little boy. In our geography class, we used to have this book called *At Work In Britain*, with pictures of Cornwall in it. I remember one of a tin-mine, another one of lambs in a fold. I always used to think how nice it'd be to be snuggled down in the sheep-fold with all the sheep and lambs. And this book told you all about the tin-mines, and how they made butter and clotted cream – and "the famous Cornish pasty". I remembered being at my desk of a winter's morning in Keighley, and absolutely craving one of those.

So off we went down there in Nineteen: me, Delia and Warwick in a little basket. Slack's had sent us our ticket, Second Class all the way! We'd to go by LMS down to Oxford, then change onto the Great Western for Truro. I remember how amazed Delia was at how magnificent the guard was, with all his polished buttons and his watch-chain, when he clipped our tickets. Because the Great Western was a real thing then, you know – the lovely trains in that yellow and brown; seats like armchairs and embroidered antimacassars for your head. And before he came into the compartment where we were, this guard tapped on the door. Delia couldn't get over it.

I remember, we travelled down with a man who told us he was going to watch the buzzards at St Hilary's, and had on canvas leggings and ox-blood boots. On the way, Warwick had a little bit of an accident in his basket – he was only tiny, you see. And, I'm afraid to relate, there was a bit of a smell, or pong. This man in leggings sat there, didn't say a word, but he took out his pipe and lit it and kept on smoking it until Truro.

Five pounds a week Slack's gave me, for one house a night, seven o'clock. You couldn't get them to come in any later. Truro was such a quiet old place, you see, everyone went to bed by about half past nine. There was a Saturday matinée, but I didn't appear for that. Saturday, they just made do with a piano.

It was only a small place, the County – though they showed good pictures. But remember, I'd been used to these great huge houses in Keighley and Barnsley with twelve hundred seats and more . . . boxes and fauteuils and whisky stalls. At the County, I think they only had three hundred seats. One little block of stalls and a titchy circle you got to by going up the stairs of the house next door. And no gangway up there. People with seats on the far side had to walk right through the projector-beam. The silly ones used to hold up their fingers and make dogs or rabbits right in the middle of Mary Pickford's face, or John Gilbert's or Pola Negri's.

They'd got no heating either. In Winter Mr Corrison, the manager, used to put a line of electric fires along in front of the screen to warm us and the audience. I'll tell you another thing they did there I never saw anywhere else. Two or three times while the picture was on, the lady from the pay-box used to go in with a big cut-glass spray full of Eau de Cologne and spray the audience with it.

I'd five in the orchestra; six if Bennett was there. "Wag" Bennett, we called him, I don't know why. He also used to play the organ in the cathedral. Sometimes I'd have him on organ *and* Gibson on piano. Flavius Maximus Gibson LRAM – we'd never to leave out the LRAM. And a lady 'cellist from Scotland, named Frew, who caused quite a bit of trouble. What it was, she'd got this habit of dragging back in three-four time. It used to infuriate Flavius Maximus Gibson because it was he gave the tempo, you see. I spoke to her about it, but she still carried on, dragging back. So one night he lost his temper, Gibson did, right in the middle of a Charlie Chaplin. He jumps up, slams his piano-lid down and hollers out. There's Charlie up on the screen, running round in a prison-suit, and down here's Flavius

Maximus Gibson giving beans to the lady 'cellist, Miss Frew. "Get out of this orchestra! And take your bloody old orange box with you!"

The next thing is, I get a note signed by all the boys . . . do you call that kind of note a round robin? So I take it along and show it to Mr Corrison, the manager. "Dear me," he says. "Have I got to give this poor young woman the sack?" If you want the truth, I think he was a bit sweet on her. "Well," I said, "if she doesn't go, all the boys will." So that Friday, Miss Frew got her walking papers.

They were a good company, Slack's, very fair to me, though I never did meet Slack himself all the time I was there. He lived in a big house near Penzance, hardly ever went out at all, just gave his orders to Corrison and the other managers by telephone. And every Friday night, with the week's takings, Mr Corrison had to pack up a great huge basket full of all kinds of medicines – and a lot of cheese – and send it by motor to Slack.

Oh, we loved it down there in Cornwall, living out in beautful countryside, right next door to a farm. We used to give fourpence a dozen for new-laid eggs. A great big bowl of cream from the diary, sixpence. And you'd got the sea *and* the River Fal. Delia could sit on the beach or go down along beside the Fal whenever she felt dispoged. That's what Mrs Gamp used to say, isn't it?

Where we lived was almost exactly half way between Truro and Perranuth. I rented a piece of land off this farmer named Blight for half a crown a week. He was a bit of an odd character and all was Farmer Blight. He'd a big black curly beard like Captain Kidd, and used to shear sheep in an embroidered smoking-cap. He played the French horn as well, or tried to. One night he came and played it under our window, quite astonishing Delia. 'Oh my goodness!' she said. "What's that terrible noise?" "Shush," I said. "We mustn't hurt his feelings." So I opened the window and we both said, "Very nice, Mr Blight."

We lived in a caravan, you see. Not any gipsy kind of a thing, though. I had it built specially by a firm at Newquay and sent over to Truro by rail. It came in on its own special trailer, in front of the guard's van. We had to have two of Farmer Blight's horses to fetch it off the platform and take it to its field.

It was a handsome thing, I'll tell you, that caravan. They let us choose any colours we wanted, and we chose cream and maroon. Artillery wheels, it had . . . a Pullman sliding roof . . . two rooms with folding Spatsmollo divan . . . lit by Aladdin lamps throughout. Delia and I had the bedroom with Warwick next to us in his cot. When he got too big for that, we put him on the Spatsmollo in the parlour-end, banked up with a lot of pillows and bolsters so he wouldn't roll out in the night.

We had water laid on . . . a spirit stove. The only thing was, we'd to bath in the sink. They'd made it so you could take off the draining boards either side, and a little folding step-ladder came out of the cupboard to go up by. Our Warwick got bathed in the sink to the age of well past four. Really, it was quite a good size, once you'd changed it all round. Delia and I even used to get in there together sometimes.

The only other thing was, having an Elsan instead of proper flush toilet. You paid a firm to come each week, take out your old chemical part and leave you a new one. Round there they called this firm The Rimmel Man. The trouble was, The Rimmel Man didn't always come. And sometimes, in a hard winter, the chemicals in the Elsan used to freeze.

We still loved it living there, did Delia and me. In the mornings in summer we'd get up early and go for walks over the fields with the dew still on the grass, over those lovely cosy old walls with grass and mosses growing on them, just like I used to see in my geography book. I remember early one morning we came across this enormous mushroom. Two feet across it must have been, just growing there in a field of cows. "Leave it, it's poisonous," Delia said. "No," I said. "It's edible. Look at its black underneath." "Are you sure?" Delia said. "Yes," I said, "I'm positive and what's more, I'm going to pick it." So I picked it and we took it home and cooked it for our breakfast, and do you know, we couldn't manage all of it!

Over four years we spent, living in Farmer Blight's field in our Pullman caravan. When we arrived, our Warwick was a baby and when we came away, he'd started school. He used to roll apples down the chute to the pigs. And he'd sit on the rug on that top step, reading his book. Even then with him it was nothing but books, books, books.

I'd never want you to get the idea I didn't love him. I *did* love him. And he loved me too – I know he did underneath. "Dad," he'd say to me when he was little, "can I come into your bed for a love?" and I'd say "Yes, love. Come on in." He was a dear little boy in lots of ways. When he thought a lot of a thing, he used to say "It's wizard, Dad." I still use that word sometimes. Have you noticed?

But . . . I don't know. I can tell you this, knowing it'll go no further. I could never quite get out of my mind the terrible pain Delia had, being torn and cut about in giving birth to him.

He never cried, you know, not even as a baby. Never cried as a little boy or seemed to get upset. Just sat there quiet, keeping himself to himself. Sort of cold, in a way. And always books, books, books.

For his sixth birthday – that was after we'd gone to Sutton-in-Ashfield – I decided to get him his first violin. I sent for the Boosey and Hawkes catalogue and tried to find one with a lion's head, like my dear old Leo, only they weren't manufactured any more. But there was a make called Valmar, very good, whose trademark – on the body – was a little flying horse. "That'll do," I thought. "He can think of his own name to call that."

So I sent for this Valmar violin and hid it away till his birthday, then brought it out, opened the case and said, "There you are, love. Are you ready for our first lesson?"

He looked at it, and do you know what he said?

He said, "I didn't want a violin though, Dad. I wanted the new annual with Teddy Tail."

Slack gave me a wizard reference – even though I'd still not met him, off in that house of his with all the medicines and cheese. He wrote me a nice note as well, saying how satisfactory Mr Corrison'd told him I'd always been, and that if I ever again sought employment in the West Country, there'd always be a position for me on the Slack Circuit.

It *was* a wrench, going. But the County was such a little

place. And I'd had this offer of the MD-ship at the Queen's Palace, Sutton-in-Ashfield, a six-piece orchestra, eight hundred seats. And nice as they'd been to us down there, Delia and I were missing our folks up north a little bit.

So that was a change in Twenty-three: on the Great Western again, then on the LMS up to Nottinghamshire. No more cream and sea breezes up there! Just cobbles and smoking chimneys and pit-heaps and miners.

We had lodgings with miners as a matter of fact. Rawtenstall, their name was, pronounced Rottenstall. The father was a pit deputy and all three sons worked at the coal face. On Friday night when they came home, their mother would have an egg custard ready. These three boys'd eat the egg custard, then stick their fingers down their throats till they made themselves vomit. When they brought this egg custard back up, it'd be black with coal dust. That was the only way they had to get the coal dust out of them.

They told us all about their lives, these boys – and, you know, it was terrible. The seam they worked was three miles underground. It took half an hour to get to in the spake, their kind of train thing. And working for hours on end doubled up, in this choking dust, and pitch black. They even had to eat their midday dinner in the dark. I remember them saying how, as they sat there eating in this pitch blackness, they could see dozens of green eyes all around, watching them. And that was the rats!

They'd originally put cats down there to catch them, but the rats proved too big for the cats. And now these cats had all gone blind from never seeing daylight. Sometimes you'd get a line of coal-trucks hurtling along, with a blind cat standing up on top of the coal.

How they killed the rats was a queer thing as well. If anyone saw a rat, he'd go up behind it and just lightly touch it on its back with a stick. The rats had such an in-built fear of the seam caving in that, if you touched one even lightly on its back, it died of heart failure.

It was the poor pit ponies Delia felt so sorry for. She was so tender-hearted about all animals. She'd not kill anything if she could help it, not even a fly. These three Rawtenstall boys told us how the pit ponies worked so patiently, dragging heavy trucks of coal along. Then, every so often, they'd be brought up into daylight and turned into a field for a few hours' rest. These boys said they used to go almost mad with joy, running round, kicking up their legs. "They don't want to go back, though," I remember the youngest boy telling Delia. It upset her all night, thinking of that.

Now here's a funny thing. In the same pit where the Rawtenstalls worked, there was a black man. I've no idea where he came from. And all through the day, everyone else looked exactly like him. Reminds me of a story they told me about all these miners at the end of the day, going to the pit-head baths, totally pitch-black, only one of them has got a – what shall we say? – a John Thomas that's bright clean pink. He's the only one that goes home to midday dinner and sees his wife!

*She* was a good soul, too, that Mrs Rawtenstall, the way she kept that home and family together. Both the older sons it was too late to do anything about. But she was determined to get her youngest, Joseph, out of that pit and away. Their father, the pit deputy, was a bit of a bad lot all round – a wastrel, a drunkard. I've seen him myself on pay-night, standing on the corner of Copenhagen Street outside the Three Tuns, throwing pennies up in the air for children to catch. The only money Mrs Rawtenstall could save was a shilling now and then that she'd slip down the side of her chair when he wasn't looking. One day, she was going to have enough shillings to buy that boy a train ticket and get him off, so he'd not die of his lungs like all the rest.

Sutton-in-Ashfield's where we were in an earthquake. And where we got our motor bike. It was a New Imperial, dark red tank, finished in double lines of gold leaf. Five hundred cc. Side-car fitted. With hood. Rear-view mirror, Klaxon horn. And shall I tell you what I gave for it? This is without a word of a lie. Eighty-one pounds, twelve and sixpence.

I'd thought I'd buy a motor bike, and I'd seen adverts for these New Imperials, manufactured in Princip Street, Birmingham. But I'd no clue how to set about getting one. It was

Frank Prue, my piano-organist at the Queen's Palace, who fixed everything up. He wrote to the New Imperial people and arranged for the machine I wanted to be collected direct from their factory. He came with me, too, to drive it away, as I couldn't drive a motor bike. Of course, that saved New Imperial the expense of dispatching it in a crate. So Frank Prue got them to remit us our train-fares to Birmingham one-way – even money for both our dinners – if we'd go and collect it personally.

I remember, when we came out of the factory into Princip Street, with Frank Prue driving and me behind, there was a policeman on point-duty. As we passed this policeman, he said, "You be sure and run that in properly. It makes all the difference."

By gum, we covered some miles on that New Imperial did Delia and I, with Warwick next to us in the side-car. All round Derbyshire – the Peak District – and up to Yorkshire, through the Dales. And to Haworth, to see the house where the Brontës lived. Delia was red-hot on all those Brontës. We often used to put up at a place in Hawes named Fineson's Temperance Hotel. And always stop for some refreshment at The Penny House, where you could see all the drovers come in. So called because a pot of ale only cost a penny.

The Queen's Palace had been a music hall – Two or Three Circuit, I forget which – but, like all of them, had gone over to Pictures and Variety. Each programme, you had three pictures and three turns. They let a screen down for the pictures, then pulled it up after intermission, revealing the proscenium arch. We in the pit played atmosphere for the pictures *and* to cue, from their books, for the turns. It'd got second nature to me by then, looking down, then up, then down. Keeping my eye on the score, the boys, the screen, or what the turn was doing, all at the same time. Thinking ahead to the next reel or the next double somersault. Your mind always up in the air and everywhere.

That motor bike reminds me of when they showed *The Volga Boatman* at the Queen's Palace, a really big picture about Russia that not only had its own special score for the cinema orchestra but its own Russian tenor who accompanied it round, singing everywhere it showed. As MD, of course, I'd to go and meet this Russian tenor off the train. I thought, "I'll go on the bike and fetch him to the theatre in the side-car."

Well, then he comes off the train at Sutton-in-Ashfield station, he turns out to be a great huge man, about twenty stone. I shake hands with him, say a few words – he doesn't speak much English – then take him out and put him in the side-car of my New Imperial. It's a squeeze, but we just about manage it. Then I hop on and roar him over the QP for that afternoon's two o'clock performance.

But when he tries to get out, he can't. He's stuck! Oh, my Lord! His face goes purple and he starts to rave and swear in Russian, and push with both hands. But he cannot get out of that side-car, and I can't pull him.

In the end, I had to run across to some men who were taking up the road. "Please," I said, "can you come and help me extract a man from a side-car? He's got to be singing in Russian in fifteen minutes." So two of these men came – great big strong chaps – and they took hold of the Russian tenor and pulled and pulled till in the end, with a terrible wrench, out he popped.

Later on, as the lights go down and he's sitting by me waiting to sing, I'm too embarrassed to look him in the eye. I look down at my desk, raise my baton, and what do you think are the first words I read in the score? "Song of the Volga Boatman. E flat. (Heaving and Straining.)"

Well, you know what came in then and stopped my career and put me out of work and nearly destitute, so I'd to join a dance band and go off to London, and finished up playing by myself on top of a plinth in Lowestoft. Talking pictures! The end of everything!

We really never believed they'd catch on, you know. There'd been sort of talking pictures for a long time, and no one thought anything much about them. Because, like I explained before, silent pictures weren't silent. They had their own musical scores . . . special sound effects, like hitting that chain with an iron staple for the hortator in *Ben Hur*. And the actors and actresses were so eloquent in their faces . . . their eyes and hands. Everyone knew exactly what was going on. Nobody *needed* hear any words.

And beautiful to look at, how they arranged the lighting and everything. A film like *Don Juan* – which we had at the QP – was more like some old master in black and white. And so subtle, the way the camera made you notice and pick up on things. Like Greta what's her name, when her wedding-ring slipped off her fingers onto the floor. And that man and his little boy in Vidor's *The Crowd*. I remember our crescendo when the camera soared away and left them, happy again and laughing at a show. I'll tell you, my boys in the pit'd be sniffing and dabbing their eyes, even though they'd watched it a dozen times already.

Now, instead, you got these horrible crude, crackly things. Folk opening their mouths like fish out of water, and the words coming a little bit later. And silly running round and pulling faces, no better than monkeys at the zoo.

As I say, we never thought they'd catch on. But then, out of the blue, they did. All the picture companies stopped making silents and switched over to sound. Even some things that'd been begun as silents were changed into talkies midway through. Didn't matter how cack-handed bad it might be, as long as the pictures talked.

So there it was in Twenty-seven – end of my world, near enough. No more pictures with special scores, and Russian tenors to sing them. No more pit orchestras. No more work.

It didn't happen straight off because, of course, the picture houses had to instal new sound equipment and that was a big undertaking and expense for them. We carried on at the QP for a few more months, showing lovely silents like *Don Juan*, I mentioned before, and playing our music to set the mood like always, and folk came in and seemed to enjoy it just as much as ever.

But you knew in your bones it was all coming to an end. Every week in *The Era* you'd see an announcement of this or that cinema company spending umpteen hundreds on new

Vitaphone equipment. And the Appointments Wanted column getting longer and longer. I remember, I had a vacancy myself in the QP pit. Crabtree, my 'cellist, left to emigrate to New Zealand. And shall I tell you how many applications I received for his position? Nearly five hundred. One was from a lady 'cellist – and, of course, they found it even harder to get work than the men. I remember the letter she wrote me, on pink notepaper with a letter J at the top. I showed it to Delia. It said if I'd give her the position, she'd be willing to become my mistress.

The axe didn't fall on us at the QP till the beginning of Twenty-eight. The General Manager – Bolting, his name was – called me into his office one Thursday dinner-time, and I knew right away what for. He said the people were arriving to put in the new projection-equipment over that weekend. We'd to play out the Thursday, Friday and Saturday programme. Then our services would no longer be required.

"It's no reflection on you, Mr Hallett," he said. "Or on any of your boys. We must follow the vogue for this thing or else lose trade." So there I was, for the first time in my life. Dismissed!

One thing I'd made up my mind very firmly about, when I'd first seen this approaching, was that come what may Delia hadn't to suffer worry or anxiety. Whatever burdens might be, must fall on my shoulders alone. As long as Delia was my wife, she'd always to feel as safe and protected as if girded about with steel.

So, for Delia's sake, I made light of it. Even though I felt the ground had been cut away from under my feet.

"But what'll you do?" Delia said. "It's getting so difficult now with all these places."

"Ooh, leave it to me, love," I said to her. "I expect I'll get any amount of offers and be suited in double-quick time. So let that be the least of your worries."

I'd no notion, you see, how difficult it really was. I thought, I'm still a young man, I've had good appointments, and hold first-rate references. I'm luckier than some. Like Henry Flack, my second violin, who was turned sixty when they pitched him out. Poor lad finished up playing for pennies on the sands at Fylde.

I bought *The Era*, *The Entr'acte*, *The Referee* and *The Stage* – every paper that carried adverts for openings in the music profession – and turned to the Situations Vacant, where you always used to find any amount of jobs, down one column and up the next, your pick of two or three hundred every week. And now, just a dozen or so, eked out among Appointments Sought. And for next to no money, some of them "Leader Violinist Required – Variety and Interlude – Excellent References Only" two guineas. They could do that now, you see. It was such a buyers' market everywhere.

MD-ships weren't to be had, unless your brother or someone worked in the front office. So I thought, "I'll go down to leader. That's all right", and I wrote off to half a dozen places. And got back not a single acknowledgement. "Oh well, I'll go to second," I thought, and wrote off again, about fifteen more letters, and by hand. Two replies only: "Regret Vacancy Filled". "Right," I thought. "I'll go to third. It won't kill me for a month or two."

I wrote off everywhere: to Manchester, Birmingham, Coventry, Liverpool. I wrote to Brighton and Eastbourne and Frinton and Southsea and Lyme Regis and Leamington Spa. Even going as third violin at a pound a week, "own dinner-clothes furnished", I couldn't get so much as an interview.

Early on, I wrote to Slack down in Cornwall, because he'd said there'd be a position for me any time. But Slack had died and the business been sold, and the new owners had shut everything down bar the County in Truro, which they'd now modernised and made over to sound. So that was another door closed.

In the end, the only thing I could see was an interval-pianist at a little picture house called The Scala over in Nuneaton, that only showed cheap Wild West things, with Jack Hoxie and them, and stank of carbolic soap. Thirty-two and six a week I got, for seven afternoons and six nights. And nobody listened. The kiddies used to throw paper darts over my shoulder.

So that Delia'd not worry, I told her a white lie. I said I was at a good place, Pictures and Variety, but she'd better not come and see me there because the comedians they had on were inclined to be a bit blue. She accepted that. But, of course, was interested in my work, same as always. Every night when I got in, she'd inquire about the turns I'd played for and how they'd done, and I'd have to invent all these names and details as I had my supper. It never stops at just the one lie, does it? Once you've told one, you've to tell another, and another.

Then I was with a dance band that played twice a week at Nuneaton Commemoration Hall. Cyril Spragge and his Four Tune Tellers. Piano, violin, and guitar in the Latin dances. I loathed every second of it, thanks in no small measure to Cyril Spragge. You'd to wear make-up that was ordinary Brown and Polson's gravy-mixing powder, and a horrible shiny silver suit. Mine had been originally made for a man about double my size. The only way the coat would fit was if Delia gathered it all up with a clothes-peg at the back.

We'd got some savings, about £200 in the Post Office. I always earned such good salaries – better ones with each job – I'd never really troubled to put much by. But no debts either, thank God. What we had we paid for cash on the nail, like that caravan and the New Imperial. And my Neuner & Hornstein violin, that I bought from Frank Prue at the QP. A hundred pounds I gave him for it, sovereigns into his hand. He was so pleased, he threw in that little brown guitar I've got as well.

Delia had gone so short when she was a girl with that terrible stepmother I never wanted her to feel denied anything. But I knew, the kind of person she was, she'd feel awkward about asking me for things. So I never actually gave her housekeeping money as such. I'd leave it in an old tail coat I had made for me when I first joined Lord and Fletcher's Orchestra. Wherever we lived, I always made sure a £5 note was in that coat, folded in the pocket where I used to put the rosin for my bow. If ever Delia needed anything for the home or for Warwick, she only had to go into our room, open the wardrobe and £5 would be there.

So, for quite a long time, I didn't let Delia know how bad things were slipping up on the financial front. I said I was getting reasonable money at The Scala and with Cyril Spragge, when really both only paid me buttons. And that £5 carried on being there for her in the pocket of that old tail coat. The only way I could do it was keep drawing on our Post Office account, which was how the whole £200 got used up. It was foolish, I know. But I didn't want her to worry.

Then I said: "Delia, love. There's no sense in keeping up a big motor bike. They're an awful bother with the petrol and oil, and a push bike's far healthier." She agreed. So that brought in a little more.

I even made a trip down to London, because I'd been told about this place off Oxford Street where musicians could go and get work through some sort of exchange, by the day or even the hour. And there were hundreds and hundreds – violinists, 'cellists, clarinettists, oboists, percussionists, all thrown out of their jobs by the talkies. Dignified men, you know. Still looking dapper as ever, till you saw their collars and cuffs. The chap in the queue before me told me we'd not much hope: to get one of the jobs from this agency place, you'd to sleep on the pavement outside the door. These men, that had played in wonderful theatres on the Number One Circuit, used to sleep the night there in boxes from the dress-factories. That's how desperate everyone was.

But what I can't understand, as I'm stood in the queue up to this employment place, is why the street looks so familiar.

After about five hours, I'm finally let in and directed to a room right on the top floor, and a man there says "Sorry. Nothing for you," hardly even bothering to look up. Then, as I turn away, I notice this big old carved wooden fireplace – and finally realise where I am. I'm in Madame Estelle's house in Newman Street, Soho, where I came and stopped with my Aunt Bertha – where she made up her beauty boxes, and praised my hands and put in her odd glass eyes, and got me Leo, my first violin. This is the very same room with the old fireplace where I used to go to sleep.

Well, I'm nearly at my wits' end with no work, hardly knowing how we'll weather through the next month when, right out of the blue, a letter comes with a Suffolk postmark, and it's from my dad. Bless my dear old dad, his heart and cotton socks. What an angel he turned out to be.

He'd retired from business in Twenty-nine, and sold both his two grocer's shops in Keighley for a good price. My mother – who I told you was an invalid – had got so bad by now, she was permanently bedridden and needed a nurse full-time. So Dad said to her, "You've worked all these years doing the books, and never complained. Choose anywhere in England you'd like to live." She said, "I've always fancied Suffolk, with those lovely Broads." So Dad had bought her a house right on Oulton Broad, near Lowestoft, and that's where he and she – and her full-time nurse – were living.

"Why don't you and Delia and Warwick come and be here, side of us?" my dad wrote to me. "I know things have got a bit tricky lately, and you'll be far better off among your own. There's a house next door to let, that I'll rent for you as you like. Mother will love seeing Delia. I've got glasshouses for tomatoes and, if all else fails, I'll pay you a wage to help me with those."

So that's where we spent Thirty-two to Thirty-eight: at "Dormers", Oulton Broad, near Lowestoft. Warwick went to school. Delia helped look after Mother – which she'd originally done, that's how we first met. I helped Dad with his glasshouses, the way I used to back when I was a young youth.

We were all right as a family, had sufficient to eat and were sheltered, thanks to Dad. But in my work, things just carried on going downhill. I'd thought there'd be more likelihood of jobs around there, being seaside. But it proved as bad as the place we'd just left. People talk about the Thirties, how difficult they were for workers in factories and mills. No one remembers what it was like for the musical profession.

One summer I was in the Lowestoft Municipal Orchestra – playing outdoors, in the Eastern Gardens – but they got on my nerves so bad, I walked out after a month. The standard of musicianship was abysmal. You could have taken all the instruments up to the top of the Eastern Pavilion, dropped them down onto the path and still got a better noise than that orchestra made when they were trying. The leader wore an orange wig you could see the canvas lining of, and while he played, he tapped his left foot on the floor. "I can forgive the wig," I said to Delia. "But not the tapping of that left foot."

Then I went with a concert party in the bandstand enclosure. A shilling an hour as piano accompanist, if you were lucky. More often, it'd just be a few pennies out of the sock. This sock on a stick used to be taken round the crowd as you played. They call that "bottling": I'll never know why.

A real tremendous bill you'd get out there! Blue comic in boater and carnation. Girl singer in sandals, with paper flowers on her hip. Flags out of coats. Joke about Mr Baldwin. Cue for Grand Finale: "He-ere they come again!"

I had the worst time of all at The Sparrows' Nest, which was a sort of dinner-dance place along the front, where I'd applied because they were supposed to want a "Director of Melody". And do you know all it was? I'd to sit up on a plinth all alone each evening in this nearly empty dinner place, from 7.30 to 10, just playing a snare drum with brushes in time to records on a gramophone.

I said, "Look. I'm a first-rate violin. I can do you piano. Get up a trio . . . give them Strauss waltzes . . . Selections from *The Merry Widow* or *Bohemian Girl*.

They said, "You're out of your time, Mr Hallett. It's Nineteen Thirty-six. *This* is what the customers want."

It was a shocking summer that year, rain lashing against the tall windows, only two or three couples ever on the floor. But my Delia came in every night and sat there, at a table down on the left. And there wasn't a moment I couldn't see her watching me and listening to every note.

Sometimes I literally was penniless. I'd read about that so often, never dreaming it might happen to me. When you put your hand in your trouser pocket, and there's nothing there. Nor anywhere else, and no prospect of it. If it weren't for Dad renting "Dormers" for us and giving me a bit for helping him with his tomatoes, I don't know what we'd have done. And every week, he'd watch till he saw we'd gone out, then he'd come in and leave a ten shilling note on the mantelpiece.

Then there was all the worry about what our Warwick

needed bought for him, after he won his scholarship to Lowestoft High School. A new blazer and cap and sports things, and I don't know what . . . Oh yes, he won a scholarship. Didn't I mention that? He was a clever boy. And always studying, like I said before, his Maths and what-not. He had no interest in music. For relaxation, he'd sit and read a book about his Physics or Calculus.

Well, I hadn't the means to titivate him up. And I was adamant we'd not to ask Dad and Mother for anything more. So Delia went to see the head of his old school, Mr Tench and explained the situation, and Mr Tench said, "Mrs Hallett, you're not to worry." Then he says there's a special bursary – kept for the really clever boys – that can buy Warwick his new school blazer and cap and sports things, and anything else he might need.

He was a funny boy, though. He didn't like the idea of taking this bursary, even though fully entitled to it. In fact, they only gave it to the cleverest ones.

"If boys at my new school find out," he said, "they'll think I've come on charity."

"Don't be silly," I told him.

"They will, Dad," he said. "They'll call me names. A charity boy or something."

"Well, you know you're not," I said. "So that's enough, and all there is about it."

In the end, I said to Delia, "I'd best give up. There's no work. I can't support my family on what I earn from music. I'd best do something else – though what, at my time of life, I can't imagine."

"Are you sure?" Delia said.

"Yes, I'm sure," I said. "Though I know you'd go on backing me up and never complaining if I finished busking to picture-house queues, Delia love."

Later that day, we were next door, up in my mother's bedroom. She'd a window with a lovely view, right over Oulton Broad. Dad was there, and I sat on Mother's bed and told them my decision to leave the musical profession and try to find some other employment.

The Dad looked at Mother and he asked me did I remember coming home to Duxford all excited and telling them I'd left Taplow's mill to go off and play for the summer at Codlin's at Llandudno.

"Yes, I should think I do," I said.

"Well," Dad said. "We didn't want to cast you down, or look on the black side in any way. But the next morning, I went into the Yorkshire Bank and opened an account for you, and paid a guinea into it. And I've been paying a guinea in every week since then, just in case a time should ever come when your music wasn't enough. So if you're decided on getting out now, that money's available. It's mounted up to almost £500."

And Mother picked up my hand on the coverlet and gave it a squeeze. Just like she used to under the table, if Dad ever so much as mentioned my joining him in the business, which she'd never stand.

And do you know what she said about that £500, and what I'd be best off doing with it?

"Put it into a nice grocer's shop."

I found a place in Bottisham, just outside Cambridge. Three hundred for the premises, a hundred for the stock, a hundred for the goodwill. We went there in Thirty-nine and left in Forty-nine to come here. Those ten years in Bottisham were what put me back on my feet financially.

That was an odd thing, too. All my years of playing music, being in theatres, knowing stage people and stage things, I'd have thought I'd been getting further and further away from how I grew up and what my father did. And yet as soon as I got behind the counter of that little shop, I just took to it. The slicing, the weighing, the packing, the totting up, were second nature. And putting a Royal Sovereign pencil straight behind my ear. Like magic, the way I slipped back into all that.

I went right through the War, with all the restrictions, the ration-books and coupons. Five years I managed everything by myself – the forms and returns and whatnot they made you do if you retailed food. And in all that time, with the strain I was under, I never got ill, not even one day. Late at night, I used to go outside, where these two big elm trees grew, and I'd stand equidistant between them, shut my eyes and recite the Taoists' Prayer. That's what I believe kept me going.

My dad said a funny thing, not long before he died. He was staying down there with us, and watching me serve in the shop.

"You're a better grocer than I was, Arthur."

"No. Never," I said.

"Yes, you are," he said. "I was good with provisions, but always too shy to say anything much to people I served. Your theatrical career's given you an edge on me. You know how to talk to them."

I wish you could have seen the garden here in Delia's time – what a show she made of it with her roses. Tulips. Daffodils. Primulas. Aubretia and night-scented Stock. Acea Japonica. Plumbago Capensis. Nice cockleshell borders everywhere. And there at the bottom, no forest but a lovely view across the fields up to Horsen Hill. Our granddaughter Patsy, when she was little, used to lean out on summer evenings and wave to some children in their bedroom all the way over at Newitt's Farm.

We came here in Forty-nine, after Dad died. By selling my shop at Bottisham and his house at Oulton Broad and buying this bungalow, I made eleven hundred clear profit. And hardly a day's gone by since when I haven't rued and regretted it.

The village had been totally evacuated in the War and used as part of a training-area for tanks. When everyone came back in Forty-five, apparently, it was a ghost place, grass and weeds growing up and millions of rabbits everywhere. Even today they're always coming across bits of shrapnel and shell-casing in the fields. There was a little boy not long ago, down Swavesey Bottom, killed by picking up a live round.

I thought "Well, it's pretty in quite a lot of ways. And convenient", which it used to be. When we first came there was the Post Office and Mrs Raymer's tobacconist. Buses to Woodbridge and Saxmundham two or three times a day from right here on the green. Chillesford Priory station just up the road. I'm not joking, honestly. For a little country place, Swavesey used to be convenient.

Warwick never lived with us here. Directly he came out of the forces in Forty-five he was off to college, living in. Then he got a job at some school down in Canterbury. Teaching maths and science – all above my head. His schools after that were always down there: Canterbury, Sevenoaks, Faversham. He chose that as his part of the world.

We saw even less of him after he married Sylvie, which I was against right from the start. But, of course, no one paid any attention to what I thought. They asked us to the wedding, but I said to Delia, "I can't watch it, I just can't." So his mother went down on her own.

Delia made a nice home of this, same as everywhere. Kept it all shining spick and span, brought on that wonderful garden. And never a single solitary word of complaint about the house being too small or not nice enough. Always the same sweet, gentle thing as ever, my wife and best pal.

We had pleasant enough times, the two of us, specially in summer, when it does get quite lovely around here. We'd go long walks all round through Butley, Eyke, Orford and Chillesford, or over the marsh paths; do fifteen miles in a day sometimes and think nothing of it. Or bicycle over to Snape or Aldeburgh or Southwold. Till that terrible thing came on, she was such a one for getting about and seeing things. I always made sure she never got worried by dogs or birds. And that she never had to go inside a chemist's shop.

I'll tell you something that puzzles me. Really puzzles me. Have you got a minute to hear this as well, or have you got to go?

All those years ago, when I was a boy at school, and a young man, and a mature man and a middle-aged man and even quite an old man, there was – how can I say it? – a certain flavour to life. You lived in the twentieth century, and that was exciting! Every year that went by, some new invention seemed to come along that was so wonderful you could hardly believe. Motor cars. Aeroplanes. Wireless. Television. Things that made people's life easier and brought them closer together and made them feel safer and more secure and happier.

I can't tell you exactly when it happened. It was when I was already quite an old man, retired and living here with Delia. That flavour of life, that I'd had for 65-odd years, suddenly changed. It was sort of like being aboard a vehicle, and feeling it stall. You weren't climbing uphill with the 20th century any more. You were sliding back downhill, faster and faster.

This village is an example of what I mean. Because, you know, these past few years, it's lost everything. First they took away the railway, then the buses. They shut down the Post Office, and Mrs Raymer's. They even shut the little school that was here. Now the kiddies have to be taken by bus, miles and miles to school every day. In winter-time, they set off in the dark and it's dark when they come home. You'd worry if you saw those little mites, walking down the lanes in the dark, with tree-roots reaching out for them.

Now I hear they've even pulled down Swavesey Hall. Up on the main road coming from Woodbridge, you'll see these big enormous gates and a line of trees down to what used to be a magnificent house, where Royalty used to come and shoot in the old days. I believe there's nothing left at the end of those trees any more but mud and a few builder's huts.

Up until Delia died, I never let on to her what a mistake I knew I'd made, coming here when we retired, instead of going back up north among our own. People down here just aren't the same. You might think you've got to know them, like I did, giving piano lessons to some of the kiddies. You can be talking to them one day when they come to collect the kiddie, all friendly enough. Then next day you'll pass them in the village and say "Good morning" and they won't even seem to want to look at you.

Almost twenty years, my Delia lived in this bungalow. And in all that time, no one across there in Almshouse Cottages so much as invited her indoors for a cup of tea.

It was Parkinson's. I nursed her. She couldn't walk, or use the toilet on her own. I had to get an invalid chair to push her around. I've still got it here, out in the front hall.

Lifting her up in bed one day, I injured my own back. Because she was a big woman, you see. I had to crawl on my stomach to the phone to call the doctor.

She was seventy-nine when she died. Remember what the doctor told her when she bore our Warwick at thirty? "Delia, you've done wonderful to live this long."

I said to her one day near the end, trying to cheer us both up: "When I asked you to marry me out in our garden at Duxford, your answer was 'I'll chance it.' How do you think it's turned out, Delia love?"

"Not too bad," she said.

She used to sit in this same chair I'm in now. I had a metal bar put across, so she could pull herself forward to look at television. The screw-holes for it are still there at the end of either arm.

So here I am, talking to you at almost ninety-seven years old. That's what I'll be, next April the 13th. My mother's birthday was April the 15th and my Aunt Nan's was April the 18th. Delia's was October the 11th.

I know I'm very, *very* old. The trouble is, I don't feel old. Inside I feel just the same as I always have. A young man, not an old one. Then I'll pass a mirror and see that face looking out at me, and . . . oh dear.

Everything's still in good order, eyesight, hearing, digestion and all that. My hand's still steady to write, and hold that bow. My memory's quite good. My mind's clear, I think. The only real trouble is what they said about Mr Chips, do you remember? It's quite a bad case of Anno Domini.

I've still got that scoliosis wrong with my spine that I developed as a boy, pushing heavy-laden delivery-bikes. Lately, it's come on a bit worse, so I can't walk much further than down to the postbox at the Cross. What I do, I get out that invalid chair of Delia's and push it in front of me. It gives me just the support I need to toddle along. I couldn't tolerate a stick. Or one of those frame things, what's the name of them? Zithers?

It can catch me out as well, say if I'm carrying a full cup on a saucer through from the kitchenette to here. All of a sudden, it's as if I'm in the middle of a high wire, powerless to move. So that's just what I make pretend. "Ladies and gentlemen," I'll say out loud, "for my next miraculous feat, I shall carry this cup of Bovril to my tray-table, not spilling a single drop en route."

Warwick comes to see me as often as he can. It's such a terrible long way to drive, from Kent all up here. He's been far from well himself, for a long time. And lately there's been some trouble with the car and its MOT test.

I know he worries about me though, deep down. I worry about him, too, in that school, what he has to contend with nowadays. If ever he speaks to a girl pupil alone, he's got to leave the door of the room wide open, for fear she'll make some allegation against him. "The boys are bad enough, Dad," he told me once, "but the girls are far worse." That's what he said, honour bright. The girls are worse than the boys.

I ring up sometimes, but don't like to in case Sylvie answers. And she always *does* answer. When he comes on and I say "Hello love, how are things?" he always says the same: "Don't ask!" Except for once, when he said, "Bloody awful!"

Patsy, my granddaughter, is working in Italy. She sent me all the cards along my mantelpiece. The inscription on one is a little bit cross. I'd written to her I was afraid she'd not recognise the garden here, the way I'd let it go. Back comes this card from Genoa: "I certainly would *not* recognise the garden after the lovely way it used to be in Grandma's time, with all her roses and aubretia . . ."

Shopping has got a bit difficult, now there are no more shops. My bread and milk come by van. He's Indian, with a broad Suffolk accent; quite nice, really. I get my paper delivered, the *Express*, which I've always read; I like its politics. The big worry is violin-strings. They aren't obtainable anywhere round here, not even Woodbridge. I've to order them by post from Randal and Teague in Lowestoft, allow four to six weeks for delivery. Half a crown each, they used to cost. Now they cost four seventy-five.

Fridays I go in the mini-bus the Council sends, to collect my pension at Orford, do a bit of shopping there. I don't like it much, sitting among all the old crows. I'll buy some Mr Kiplings, honey to put in my tea, perhaps some bananas if they aren't too dear. It's one of those supermarket places, though I can't see much super about it, really. I'll often buy a packet of biscuits, fetch it back here and open it, and every one in the packet'll be broken. In our shop in Keighley, broken biscuits were a spoiled line. We practically used to give them away.

Dr Rich comes once a fortnight, gives me a look-over and stays for a bit of a talk. He wants to get me a home-help, but I'm not keen. Things would only get shifted around and turned upside-down. I know it's a pickle, specially after the way Delia liked to have everything. That little broken couch – where the guitar is – used to vex her. "We must get it a new castor and its leg mended," she kept saying for years. Now she's gone, for some reason, I don't quite like to do it.

The vicar calls in every so often, though I don't ask him to. That Taoists' Prayer expresses all I feel in the matter of worship. They have what they call a team ministry now, based at Aldeburgh, running all the churches by rota. I believe St Peter's here only gets a service one Sunday in four. This present vicar's an old army man. You can always tell, can't you? I don't think he's much bothered about my soul, but he does like my handwriting. I can still do that copperplate I learned in Taplow's foreign invoice department. If they're having a sale-of-work or a coffee do, he'll drop in a hundred blank cards and I'll write them out for him as invitations.

I do get a bit nervous sometimes here by myself, what with everything you read about these days. I'll think, "Don't be silly. Why'd anyone want to be bothered murdering you? You've nothing of value, just some old sticks of furniture and a violin." But that doesn't stop them any more, does it? They'll do it for 20p, a handful of sweets or a pension-book.

And there are so many new things you've to start worrying about, aren't there? Like all this dreadful Aids business. I see even nuns are going down with it now, through transfusions of infected blood. I used to quite enjoy giving mine, when that van thing toured the villages. I'd stay for a cup of tea, a biscuit, a lie-down and a bit of talk to the nurse. And all that time I could have been contracting Aids.

I look at television quite a fair bit, though that set's not too grand a performer any more. He'll last me out anyway, old Ferguson. I love a good play, if you can find one. And the orchestral concerts, but not this modern shiny-light jingly-jangly stuff. I'm not saying it's bad: I just don't understand it. And some of the dancing tends to get on the suggestive side.

What I do enjoy, though it's silly, is something they put on for kiddies in the afternoon. Do you follow the adventures of Wonderwoman? She's a card, really, the way she goes wooshing here and there, shinning up high buildings and throwing all these bad men about. I'll sit and watch her, and sometimes think to myself, "*I'd* like to know someone like that."

Delia was the only one for me, and there was none after. But occasionally I think it'd be nice if, one day, Wonderwoman were to woosh into here, in those red boots and that starry-stripey cloak of hers, and carry me off in her arms.

I'll tell you what keeps me going. It's the same thing as all through my life. It's when I open that case, take out my Neuner and go to that music-stand. It's when I put my handkerchief on my shoulder, rest my cheek, look along that little dark road of strings, stretch my fingers out and bring up my bow. After all this time, it still makes me so excited, I have to catch my breath.

I'll shut my eyes sometimes, and feel the years drop away as if they'd never been. I'm back in that pit in the dark; the lovely hubbubby dark. I'm at my light, watching a scarlet curtain that shimmers silver all along its folds. My baton's raised. Our warning bell rings; up shoot the tabs. There it all is, brighter than day, with the Corps de Ballet: "numbers six, four and nine, watch lead girl for change." I can feel that cool air on my face, made of rouge and pomade, feathered dresses, gold slippers and loveliness.

I can see them all come out there as we play their cues . . . Vesta Tilley . . . Eugene Stratton . . . Marie Lloyd . . . George Lashwood in his opera cloak, sipping his tea . . . the Chinese acrobats, sliding down to the stage by their pigtails . . . Amandus as Pope of Rome . . . Bryn the Terrible . . . Coram the ventriloquist in his Guardsman's uniform, and that little soldier doll in his breast pocket, lit by the one pin-spot. I can hear what they said to each other, just before the little doll lifted up its bugle and played "The Last Post":

"Sir, do you think I'll ever be a *real* soldier?"

"I'm sure you will. Someday."

"Sir?"

"Yes?"

"Is 'someday' the same as 'one day'?"

I've been playing something lovely for myself, this week, Beethoven's "Spring Sonata". And I'll tell you a thing I just can't understand. Now at this silly age of ninety-six, I seem to be playing better than I ever have in my life.

Well, we've talked a good long while. And you've heard a few things. Not for quotation, of course, and in the strictest confidence.

I'm not a bit afraid, you know. It's just like going downhill, over jumps, towards the edge of a precipice. You know there can only be one or two jumps left before you go over.

I'll go to bed tonight, quite happy. Fold everything up neat, put my keys where Warwick can find them easily if anything should happen. Then get into bed, next to Delia's place. Think of her a little bit, then say the Taoists' Prayer, like I used to late at night in Cambridgeshire, between those two trees:

"I know Thou carest for me as for all things. With every part of Nature, I am in Thy hands. Whatever may befall, I trust Thee utterly . . ."

We'd better stop now. These units notch up so fast, don't they? We don't want to get a shock when the bill comes in.

When I say cheerio to you in a moment, I'm going to use a term we always did in Yorkshire, even man speaking to man. I want you to know in advance there's nothing peculiar about it. It's just a term of affection, to denote our friendship, and your being in my confidence.

Goodnight then, love. Thank you for phoning me. Goodbye, love.

Goodnight.

# Living Doll

You had to be in early at *Eye* magazine to see Dolly Pilchard. Her shift began at five-thirty and when she finished, just before nine, only Derwent the graphic artist was likely to be at work in *Eye*'s fourth-floor concourse. Few other than Derwent even knew she'd been there, let alone how she occupied herself among the open secrets of Britain's greatest Sunday colour supplement.

Dolly was equally unaware of *Eye*'s vast pre-eminence as she vacuumed the yellow carpet tiles, polished the black work-tops and emptied wastepaper tins – that so many Sunday rivals would have paid fortunes to sift – into the cleaners' communal plastic tub. She did not speculate why the early-morning debris should so regularly include a squad of empty champagne bottles with corresponding greasy glasses and rocketed corks. Once a month or so, after some special editorial achievement, she would find the whole concourse a sea of bottles, ravaged food, broken glass underfoot, and three or four desks still pushed together after their use as an impromptu discotheque floor.

Whatever the mess might be, Dolly set about taming it with her same illimitable stores of elbow grease. The only comment that ever passed her lips was a murmur, not wholly censorious, of "High jinks . . ."

Derwent the graphic designer, though surly and friendless, had long ago been taken to Dolly Pilchard's Cockney heart. Each morning when he arrived, a tartan Thermos of coffee stood at his drawing-board with three shortbread fingers beside it on a square of kitchen-roll. "He ain't got no Mummy," Dolly explained to the other cleaners, "so I'm like his Mummy to him." She brought Derwent presents back from all her holidays and, each Christmas, made his own small pudding alongside her family one.

"I put a nice drop o' brandy in," she always reassured him. "*And* I put in Russian stout." Her wink suggested infinities of Soviet good cheer.

She was small, stoop-shouldered and thin with a dour little face that, in the ordinary way, suggested anything but over-the-top hilarity. Her hair was steel-wool grey, tied by a surprising, youthful ribbon at the back. In winter, with her overall and the long cardigan-halves beneath, she wore stylish, almost skittish fur-trimmed ankle boots.

Her nature in all things was impulsive. On many mornings as Derwent came through the concourse, Dolly greeted him by wordlessly raising skirt and underslip to reveal broken stockings and deeply-grazed knees. The explanation was always the same. Running for her bus from Walworth before dawn, she had launched herself through the air to catch hold of its rear platform rail, and missed. One memorable morning, Derwent found her at work looking like a Cruikshank drawing of Marley's Ghost, her face bound round by a bandage securing a thick topknot of lint.

"Dolly . . . what*ever* have you been doing?"

"Call me a fool," Dolly said, shutting her eyes stoically and rubbing with her cloth. "'Go and put the stepladder in the bath, don't I? and climb up to change a bulb, when there's all ice in the bottom of the bath. Straight on top of me barnet I went! I was in double agony! Mr Pilchard had to go next door and get the nurse lady to come and put a dressing on me. I've fell on me head other times an' all – climbing on a stool to unbolt that back scullery-door, 'cos *he* can't do it with his leg. 'Must be how I get rid of all the mad blood in me."

Janice, the new Picture Desk secretary, became Dolly's other early morning confidante. Janice had previously worked for a solicitor, and maintained a punctilious nine o'clock start, even though her new boss would not appear, and no Picture Desk phone ring, for a good hour and a half yet.

She was a solemn little girl of sixteen, with attitudes in every way calculated to win Dolly Pilchard's approval. She, too, received coffee, home-made shortbread and, in time, the secret Dolly had come upon during her hours alone in *Eye*'s executive suites.

135

One morning as Janice was unpicking her headscarf, Dolly came up, gripped her elbow and gave a meaningful jerk of the head. Janice let herself be propelled into the Editor's office, with its freshly vacuum-ruffled carpet and savoury smell of Min Cream.

"This is Mister Simon's," Dolly told her in a high-decibel whisper.

"Yeah, I know."

"I used to do for him before he was here — when he was still up on the fif' floor."

"Mm?" Janice said, mystified.

"Look," Dolly whispered, tightening her grip on Janice's elbow and pointing to the small refrigerator set into a recess under the wall-length work-top.

"That's Mister Simon's fridge, that is . . . and do you know what. He's got *grub* in it! Look." She flicked open the fridge door and quickly shut it on the dense array of boxed cheeses, pâtés, yoghurt, Perrier and white wine.

"High jinks go on here you know, Janey," Dolly murmured with narrowed eyes. "You wait . . . you'll see. There never was such a place for high jinks."

This was 1969, when *Eye* magazine stood at the zenith. There had been nothing like it in Fleet Street before. There would be nothing like it ever again.

The derided editorial experiment of a few years before had turned into a Golden Goose that just couldn't stop laying. No other Sunday supplement — not even the *Times*'s — generated advertisement revenue on such a gorgeous scale. What had begun as merely the *Sunday Independent*'s "colour section" now totally supported its parent newspaper and upstairs neighbour at Constellation House. The "*Sunday Indy*" had the prestige, under its crusading Editor, Jack Shildrick. But *Eye* mopped up the millions as the very glass and mould of affluent, "swinging", butter and cream-sluicing, Beatle-crazy Britain.

The *Sunday Independent*'s proprietor was a canny Scot, wise enough to keep any Golden Goose firmly under his coat. *Eye* magazine, consequently, was a thing apart from the paper, its

Editor not answerable to Jack Shildrick like other departmental heads, but direct to the proprietor via his chief executive, Sir Dudley Fox. Shildrick had no direct control over his paper's most glamorous, high-profile element.

In the seven copper-faced floors of Constellation House, *Eye* was a law unto itself. The proprietor imposed only one house-rule, that it should continue generating its stupendous revenues. Provided it did so, editorial freedom was absolute. It could use and, if need be, waste the most famous writers, photographers and illustrators. It could send people anywhere in the world, for whatever reason. As long as those 18-carat eggs kept dropping into the ad-manager's nesting-box, no one could interfere.

Its separation from the black and white paper, and Jack Shildrick, was as vast as if oceans, not just one staircase, lay between. Emerging from the lift at any other floor, one heard the clatter and hum of usual newspaper production. At *Eye*'s fourth floor, one met only luxuriant silence, possibly broken by the distant pop of a cork and freshet of happy laughter.

Simon, its Editor, was a middle-aged patrician with a Zapata moustache who smoked three Romeo y Julietas a day and dealt with his only taskmaster, "Sir Dud", in their common tongue of Eton and Balliol. Simon had edited *Eye* since its inception in 1963. Each dizzy up-turn in its fortunes had taken place amid his generous guffaws, perfumed by the aroma of his cigar.

For those on the fourth floor, in that marvellous money-clinking cloud, every rule of Fleet Street had been turned upside-down. Instead of hurry and panic there was languor and laughter. Instead of pale ale and cottage pie there were four-hour lunches at Chez Victor. Instead of ranting News Editors there were young men from Cambridge in pink shirts and Rupert Bear trousers, with names like Edward, Jules and Nick. Instead of constant, striving fear there was job-security such as had previously been enjoyed only by medieval calligrapher monks.

Each day in *Eye*'s concourse began like a holiday, among fresh scents of soap suds and furniture-wax. Ahead, for nearly everyone, lay pleasant hours of looning, lechery and lunch. And then, more often than not – triumph and pre-eminence being so taken for granted, they were almost boring – a six o'clock champagne party.

Simon's "ideas lunch" took place in his office on alternate Wednesdays. More infrequently there were "ideas breakfasts" at The Connaught and "ideas dinners" at The Garrick or Gay Hussar. But ideas lunches were a fixture – the closest thing to routine for *Eye* executives as well as quintessential expression of its lovely, carefree life.

At 12.45, a procession of boys and girls in black – from "Nosh Soonest", Islington's most trendy food-to-your-door company – began carrying foil-covered dishes, shrink-wrapped quiches and pies, French loaves, Royal Worcester plates, silver cutlery, glasses and red and white gingham napkins into Simon's office. Both his secretaries also became visible, gathering chairs to augment his luxurious black leather suite.

From cubicles and loose boxes down the concourse, the Deputy Editor, the Art Director, the Picture Editor, the Fashion Editor, the "Design '69" Editor, the two Associate Editors, the Consulting Editor and the Special Projects Editor obeyed the unspoken summons. Here and there someone lingered who, at this zero hour, had suddenly found urgent need to make a loud, dramatic phone call to New York.

By 1.15 no one remained in the concourse but Janice at the Picture Desk and the two female sub-editors, whose unremitting workload generally stopped them going out for lunch.

In Simon's office, the polished black work-top was now covered with rice salads, a sculpted game pie, green and red-veined quiches, baskets of fruit, a whole Blue Vinney set about with cheese clublets, and a dozen each of Muscadet and Nuits St George. Supernumerary items, like stuffed olives, Normandy butter and Perrier, could be had from the refrigerator underneath.

The first fifteen minutes passed in concentrated spooning, hacking, cork-extracting, pouring and a smilingly fierce mêlée to secure one of the low-slung leather armchairs rather than the armless straight ones ranged in a semi-circle round Simon's desk. The Features Editor dropped a large piece of game pie onto the immaculate red carpet. "Christ, I'm sorry," he said, pushing back his boyish quiff and trying to rub the residue of pastry and meat into the pile with his foot.

Not until the dessert stage did Simon get to nominal business by popping a grape into his mouth, looking round the semi-circle and saying: "Right, you young rips . . . what's the gossip?"

The gossip, as usual, centred on Jack Shildrick, otherwise "Mighty JS" – his facile enthusiasms, his laughable Mancunian naïveté and philistinism, his repeated attempts to influence *Eye*'s content as though it were just another department of the newspaper.

The Art Director began, in what was agreed the best impersonation of Shildrick's gritty, over-excitable Northern voice.

"You know what he's supposed to have said about Lartigue's photographs of the rain forest pigmies? 'O, bloody hell, not *another* load of black tits.'"

"Oh God, the man gets worse and worse . . ."

"He rides a motorbike now, you know."

"Oh, no!"

"He does – a bloody great Bonneville 1800. And wears all the leather gear."

"Not that one by the front entrance . . ."

"Yes – the commissionaires have to keep an eye on it."

"Did you hear Jules's line about him? Go on Jules."

"I just said you can always see on Shildrick's face a perfect impression of the last bottom to have sat on it."

"I have to tell you we've received some more ideas from Mighty JS," Simon said amid the gale of laughter. "Written in a style I can only call late 20th-century Dictaphone . . ."

Nursing his wine against his chest, he opened a blue cardboard folder and indulgently drew out a two-page foolscap memorandum. In his own very passable Shildrick voice he read aloud:

"I've just seen a horrifying report on the state of Britain's teeth. It says that six out of ten people are going to lose their teeth by the age of forty-five. I think you should do a big colour special on everything appertaining to teeth. Derek could do smashing graphics to go with it – charts and graphs showing things like the decline in infant tooth-decay, the general fall-off in dental health since the War, etc. How often should people clean their teeth? What's the best kind of toothbrush to buy? ... I think it could be a belter for our big Spring circulation push ..."

There were Shildrickesque murmurs of "Ee!" and "By the 'eck!" The Art Director – who before lunch had been laying out Bill Brandt photographs in running uncaptioned spreads – showed studied unemotion at the prospect of the "smashing graphics".

". . . It's the same old story. He wants us to be *Woman's Own*."

"More reader service," murmured another Shildrick voice in a wearily familiar Shildrick phrase.

"Show it with charts."

"My wife . . ." Simon resumed reading.

"Oh God – not t'wife again," the Fashion Editor moaned.

". . . My wife says that a thing very few people know how to do is lay a table properly. There's more to it than you'd think – placing cutlery in formal setting, positioning flowers so as not to block views etc. I think you could do a nice little visual piece called something like Secrets of Silver Service . . ."

"*What?*"

"He can't be *serious!*"

"A table's about the only thing *he's* ever likely to lay," the Fashion Editor murmured, sweeping crumbs from her Foale and Tuffined lap.

"There's more . . . 'Both my daughters are going potty over a new pop combo called Amen Corner . . .'"

"'A new pop combo!'" the Feature Editor gurgled. ". . . Oh God, Derek, I'm sorry. I've kicked over your wine."

"Red or white was it, Jules?"

"What else have we got," Simon said, glancing quickly through the remainder of Shildrick's memo. "Natural childbirth . . . Window-boxes . . . Whatever happened to Esperanto . . . Looking ahead to the Common Market . . . Anne the sportsgirl Princess . . ."

"God!"

"I still can't believe it! Secrets of Silver Service!"

"Remember when t'wife wanted us to do Getting to Know Your Knitting Machine . . ."

"Well, what's the view?" Simon said, glancing round the semi-circle. " 'Thanks but no thanks' – right?"

The movement that banished Shildrick's two-page memo brough out a rainbow-and-silver box of Romeo y Julietas.

"So what have we got on the way?" Simon said, contentedly puffing blue-tinted smoke. "Toby?"

The Deputy Editor took a cigar from the box and passed it on.

"I'm still chasing David Niven, Nureyev and President Mobutu."

"Jules?"

"We've got The Curse Through the Ages ready to go . . . just need to shoot a cover picture."

"Who are we lining up for that?"

"I've asked Diane Arbus. She thinks she might be able to, but she's not sure. I'm going over to see her in LA next week."

". . . and Edna O'Brien's agreed to write What Did Christ Really Look Like? I'm going to ring her agent this afternoon."

"Jessamyn, you're off to Milan when?"

"Thursday."

"Are you and Hockney travelling together?"

"No – he's coming on from Paris."

"I thought a few of us boys might pop out while you're there – look in on the Collections, have lunch. Might be a nice little jolly."

The concluding business was dealing with a pile of ideas sent in by outside freelance writers and photographers. This took very little time. No one who did not already work for *Eye* was deemed good enough to do so – unless they happened to be a pretty girl in a mini-skirt, encountered by one or other of the young rips at a party. The Editor's own commissions in this field stuffed a fat, atrophying folder in his outer office files.

"Oh, Simon – I meant to ask you," the Features Editor said as the meeting broke up. "Am I still supposed to commission that piece about the mac-flashers on Wandsworth Common?"

"Yes dear boy. Go ahead."

"Kingsley Amis might be good . . ."

"I thought Sir Dud wanted us to cut down on sex," the Fashion Editor said.

"Ah, but this is *sad* sex. He doesn't mind *sad* sex."

The young rips dispersed, as ever, amid laughter.

Dolly Pilchard knew them all and spoke their names – mostly – with awed reverence.

"Mister Simon . . . he's a lovely gentleman, isn't he? I used to do for him when he was up on the fif' floor. And Mister Toby and Mister Jules . . . and Mister Derek." She jerked her head at the Art Director's wall with its massed posters of current visual influences: Alma Tadema, Karl Marx, Ho Chi Minh, Charlie Chaplin, Yukio Mishima.

"Shall I tell you what I call that Mister Derek?" Dolly whispered, gripping Janice's elbow and looking down the empty concourse.

"I call him . . . A poof!" she burst out, ducking her head, waltzing backwards and laughing on a strange, unearthly, ungovernable note:

"Hooo hooo hooo! Hooo hooo hooo-ooo!"

Janice had become a regular in the colloquy each morning at that empty hour of nine, while Derwent worked morosely at his drawing board, and Dolly conducted her last flick-round with a pulled-out soft cloth, as lethal to truant specks of dust as a frog's tongue is to flies.

It was while these finishing touches were made that Janice heard of the operation for stomach ulcers in the Forties which had changed Dolly from "a big woman" to her present smallness and boniness.

"I was in double agony," she said, pausing with a wastepaper tin and closing her eyes in almost hallowed remembrance. "You should have seen what I was coughing up, Janey . . . like all these great big lumps of wet beetroot . . ."

"*Please!*" Derwent murmured over his stencil.

"Gawd's truth," Dolly said, mistaking his tone for incredulity. "Like great big lumps of wet beetroot, they were, with great big dollops of double cream. Four operations, I had. And when I come out, I was the way I am now – a spent husk. I say to Mr Pilchard sometimes, 'What a shame you still ain't got the big woman you married. You married a nice fat turkey and all you got now's a scraggy old crow!'"

In time Janice learned of the world Dolly returned to each mid-morning on the 118 bus – of Mr Pilchard and the tin leg he'd worn since 1917; of her second son's wife, admittedly Belgian but revered by Dolly for her gentility and spotless home. None, though, received homage on the scale of her elder son, now in his fifties but still content to live with her and Mr Pilchard in Walworth.

"*He* knows which side his toast's buttered," Dolly said proudly, rubbing away the stigmata of collided wineglass-rims. "He knows he's still a baby to me. I does all his shirts nice for him . . . makes his bed. I done him his favourite pudden, Sunday . . . nice steak-and-kidney pudden with a drop o' Guinness in. When I leave off here, I'm goin' down Leather Lane to get a skate's eyeball for his tea."

"A *what*, Dolly?" Derwent said, closing martyr's eyes.

"Ain't you never had a skate's eyeball? Lovely grub it is. He likes all that . . . pig's trotters, faggots, stewed eels and mash. 'Old Mum can still cook,' he says. He knows he's all right with his old mum."

Janice heard many stories about this favoured child, some filled with adoration of his evident laziness and obtuseness, others revealing Dolly's partiality to any violently humorous contretemps.

"The other day he's had a few dinner-time, so he decides to go down the Labour Exchange and make bother. In he goes, up to the counter, bangs on it – and he's proper pie-eyed. 'I want some 'elp!' he shouts out. And two blokes . . . *two* blokes!" Dolly cried, clutching Janice's arm. "They *both* come round the counter and chuck him out on the pavemint! Hooo hooo-ooo!

"His chest ain't strong," she added tenderly. "That's why he's had to be off work all these years. But he knows I'll always look after him, Janey. 'Cos he's my baby. When I had him, I never even knew where babies come from."

Her expression made a smile twitch even behind Janice's proper little fingertips.

"Gawd's truth, I never did," Dolly insisted, wide-eyed. "I just thought I'd got the belly- and back-ache. I carried him all nine months, not knowing he was there. The night he was born, I'd met Mr Pilchard at Gatti's in Westminster Bridge Road – what we called the fleapit, 'cos you could get in for twopence. Mr Pilchard says, 'Here, you look seedy gal, you better go home', 'cos we was still living with our separate mums then, we couldn't afford a place of our own.

"It was my mum who realised what was what and sent me in to St Thomas's Hospital. And even when I come round after he's born, I *still* don't know. I said, 'Here, Nurse, ain't that lady's baby makin' a noise' and she said 'It's not that lady's baby. It's yours.'"

"And now he gets spoiled rotten," Derwent commented drily.

"I guess I always did love him that extra lump 'cos he was such a surprise," Dolly agreed. "I used to take him everywhere – hopping down in Kent, when we all used to go off in those trains for two or three months. He'd stop in a little basket under the lean-to while we was all picking hops. I can show you a photo of him standing up in a bucket, waiting to get washed.

"But, Gawd's truth – strike me dead if I lie – I started out as a married woman not knowing where babies came from. I soon caught on, though," Dolly added, waltzing backwards, in a voice shrivelling like touch-paper:

"I never knew where he come from. But I knew where the next bloody one come from! Hooo hooo hooo-ooo! Hooo hooo Hooo-ooo!"

Janice was getting married in eight months. That – and the greyhound she and her fiancé owned – totally occupied her mind. Though not yet seventeen, she was far too grown up for nearly all aspects of the wonderful Sixties life that teemed round her on *Eye*'s Picture Desk. She sat there as at the solicitor's previously, a neat, upright figure, answering the three phones, filing contacts and transparencies, untouched by the super times everyone else was having. The internationally-fêted war photographer who tried to make all the secretaries turned away with a shrug of despair after fifteen minutes perched beside Janice. As she would say in her wise little voice, she "wasn't interested".

From that premature nine o'clock start, her working day and the magazine's continued resolutely unreconciled. At lunch she took an hour exactly, spooning yoghurt. When the Picture Editor returned from lunch around four, Janice had his lemon tea firmly waiting for him. Because she came in at nine she left at five – an irregularity tolerated like any other at *Eye*. Below in Fleet Street her fiancé waited in his Ford Cortina, pushing the passenger door open as he saw Janice approach. Life on *Eye* was just beginning as the two of them drove off together towards Watford.

"Not *another* party," Janice said, untying her headscarf on a bright winter morning. Sunshine poured through the slanted windows onto a concourse only just restored to order. Empty green and black bottles formed an open-mouthed queue around the stationery cabinet. In the tea-making alcove, several score freshly-washed glasses stood up-ended on clean teacloths. Four desks had been dragged out of line and pushed together to form a Roaring Twenties-style dance floor. Dolly, with soft cloth and Min, was scouring at the footmarks on their combined surface.

"I dunno what they get up to," she said, without rancour. "You should have see it when I got here at five. Chairs knocked over, filthy dirty plates everywhere, broken glass on the floor . . . I could have cut meself, easy. Proper high jinks."

"Do you know what it was, Derwent?"

"Some sort of launch-party, I gather," Derwent said, barely looking up. He was at work on a finely-detailed drawing of a car chassis for *Eye*'s imminent "Motormania" issue. His curt voice and bitter face came from foreknowledge of the display his loving draughtsmanship would receive. Technical illustrations were never more than inserts among *Eye*'s running spreads of wonderful photographs.

"Janey . . ."

Janice turned to see Dolly standing away from the desks, her skirt and underslip ruefully upraised.

"Oh Dolly – not *again*!"

"Straight on me nose," Dolly nodded. "I see it pullin' away just as I come round the corner . . . and there's not another 188 for twelve minutes. 'Missed the rail, didn't I, and went flying with both me bags. I was in double agony! Two fellers had to come and pick me up out of the road."

"Are you all right?"

"'*Course* I'm all right," Dolly said, rubbing vehemently at the desk-tops. "Take more to put a crimp in me than a few old scrazes."

Janice sat outward on her typist's chair, sipping coffee which had a rich, curdled flavour owing to Dolly's preference for "hogmanised" or, sometimes, "humanised" milk. She was a pleasing sight to Dolly with her decorous zip-fronted dress, clean tights and orderly gold charm bracelet. Not like some of those other minxes, in skirts so short you could nearly see their bottoms. And dirty! Dolly had seen the mess they left – rotting cartons of milk, teabags left like dead rats on spoons – and wondered what kind of homes they went back to at night.

She took an almost sisterly interest in Janice's wedding plans, and kept eagle-eyed watch on her daily voyage through Leather Lane market for useful bottom-drawer items like towels, pillow slips, dusters and knitting wool.

"I see some lovely shammy leathers down there yesterday," she reported, tilting back the stopper on the Min. "One whole stall, nothing but shammy leathers . . . beautiful quality. I'll get you one when I go down there later if you like."

"Ooh yes. Ta, Dolly."

"I start me puddens for Christmas today," Dolly continued as she returned to the sink and began to dry the glasses set to drain. "'Soon as I get home, give Mr Pilchard his dinner and have me rest, I'll start on 'em. *You* can 'ave one an' all Janey, same as I make for Derwent. I put brandy in 'em, *and* I put in Russian stout. You ask Derwent . . . he didn't like Christmas pudden till he had one o' mine."

Derwent looked up briefly and murmured an embarrassed "Very nice". This made Dolly dart over and hug his crewcut head to her pony-tailed one.

"He ain't got no Mummy, see," she crooned into Derwent's

ear. "So I make him his own little pudden in its own little basin. Don't I, my little bit o' cobbly cheese? Don't I, my little waxy-waxy?"

"Dolly . . ." Derwent almost laughed. "I'm a married man . . ."

"Here, Janey . . . I'll tell you what. You want to go down the Canteen of a Saturday, while they're printing the paper. They have a big market, the printers do. You can get anything . . . tablecloths . . . woollies . . ."

Dolly broke off and made herself inconspicuous as people came into view at the far end of the concourse. Not *Eye* people but half a dozen strangers, male and female, led by a small man in a conventional blue suit with hair unfashionably short and flat on top.

They came slowly down the concourse, looking into each office as if assessing its proportions. In the murmur of voices the blue-suited man could be heard saying "Oh aye, that's no bother . . ." and "Aye, we can have that done soon enough."

As they drew level with the Picture Desk, the blue-suited man smiled pleasantly at Janice.

"Simon not about yet?"

"No, not yet," Janice replied.

"Tell him I'd like a word, will you? When he's got a minute."

"And your name was?"

"Shildrick," the blue-suited man said, almost apologetically.

"O.K." Janice said, writing it down.

The blue-suited man picked up an empty wine bottle, examined it thoughtfully, replaced it beside the stationery cabinet and followed his party through the swing doors next to Simon's office.

"Do you know who that was?" Derwent whispered across, looking almost nauseous with excitement.

"No."

"Mr Shildrick . . . the Editor of the paper!"

"Oh," Janice said, unimpressed.

"Not much meat on him, is there?" Dolly Pilchard commented.

★

Three unforeseen events gave Jack Shildrick the power to get his hands on *Eye* at last. The first, and most crucial, was that Sir Dudley Fox, its long-time protector and buffer against Shildrick, had finally indicated readiness to retire. The second was a drop in ad revenues, small enough yet so alarming to the proprietor, he could easily be persuaded to sanction a fresh editorial approach. The third was management's discovery, in this new draught of fiscal awareness, that *Eye* spent £50,000 a year on champagne and that last month a group of its senior executives had flown to Milan, apparently for no better object than to have lunch together. Even for 1969, this was going too far.

The coup de grâce came with lightning suddenness. Called to Shildrick's fifth-floor office for what they presumed merely a theoretical chat about next Spring's plans, Simon, the Deputy Editor and the Features Editor were removed from their jobs en bloc. In the next office, the new Editor Shildrick had already appointed and briefed, waited with some of the new editorial team to talk to him straight afterwards.

The knifing was timed to happen at six-thirty on a champagne-less Friday, when all *Eye*'s other young rips had left for the weekend. Later that evening Simon rang the Fashion Editor and told her he was "moving". That was the extent of the news passed round by phone on Saturday and Sunday, from Bayswater flat to Suffolk country cottage.

On Monday morning they gathered in shell-shocked silence around Simon's desk. It was the first meeting some of them had ever attended here without assistance from Nosh Soonest. The long work-top, empty of dishes and bottles, had been polished to a wet liquorice shine. Not even coffee was offered. Suddenly the cupboard seemed bare.

Simon told them his successor's name, smiling gracefully to see what a spasm passed over the assembled faces.

"You can imagine . . . she's absolutely thrilled to have got the job. And, who knows, it may work," he added. "Fleet Street's first woman Editor . . . And she *has* had a very big success with *Woman and Leisure*."

"Jesus wept," the Fashion Editor sighed. From the rest there was only bleak silence in contemplation of the newest bottom to leave its mark on Shildrick's face.

"He's offered me the paper's new Travel section," Simon went on with a good show of heartiness. "Jules here is going into the Newsroom and will, I'm sure, do a super job. As for Toby . . ." His tone brought sudden awareness that the Deputy Editor wasn't present. ". . . well, Toby's decided it's time to move on."

"Was there ever any question of Toby being Editor after you?" someone asked.

"No," Simon replied brusquely. "Anyway, as some of you already know, great plans are afoot. A whole new section at the front . . . customer service and consumer items. Lots of nice interesting little bits, to quote Mighty JS. Plenty of charts and graphs. He thinks we've been criminally wasting the talents of that boy Derwent in Derek's department. They plan a major relaunch for Spring . . ."

"Under a new name?"

"Yes."

"What name?"

"*The Roving I.*" Simon enunciated carefully.

He glanced at the Art Director, seated on both hands on the work-top, expressionless and non-committal as always.

"Derek will still be here, of course . . . no doubt making it all look more tasteful than it otherwise might. The rest of you Shildrick hopes will mesh in with the new team, as he puts it."

"Is it true about no more pieces longer than a thousand words?"

"No more pieces longer than a thousand words," Simon assented in his Shildrick voice. "No spreads longer than two pages. Lots of nice interesting little bits."

They dispersed, talking together in low tones like a bereaved family rather than the back-stabbing pre-Bismarck robber barons they had formerly been. Mutual sympathy even extended to the Special Projects Editor, normally stabbed in the guts as freely as in the back, who at this hour of crisis was half way across the Atlantic on a free facility flight.

When they had gone Simon sat for a while, staring at the

place on his desk where so many wineglasses had stood. As it happened he was not so very sad to be withdrawn from the clamour and pressure of his young rips. But tradition must be served to the last. Drawing towards him a clean page-layout sheet, he began to draft the announcement of his leaving party.

Change was affecting every level of the *Sunday Independent*.

When Janice arrived two mornings later, Dolly beckoned her through the Art Director's doorway and round the corner to the light box surmounted by posters of Lana Turner and assorted Japanese in jockstraps, Nazi helmets and motorcycle goggles.

"I've already told Derwent . . ." Dolly whispered deafeningly. "They're laying forty of us cleaners off at the end of the month. No one's meant to know yet, but I wanted to tell him and you."

"Oh, Dolly . . . you're not leaving!"

"Redundancy, isn't it," Dolly said, winking and tapping the side of her nose. "Forty of us had the chance and we're taking the dibs while it's going."

"Doll-ee!" Janice wailed.

"I wondered if I ought – 'cos, you know Janey, no one else'll do this place like I do it. Gangs of contract cleaners they're supposed to be bringing in for the whole building, and you can bet your bottom dollar what that'll mean. A dirty mop in a dirty bucket . . . and no elbow grease. I know them cleaning gangs."

"What'll we do without her?" Derwent said from the doorway.

"You'll miss my coffee of a morning, won't you – and Janey here, she'll miss hers. But I shan't forget your puddens," Dolly said. "I'm getting the Russian stout on my way 'ome this very day."

She darted across to rummage in the holdall she'd left on the Art Director's work-top.

"Here, Janey – here's the photo I said I'd bring of when we all used to go hopping down in Kent." She handed Janice a tiny veined snapshot of a child standing in a bucket, with an aproned, pony-tailed girl behind him, squinting out from the blazing sepia noon of long ago.

'And here's one of me on holiday ... the place down in Cornwall where me and my friend always go. It's called Seaton Valley Holiday Camp."

This was a colour snap of Dolly by herself on a dance floor, summer dress and foamy petticoat gathered up in both hands.

"Dolly – you're doing the Can-Can!"

"That's right," Dolly agreed. She gave a wink, elbowed Janice, and her voice dropped to an entirely different register.

"We have a knees-up!" Dolly Pilchard almost growled.

The news somehow reached Simon that on the day of his leaving party, Dolly Pilchard would be at Constellation House with forty axed cleaners collecting their redundancy cheques. She must be invited too then, he decreed. He was full of such gestures in these final days – to his staff the epitome of magnanimity and sportsmanship. It was known he had already taken his successor to lunch at the Caprice and generously passed on all possible wisdom from his six years in the chair. Sub-editors who took in the last page proofs he signed, already felt nostalgic for the scent of his cigar, the italic neatness of his initials, the learned little jokes he would make about misprints or infelicitous phrasing. In his outer office his two secretaries – who'd elected to move with him – were sorting out files estimated to contain some £100,000-worth of unused profiles and humorous sketches, in large part commissioned from pretty girls at parties.

Dolly, in turn, invited Janice and Derwent to the cleaners' farewell ceremony in Constellation House's subterranean Executive Canteen. Since Derwent had work to finish, Janice made the journey alone, down through nether regions of Cashiers and Bought Ledgers to the white-tiled entrance off the newsprint delivery-bay. It was a far larger function than she'd expected. About a hundred people, outgoing cleaners and their families, stood around the mosaic pillars or sat in directorial banquettes under murals showing scenes from Mediterranean harbour life.

"Here she is – my little Janey!" Dolly cried, springing out from the crowd with a plate of sandwiches in each hand. She had removed her overall but otherwise was as usual, in blouse, long cardigan, pink hair-ribbon and fur-topped ankle boots.

She gripped Janice's elbow, vouching for her as colleagues turned round. "S'all right gals. She's just like us – rough! Here, where's my little Derwent, then?"

"He's coming in a minute."

"Go on, have a sandwich," Dolly urged, driving one of the plates she held into Janice's midriff. "There's little patty ones and little fishy ones – no crusts. Go on, get stuck in gal. It's all free!"

Janice sat in a banquette with Dolly's Belgian daughter-in-law, a dignified, well made-up woman in a sky-blue coat. Dolly herself preferred the role of hostess rather than guest, darting in and out of the crowd with plates of sandwiches, vol-au-vents and crisps.

"You can never get her to sit down," the Belgian daughter-in-law observed with guttural kindliness. "Just the same at home, she is. Alvays got to be on the ving."

"Where's Derwent got to, then?" Dolly said, reappearing with a fresh plate. "Here – have one o' these little patty ones. Go on!"

"Thanks Mum," the Belgian daughter-in-law said, taking a sandwich and holding it cautiously next to her patent-leather bag.

Sir Dudley Fox's successor-designate as Chief Executive had come from the seventh floor to present each cleaner individually with her redundancy cheque. Beside him the cleaners' union "Mother of the Chapel" called out the names from a list, floor by floor. When the fourth floor was reached, an outsize plastic-wrapped bouquet unexpectedly materialised on the VIP's pin-striped arm. ". . . and not forgetting . . ." the Mother of the Chapel said ". . . our dear little Dolly." Cheers and whistles broke out as Dolly stepped forward. She returned with the bouquet, one arm raised in a backward gesture of farewell, as stylish as some great actor leaving the stage after umpteen encores.

"Too free-hearted, that's her trouble," the Belgian daughter-in-law said to Janice. "That redundancy money, she'll give it all away, I bet. Anyone asks, Mum give it if she got it. Too free-hearted, she is."

The Mother of the Chapel joined them, smiling tearfully.

'That's forty I've seen off today," she said. "Shocking, isn't it? Even little Dolly, who's give me her *Mirror* every morning for twenty-two years . . . and always cheerful and pulling our legs . . ." She took out a tissue and dabbed her eyes. "It isn't going to be the same."

The Art Director kept up *Eye*'s old atmosphere to the last. As preparations for the party went on around him, he leaned on his work-top on the telephone while absently leafing through the portfolio of the young photographer who'd come in to see him. After ten minutes or so, he hung up, closed the portfolio and slid it back to the young photographer with a single word:

"Goodbye."

All the major contributors to *Eye*'s success and prestige had been bidden to say farewell to Simon and his Golden Age. They included several major novelists, the half-dozen leading British and American photographers, TV celebrities, noted academics, and a gaggle of the top fashion models who owed their careers to having appeared on *Eye* front covers. Such was the party's invariable style that its reason seemed hardly sad, let alone ominous. The invitation – a traditionally clever Art Department mock-up – showed Simon's face superimposed onto the nude reclining figure on Manet's "Déjeuner sur l'herbe".

The throng in *Eye*'s concourse from six o'clock onward, seemed as brilliant and untrammelled as ever. Down one side stretched a buffet tended by the black-clad minions of Nosh Soonest. Down the other clustered a white-necked army of Pol Roger. Corks popped, foam sparkled and gold bubbles arose in vertical streams, as if life hereabouts were still the same sweet, carefree song.

Simon stood a little apart, flanked by his two outgoing young rips, receiving handshakes, arm-grips and murmured sympathies with that same gracious, sportsman-like smile.

". . . Of course it won't be so obviously enjoyable," his voice could be heard repeating. "That's the trouble. *No* job could be as enjoyable as this one's been . . ."

"Actually Simon, I've got rather a good idea for a travel piece. How big's your budget on the new section going to be?"

"Patrick!"

A chorus of welcome greeted *Eye*'s famous war photographer, who'd flown back specially for the party from Saigon. With him, rather unexpectedly, he brought a desk-top blotter, pen-holder set, address book and sundry mud-stained inter-office memos, copy letters and expenses-sheets.

"Do these belong to anyone here?" he said. "I found them lying on the pavement as I came in."

"Aren't they yours, Toby?"

"Christ!" the Deputy Editor exclaimed. He took his retrieved possessions and plunged away to his office. Through its glass wall, one of his several ex-mistresses on the magazine could be seen, flinging other detachable objects through the open window as her personal gesture of farewell.

It was typical of Jack Shildrick that he should come downstairs to join the party, bringing the new Editor of what would no longer be *Eye* magazine, and the team that would effect the transformation. Suddenly there they all were across the room, in a clearing of anomalous colour and voices that didn't fit. A hundred eyes obliquely fastened on the new guiding spirit of Britain's greatest Sunday supplement. They noted her bright red chiffon dress and the gold ringlets that grew in abundant scrolls around her pointed, vivacious little face.

Equally typical of Shildrick was his apparent unconsciousness that he'd just done wholesale butchery, and his progress round the room with that familiar anxious, insouciant air, inviting any bottom that wished to place its fleeting impress on his countenance. "Who should I get to be Cookery Editor?" he asked one group. "Do you think we should have a children's section?" he asked another. Whenever faced by someone condemned to "mesh in" with the new team, he employed the same match-lessly disorienting line. "I'm told you're the only person round here who ever does any work."

"Patrick . . ." Simon said, drawing the war photographer towards the red chiffon and gold ringlets. "Come and meet your new Editor."

The photographer talked for some minutes in passionate undertones about the situation in Saigon, the corruptness of the Thieu regime, his recent injury in a landmine blast and his plan, next week, to fly with the B14s on a bombing mission over Haiphong.

Then the gold ringlets shook coquettishly.

"I'm not really that interested in foreign stories," his new Editor said. "I'm more a touchy, feely, smelly sort of person. There's something you *could* photograph for us, if you like. We've got a super title for it – Secrets of Silver Service . . ."

Alone by the desk-top of bottles, Simon suddenly felt his head encircled by an arm and pulled vigorously downward.

"Ay-lo, Mister Simon! Ay-*lo*!"

It was Dolly Pilchard, tiny in the canyon of turned backs. With her stood Janice, holding an outsize plastic-wrapped bouquet.

"Ay-lo, Derwent!" Dolly cried, spotting him through the crowd. "Why wasn't you at my do, down in the nobby part?"

"I'm sorry . . . I had to go and see Mr Shildrick . . ."

"Eh?"

"Mr Shildrick wanted to see me . . ."

"We fell over," Janice said with a rueful little smile. Dolly nodded wholehearted agreement, raising her skirt and underslip.

"Those bloomin' highly-polished stairs! Straight on me nose I went. Janey here couldn't hold me. I was in double agony!"

"There you are, Dolly dear," Simon said, at his most winningly gallant, handing her a glass of champagne.

"My Mister Simon . . ." Dolly said, gazing up at him with fond eyes and cheeks which, it could now be seen, were flushed as with high fever.

"So glad you were able to come, Dolly dear."

"Ladies and gentlemen!" the Art Director shouted, hammering for silence with a type-scale. "In a moment there'll be a little something for Simon – but first the film-show." He was standing at the projector he used to view photographers' transparencies. Across the concourse, a white screen had been unrolled on a stand. The hubbub died as the overhead strip lights went out.

". . . I'll keep hold of me bag," Dolly Pilchard's voice clearly said.

The slide-show that followed was all of Simon, on many convivial occasions during his editorship. There he was with the young rips in his box at Lords; in his box at Wimbledon; drinking champagne from a Daimler boot in the car park at the Twickenham Varsity Match. There he was at lunch after lunch, at dinner after dinner, viewed down the white avenues of food and drink, always presiding, consuming and blissfully guffawing. Laughter over the opening slides dwindled into nostalgic silence. It was like watching scenes from some magic, irretrievable Edwardian afternoon, instead of just the week before last.

When the lights came back on, a tissue-paper-covered board and a shiny red package had appeared in the Art Director's hands.

"We got these for you, Simon . . . and we want to say we're all desperately sad to see you go."

"Hear hear," several voices murmured emotionally.

The board was a leaving card – another clever Art Department mock-up – bearing everyone's signature. The parcel contained an electric chess-set and a corkscrew. Simon looked at the card first as politeness required, smiling at its irreverence. He then delivered a speech so brief, only the people nearest him realised that was it.

"The last six years have been a ball. Thank you all for coming to the party."

"Simon Bonham . . ." the Art Director added lamely, holding out the ring of projector-slides. "This is your carousel . . ." There was an awkward pause, as the Golden Age finally petered out. The crowd turned inward on itself again. A bright new executive resumed "We've got a scrummy thing for the first issue all about teeth . . ." Then a wholly unexpected voice spoke up.

"I got a little ditty I want to sing!"

Dolly Pilchard advanced into the space before Simon and the Art Director.

" 'Don't mind, do you Mister Simon?" she asked him with her utter aplomb.

"Dolly dear – of course not. Be our guest."

"I made it up meself," she said, turning back to the company. "It's a little ditty 'cos I'm never coming in here to clean no more."

Unfastening the bag on her arm, she took out a folded piece of paper. The brilliant company watched as if mesmerised. "Here's my little ditty," she said, unfolding it. Without further preamble she began to sing:

"Goodbye – to all my cleaning days. Goodbye – to all my cleaning ways. Goodbye – to all those friends so dear. Goodbye – to friends both far and near . . ."

The melody was that of every soulful Cockney ballad ever sung round a pub joanna on a gas-lit, smoky-mirrored Saturday night. The voice was like a child's piping the words up, unabashed. As she sang, she smiled and held out her arms to them all, her unclasped handbag swinging from the left arm.

"I leave yee-ou – with a kind sweet heart. But even – the best of pals must part. So Goodbye – to all my cleaning ways. And Goodbye – to all my cleaning days."

She held the last note a long time, her arms still outstretched to them all. There was a small fidget of applause, then nonplussed silence.

"Carm *on*!" Dolly shouted reprovingly. "What's all the long faces for? Let's get a sing-song going, eh?"

She darted to the nearest spectator – a highly-wrought Hampstead lady biographer – took both her hands, pulled her forth into the arena and, swinging their arms in time, began, "If you knew Susie, like I know Susie . . . Carm on gal! I can't 'ear yer."

She broke off singing and glanced round the company, puzzled by their obdurate unanimation. Then, with a sudden flash of insight, she understood.

"I know what you lot want!" she said, wagging a finger that was not wholly censorious. "*I* know what you want! You want the Can-Can, don't yer?"

In an instant she had skipped onto a chair, and from it to the adjacent cleared desk-top. The brilliant company still watched mesmerised as skirt and coffee-coloured slip arose from laddered and dusty, indefatigable knees.

"You watch . . . *I'll* do yer the Can-Can!" Dolly Pilchard shouted.

Simon made a conquest that evening, as usual. She was the new secretary in the Production Manager's department. She had long honey-coloured hair and eyes whose hand-drawn lashes formed two starfish of vehement innocence. She wore a virtually transparent crocheted mini-dress. "Why don't I take you to Boulestin?" he exclaimed, as one struck by an unprecedented idea. Faint weariness at the thought of what lay ahead quickly passed. He went into the office that was no longer his, to call his wife in Richmond and say he'd be late again.

The conquest sat and waited as he brought Dolly downstairs, manoeuvring her bouquet after her through the lift-doors. He disengaged her from the neck of the late-night commissionaire, steered her out into Fleet Street, lowered her on to the marble step that ran the length of the buildings, placed her bouquet beside her and gently withdrew his head from her arms.

"I'll never forget you, Mister Simon," she murmured. "Sorry I've got in such a collapsable state . . .

"Didn't I do the Can-Can for 'em, though?" she added, more to herself than Simon, with a reminiscent chuckle. "Didn't I dance and show me drawers, eh? I dunno what the old man's going to say. I've still got the bit of haddock in there I bought for his tea. O, knees up Mother Brown," she began singing down on the step, kicking up each leg in turn like a Tiller Girl.

A taxi soon came — as luck would have it, with a pleasant young driver. He smiled round from his cab while Simon inserted Dolly, her bags and bouquet. "You can all come over . . . the lot of you. I wouldn't care," she told him as he leaned in, making everything secure. "Ask Janey to fetch yer all over one day . . ." The taxi ticked over louder, bracing itself for its long voyage into SE17.

"Little Janey'll fetch yer all over . . . Any dinner-time . . ."

Simon watched the tail-lights recede until they merged into the chaos at the turn to Blackfriars Bridge. He patted his pockets, sighed and looked up at the seven garish floors of Constellation House, where contract cleaning-gangs were already at work. He sighed and walked towards the figure in piebald fun fur, awaiting him in the brightly-lit entrance hall.

# Only the Lonely

Almost the first thing he could remember was going to bed at night and being afraid of ghosts. Long before real life had fully defined itself, ghosts were vivid and active in his mind. When he shut his eyes there they were, teeming in the world opened up by the drawing down of his lids.

There were lines and flashes that changed into figures on horseback, riding past in endless vertical review. There were points of light that became disembodied heads, rushing towards him with malign velocity. There were zigzags that became faces, snarling or leering in triumph at his helpless bed-bound state. Worst of all was the face wrapped in white bandages with no eyes, no nose, only its scarlet, grimacing mouth.

His parents in those days kept a small hotel built on the site of a medieval priory. He often heard them talking about the ghost of a grey monk, reputed to haunt the corridor where his bedroom was.

"Leave the door open, *please*," he would beg Kathleen, his nanny, after she'd kissed him goodnight.

"It is open."

"*Wide* open. Bumping the spare bed. *Please*."

His eyes clung to the light round his half-open door, fighting against the moment when his lashes would meet and the universe of ghosts be revealed to him again. Here they came from their purplish dark – the horses, the dancing heads. Here now, too, came the grey monk, gliding past the end of his bed and his curled-back toes to disappear into the wall above the wash-basin.

He was three years old, and already suspected his home wasn't a happy one. He seldom saw his mother and father, preoccupied as they were with running the hotel. Their bedroom was opposite his in the grey monk's corridor. Sometimes far into the night, he would wake to hear their voices, shouting furiously. Once he heard screaming, followed by a noise like breaking glass.

He shut his eyes and burrowed under the clothes, preferring the dread that waited there. The faces swirling round him seemed to grin more malevolently. The bandaged head laughed with its red mouth.

The terrors multiplied when he learned about death and graves and skeletons, and Jesus dying on the Cross. All the stories attesting to God's kindness could not dispel the horror of Heaven, scarcely less than that of Hell. He wished Kathleen would not tell him the prayer that said "If I die before I wake, I pray the Lord my soul to take." He pictured a soul as white and flaky, falling off bones, like the fish he couldn't eat up at lunch.

It appalled him to discover how many dead people there were – the forests of gravestones and crosses marking huge potential access for ghosts back into the world. He guessed what spite the dead must cherish towards the living, and how they must long to pull him down to join them in their kingdom of bones and mould.

He told no one of his fears, even when there was someone to tell. If he mentioned the subject it would be obliquely, as if seeking information for a friend.

"Mummy, do you think a ghost could . . ."

"There are no such *things* as ghosts!"

"Yes, but just supposing a ghost . . ."

"I've *told* you! There are no such things as ghosts."

Now he could not count the awful things that rushed on him when he shut his eyes. There was "the girl in green", murdered in a Paul Temple radio serial, her clothes somehow more terrifying than the blood trickling out of her mouth. There was his own great-grandfather, chin-bearded and yellow, scowling from an oval album-frame. There was even the recently-dead King, a ghastly postal order profile, at whose State Funeral the Naval pipes had seemed like squeals of resentment from all those unwillingly banished under ground.

He was seven years old, and knew beyond a doubt that his

home wasn't a happy one. The screaming and shouting late at night now went on almost continuously. Once he got up, tiptoed to his door, opened it and looked out. His father and mother were in the passage, fighting for possession of a double-barrelled gun. Neither saw him standing there.

Their last home as a family was a flat in a rambling old house at the end of an unfrequented lane. Directly opposite was a sunless churchyard, filled with shadowy memorials to people dead a hundred years and more.

He would often be left alone in the flat at night with Hercules, the old labrador, for company. The flat had many loose floorboards that creaked loudly underfoot. Night after night he lay rigid with terror beneath the bedclothes, wondering if that last creak had been Hercules or the dead from across the lane, coming to claim him.

He began to be left alone by day as well as night. More and more when he woke in the morning, there would be no one at home. He would get up, feed Hercules and see himself off to school. He would walk back from school in the afternoon, along the cobbled footpath to the churchyard and an empty flat.

He had no friends to play with after school. It was no good making friends if you couldn't invite them home to tea.

In the evening he would walk down to the seafront, past guest houses emitting a sociable odour of gravy, and pubs welcomingly throwing open their bar-doors. The late sun threw his shadow ahead of him on the pavement, thickening his sandals to club-feet, each with its wildly elongated curly strap.

The busy esplanade felt strangely remote, as if he viewed it through deadening glass. For he knew he did not belong here, even though apparently condemned to walk here for all conceivable time.

He would move through the holiday crowds like one invisible, making no mark, leaving no trace. Each summer evening seemed a chill eternity, staring from the outside at familiar things that were unreachable; seeming to have no substance but his own shadow, and a sigh.

In all these years of haunting empty rooms and unseeing crowds, he never for one moment realised his own utter loneliness and unhappiness. He just thought this was how it felt to be alive.

He was wrong. He knew it from the moment he took the first tentative hold on his own destiny. At once, the drab little coffin of misery shattered around him. He began to dig his way, with ever more strength, towards the sun.

In adult life he became successful, confident and – most miraculous of all – excited. The boy who had looked at summer sticky buds and despaired became a man who welcomed each morning like the first of the holidays.

His twenties passed in zestfully making up for lost time. He stocked his life with friends, inviting them home to tea at every opportunity. He lined his rooms with books full of the stories he'd once longed to have read to him. His life took on the calmly methodical joy of a painting-by-numbers, each blank segment filling with the colour and vitality now at his command.

Darkness was an element conquered with all the rest. Darkness now was where one made love, then talked. Or where one slid to sleep alone, looking across at a bookshelf, lulled by the warmth and understanding collected there.

To think of ghosts became a measure of his own security, sharing another's breath, invulnerably tangled in other arms and legs. He'd shut his eyes and stare defiantly into that old, terrifying universe of flashes and whirls, daring the white-bandaged head to come and get him.

Not that he stopped believing in ghosts. Quite the contrary: he believed in them with all the logic and reason of his newly-settled mind.

"There's just got to be something in it, hasn't there?" he would say when the subject came up at dinner parties. "People have been going on about it for so long . . . and there's so much documentary evidence. If by ghosts we mean feelings or emotions that stay around, I can believe in that. If we can accept the existence of radio waves, why not ghosts?"

"Have you ever seen one?" he would sometimes be asked.

"No," he would answer firmly. But never mention for how

many hours of unfulfilled dread he'd expected to, in the grey monk's corridor or in the sepulchral flat opposite the church-yard.

The single visitation he could say he'd had was a negative one – as if Heaven were corroborating what grown-ups used to insist about there being "no such thing".

When he was twenty-nine his father died, slowly and agonisingly, of throat cancer. That September was lovely in Berkshire, with smoke from burning cornfields drifting over gardens full of drunkenly overblown roses. The Queen was on a State visit to the Shah of Iran. He watched it on newfangled colour television, next to the shrunken figure in the hot, crumpled, pitiless bed.

"These drugs I'm taking give me awful nightmares," his father whispered to him one afternoon. ". . . horrible faces rushing at me . . ."

He sat there all through the final coma, until the ghastly snorted breathing abruptly cut off. He leaned and looked into his father's face. Nothing was there. He was looking at something gone away.

That night, after the room had been cleared, he slept there on a camp bed. It was in some obscure way a challenge – show me. He fell asleep at once, and slept dreamlessly. The room almost rang with its emptiness.

Once or twice, in later years, his social circle briefly overlapped that of the spirit world.

While working in East Anglia he became friendly with the landlord of a country pub reputed to be haunted, as is virtually every pub in East Anglia.

The landlord was a tough, unsusceptible character who accepted the haunting with the same testy resignation as coach parties and VAT.

"When I come into this bar of an evening to open up, I know they're here . . . I can feel them, sitting all along that bench under the dart-board. 'Go on, get off with you,' I holler, and out they go, through that wall. I've discovered it's where the door of the old Snug used to be . . ."

In London he met a photographer who'd got involvad in psychic investigation after renting a studio haunted by an old lady. The photographer had been taking girlie pictures at the time, and each morning would find the previous day's prints angrily stuffed into the dustbin.

"So you've actually seen one, have you?"

"Oh yeah," the photographer said nonchalantly.

"What – in an old house?"

"You can see them in an old house. Or a brand-new house. Or in the open air."

"Really?"

"Yeah . . . in a few dry leaves or a bit of broken glass. A patch of oil on a puddle."

"And are they ever dangerous?"

"No-o. Well . . . there's a few, what we call boisterous spirits, that can cause trouble. And you might get a nasty one where there's been a sex crime. But as a rule there's no harm in them."

"And they do go if they're exorcised?"

"Mostly you don't have to go that far. Just tell 'em to clear off and they do."

Other stories reached him down the years, at second and third hand. There was the woman who regularly awoke in her Sussex manor house to find a girl in a Victorian nightdress at her bedside, staring at her. There was the chimney-sweep at Hampton Court Palace who couldn't leave his brushes unattended for five minutes without finding them scattered all over the floor. There was the couturier, haunted by a termagant Fashion Editor, whose dressmaking forms would be furiously knocked over if he slackened work for one minute on his next collection.

Invariably the person visited would be sane, sceptical, down-to-earth; the very opposite of a weirdo or crank. In many cases, realisation it had been a ghost did not come until some time afterwards.

He heard stories about ghosts in predictable locations, like ancient inns and cottages, but also in brand-new Council maisonettes, tower-block flats – once even in a trendy Thames-side shop selling French cookware, dried flowers and lavender bags.

He heard of ghosts that were mischievous, fractious and destructive, but also of those that seemed friendly, benevolent, even comforting. And – most commonly – of ghosts that, far from wishing to disturb or terrorise, seemed diffident, apologetic, even rather sad.

But never once, in the realm of believable encounters, did he hear of any ghost that threatened any living person harm.

Whatever injury the supernatural world could do the natural one had, in any case, been eclipsed by the injury it was doing itself. His middle years coincided with the wholesale transference of human fear from the unknown to the all too plainly obvious.

Looking back from his thirties and forties, he realised that the dreads and terrors of his childhood had underscored the safety and security of that world. He remembered how the hooded heads which tormented him at night used to dissolve with morning – how the fear of a race of murderers, setting forth to slaughter children after dark, could be comfortably laughed away amid sunshine and sticky buds.

Today those same hooded heads massed in broad daylight, in Belfast and Lebanon. The union of child-slaughterers embarked nightly on its methodical work. Every phantom of the quiet Fifties' dark had become accepted fact.

He saw how lightly modern children regarded the totems of his juvenile fear. Dracula and Frankenstein's monster were now merely mascots for T-shirts or crisp packets. Far worse horrors could wait in a walk of a hundred yards from their homes to the corner letterbox.

He remembered how excruciatingly he had feared Death when it appeared a minority pursuit, limited by those forests of marble glimpsed from passing trains. Now it was a world craze, its possibilities multiplying every hour, if not from newly-inspired cruelty then from newly-invented disease.

His own attitude to it grew more relaxed the longer he realised he'd managed to stay alive. His most frequent thought about dying was how strange it would be suddenly to have all in common with everyone in history, from Genghis Khan to Fred Astaire.

At times, as he grew older, the thought of oblivion seemed

almost inviting – to float in blind tranquillity, like a cell under a microscope, heedless of the centuries drifting past.

Then, too, he would think of ghosts as he now understood them: beings, for some reason, barred from that eternal slumber, condemned to stay and gaze at the living world as through a shop window, longing to join in, mystified by the constant discovery that they couldn't.

He realised now that they were not to be feared, only pitied. What he couldn't understand was why, in the deepest parts of himself, he pitied them so much.

He never married, though he loved children, often preferring their company to that of grown-ups. Ruthless as he was in all other departments, he could never endure to see a child in tears.

In his forties, he started going out with a busy Fleet Street journalist, and so came to the final haven of his unlooked-for happiness and fulfilment.

One night, they returned from a party to her house. He went straight up to bed while she played over the messages on her telephone answering-machine.

A few minutes later, she called him down to the drawing-room, where she had her desk. "Something rather horrid's happened," she said. "I think I've had an obscene phone call."

She played back the message-tape. In between staccato colleagues' voices there was a longish interval, crackling as if on some different wavelength, filled with a barely audible, halting sound.

"It's heavy breathing, isn't it?" she said.

"It sounds more like someone crying," he said. "Play it again."

She did so.

"I'm sure it's someone crying," he said. ". . . the sort of quiet crying when you're totally heartbroken."

The mystery was never explained. He kept to himself his suspicion that the answering-machine had picked up a ghost.

The sound stayed in his mind, troubling him so much that he began to wonder whether, after all, he might not possess some slight psychic power. For he could so well imagine how that kind of heartbroken ghost might feel. He could almost sense the floating cold, the puzzled pain of seeing life as through impenetrable glass. And crying to realise you had no substance: only your shadow and a sigh.

He did not fully understand until he was almost fifty.

Quite famous now, he was asked out of the blue to present the prizes at his old school's speech day. He meant to refuse, since it would mean going back to the place where he'd grown up. She persuaded him to take her along and make a weekend of it.

As they walked along the seafront the first evening, she looked around her in amazement.

'*This* is where you had all those ghastly times! It's so pretty and welcoming.'

Much had changed in forty years. But there was still the same wide, reddish pavement with the cracks that were etched on his memory. An old instinct made him half shut his eyes and imagine he was flying in a plane over reddish fields, bisected by erratic roads.

He looked at his own large, firm shadow, thrown ahead of him by the late sun, with another walking beside it.

He remembered the smaller shadow on its own, treading the evening eternity with its sleepwalking legs and wildly-elongated curly sandal-straps.

He felt a spectral breath of sunshine with no warmth, summer air with no hope. He glimpsed phantoms of faces turning to look at him, then looking right through him.

And in that moment saw the full measure of his deliverance.

Later there was dinner by candlelight with more new friends. Beside him sat the person representing the furthest he could travel from those other times.

Between bursts of laughter, he turned and took her hand.

"I realised something this afternoon," he said. "This is probably going to sound quite ridiculous . . ."

"It won't."

"I couldn't understand why everything seemed so new as well as so familiar. I felt I was seeing it all for the first time as a living person. Do you understand?"

"Yes."

"I know how a ghost would feel. Because I used to be one."

Not long afterwards there happened to the grown man what the small boy had lain and dreaded through so many hours of uneventful dark.

He was alone, but happy, preparing for bed in an unfamiliar room. Over by an old oak linen press he became aware of something standing and watching him.

He did not run, or even recoil.

He walked across, hands outstretched.

"Hello," he said. "Is it awful? Never mind. Tell me about it."

# Rats in My Kitchen

PT saw them long before they reached the cabin. There were two in the car, a red Pinto – the kind Englishmen liked to rent – bumping up the track around the ploughed hill, scattering dust, chickens, and the brighter red cardinal birds. At the top they drew in behind PT's old pick-up truck. Both got out slowly, like nervous cops, using the car-doors for cover. One carried a large tape recorder, the other wore two Nikons and a canvas fisherman's bag which he pushed behind him as he stooped to lock the car. PT heard his loud yelp to feel static electricity, carried from some big city motel, still burning far into the poor lands of Tennessee.

"This must be it," they told one another uncertainly across the car. For the road stopped here, above a barren slope where lumps of torn newspaper leapt and somersaulted. There was nothing beyond the cabin, with its earth wall, its tin roof, its strong points of wire and matchboard, all poised at the summit by some whim of the weather. A long, singing moan reached their ears from the wind in the deep-rutted earth. Yet again they conferred, and agreed: this ought to be the place.

The cabin door, beaten on hesitantly, opened a fraction to reveal a child, no more than five years old, barefoot, with hair gathered into little beribboned stooks.

"Is Ol' Black Rock in there, please?"

The child didn't answer, but only smiled indulgently at the voice's timbre. The door pushed wider to disclose PT, a figure altogether reassuringly of this world.

"We called from Memphis," one Englishman said. "Jim Tarbutton sent us – from Kazoo Music."

"Sure. C'mon in." PT said, turning away the child under his hand. Grizzled grey fringed his powerful neck within a raised black-and-white plaid lumberjack collar. Across his barrel-like T-

170

shirt could be seen part of some printed slogan. He stood aside for them, stretching the bracelet of the rather elaborate chronometer on his wrist.

The cabin had one room and eight inhabitants. Three children played on the dirt floor; at a single post in the centre, two young men leaned, intensely dolled-up in patent leather shoes and velvet caps, chewing gum they had not the means to purchase, snapping fingers to a rhythm they only hoped to hear. A young woman in a long pink ballgown was clearing pots and dishes, helped by a girl.

"We just got through eatin' breakfast," PT explained. He had sat down on a small bed along the inner wall. "Where you all from, you boys?"

The Englishman with the tape recorder opened it briskly, by unfastening two clasps. He had a warm, soft, vibrant, disinterested voice.

"I work for radio, PT. In London – you know? We met before, if you remember, when you and Ol' Black Rock came over with the Blues Caravan. That sure was a great show."

"Yeah?" PT said, on a rising note of indifference. Mostly they said they remembered some show or Blues Caravan someplace, which was more than PT could do. Bright lights, a big, cold stage, were all PT remembered of London. And getting money, and a bottle.

"I'm putting together a big radio special, PT – Blues and Country Blues, right from the beginning," the Englishman said, unravelling a large microphone. "Steve here works for *Radio Times*. You know *Radio Times*?"

"Mm-hm," PT assented. "You want to do interview with Ol' Black Rock?"

"Right." The Englishman seemed relieved to find himself understood. "Is that okay?"

"No problem: he be right with you," PT said. "He ain't been feelin' so good."

At the end of the cabin was a curtained recess, from which Ol' Black Rock now walked, helped by the young men and children. He was nearly all brown bones now, both eyes stuck fast with a thick yellow blindness, yet he crossed the floor delicately, unaware of his helpers. He wore two parts of an ancient grey suit, made sleek by decay, and his clean white shirt cuffs, folded back with almost conscious elegance, revealed a hospital plastic identity-tag worn on one skeletal wrist like a lucky charm. He was guided to a chair, near the door, whereupon his limbs arranged themselves as from memory in an attitude of sitting. A cigarette groped its way to between his lips.

"And you knew Blind Blake, isn't that right?"

The Englishman cupped the microphone under Ol' Black Rock's race, closer still lest the tape spools failed to catch that eerie, croaking voice in which all fences between the words had been blown down.

"Yeah. Blind Blake. We knowed him."

"And Blind Boy Fuller?"

"Yeah. Blind Boy Fuller. We knowed him, too."

"– and Barbecue Bob?"

"Yeah, we knowed him. Barbecue Bob."

One of Ol' Black Rock's teenage sons, meanwhile, sidled up to the photographer and inquired nonchalantly: "What you all drinkin' today?"

"– he had a barbecue stand; isn't that right?"

"Yeah. Barbecue Bob. We knowed him."

"– I could go git it down at the liquor store," whispered Ol' Black Rock's son. "Just a six-pack o' beers."

The victim, understanding, groped behind his camera; a five-dollar bill changed hands. They took PT's truck away to fetch the beer.

"And Blind Lemon Jefferson, you know?"

"Yeah. Blind Jefferson."

"When you were on Beale Street?"

"Yeah. Beale Street –"

"But he came from Texas, didn't he?"

"Yeah. Texas. We knowed him . . ."

"He was good with that knife, you know," murmured PT from the bed.

"Yeah." Ol' Black Rock nodded. "Yeah. We knowed him."

"– he was blind, man," PT said. "But he could take that knife, man, and cut you all to pieces. He'd catch where your voice was. Take a knife, he could, and cut you all to pieces –"

"– sorry, PT," the Englishman said. "Could we try to keep the background noise down? Otherwise ... you know ... the recording ..." He leaned forward again, through the children, to Ol' Black Rock, glancing timidly at the sound-level.

"And you knew Memphis Minnie, too, didn't you? Isn't that right?"

This cat fooled me, PT thought, just as he thought most every day ...

This cat fooled me good. I must have been 'leven years old, he was round thirteen, fourteen. He'd come down around Snake Hollow, playin' for our country picnics, getting 'round two dollars for the engagement. Playin' was awful cheap then. My Mom, she'd take out the beds in our cabin to make room, and set a table 'cross the kitchen door. My Mom would cook catfish and sell it, and they'd sell that ol' moonshine whisky, maybe git to shooting craps in the barn. Late at night, it'd start to git rough. Somebody'd go shoot out all the lights.

I seen this guy at early mornin', comin' 'cross the fields, swingin' that old guitar. He seemed to me like a big city man back there in Twenty-nine. He heard me playin' that harmonica – I had one o' them that cost a dime.

He say, "Look man, you oughta come to town with me. Hitch your mule to the fence, and let's go."

I said, "You got to ask my Mom."

She said, "Okay, but you all gotta bring him back tomorrow."

So we went on down to Memphis. Nex' thing I know, we was in Arkansas. And we bin runnin' ever since ...

"You and PT rode the freight trains, isn't that right?"

"Yeah," Ol' Black Rock nodded. "Rode the freight trains. Me an' PT rode the freight trains."

"Riding the boxcars?"

"Yeah, ridin' the boxcars. Me an' PT, we rode the boxcars."

Best was when you'd get to ride top deck. On the roof, that means. You'd ride the bumpers, maybe, in between the cars.

Some nights, man, 'f you was pressed, you'd ride them iron rods they had lyin' long underneath. Him an' me, we'd lie together, ridin' them boxcar rods.

O man, we had us a good time, runnin' all over with Jimmie Rodgers – he was a good hobo, you know: he could do the beggin'. Nights, we'd git in one them hobo jungles by the railroad side, and they'd have some big pot cookin' with ever' kind o' meat in there that could be named. Turtles, man, they'd cut up for the pot. They'd have some ol' tin cup, you know – pick up an' dip an' pour into your cup. We'd set there, man in the hobo jungle, an' git snug, and someone'd go git a bottle o' that whisky, that ol' moonshine, poison whisky, and we'd git half juiced-up there.

This cat used to be awful bad 'bout fightin', you know, while he was gettin' round. Why they gave him the name Ol' Black Rock was 'cause of an ol' black rock he toted in his pocket. He'd git to drinkin, and goin' with some woman, and he'd want to bull-do her, then some other guy step in there. This cat'd chonk him with that ol' black rock – knock hell outa the other fellow, then take off. Man, he light on his feet, but he sho' hit you.

Memphis used to be awful bad 'bout stickin' you up, on Beale Street, there. Stick-ups and bank robbin'; armed robbery. Confidence, O man: one of the confidencest places in the world! Droppin' the pigeon, they done. Some guy come outa the bank, an' you'd confidence him outa what he got. We see all that stuff worked. We was musicians – those smart guys, they thought we's on the sunny side. Some sharp guy, he'd come up and say, "Here's twenty dollars, man, put it in your pocket." Him an' me, we'd git half juiced-up, start playin' there on Beale Street, the people come gangin' round. That was what the sharp guys wanted, so they could clip them pocketbooks.

This cat – he could sure hide money! I'd always be gettin' my pocket-book clipped, but this guy hid his in his shirt-tails. This guy had money tied up in his shirt-tails.

O man, the drinkin' we done back there. The fightin' an' the runnin', man! This guy been hoboin' six to eight months, an' he 'spects his girl friend to be the same thing. He say, "Where's all them little clothes I bought you: where they at?" And some bad guy sittin' on the bed. He'd always push me in! He'd say, "Go on, git the guy, PT, go git him!" And I was astoundin' nimble at that time. I'd really catch the guy an' handle him pretty good, 'fore I do too much an' have to leave town.

I done time, man. Ain't nobody ain't done no time in the penitentiary. If people try to hurt you – maybe git to rap at you with a knife – I'd find me that ol' scattergun, man, and – boom! They try to hurt me: I boom. I musta boom three, four guys, man, that tried to hurt me.

Two children crossed the cabin bringing Ol' Black Rock's guitar. It was an instrument devoid of history: no Ultratone or Nick Lucas Special, only a cheap, flat, mass-produced Japanese model, wired to a splintered wooden frame in which an old radio loudspeaker kept loose company with some feebly-glimmering valves. They fed the guitar to Ol' Black Rock, who grasped it like a drowning man, blind eyes cast to Heaven, while his fingers staggered over the frets. Children clustered round, picking and testing; a tattered cord buzzed through the valves. PT, on the bed, had tipped a small harmonica from his pocket.

"Railroad Bull – you remember that one? Made that record in Nineteen Thirty-seven. Let's hit 'em a lick on it, Black Rock."

The tape recorder was a BBC-issue Uher, guaranteed reliable in any outside broadcast situation. But here, on a three-legged stool in Tennessee, the tape recorder faltered, as if at the behest of draughts, as if called on to register psychic disturbance. That was the effect of Ol' Black's voice, unearthly, metallic, from a long-dead tongue; of the guitar which furred and buzzed on one lone, crouching chord. PT, over at the bed, blew intelligible Blues perkily into his cupped hands, one thick leg stamping time. And the tape spools made a show of doing their work. The photographer moved in closer to Ol' Black Rock's chair. Senses laboured yet could not see, as that blind yellow eye plainly saw, the bodies of rags in ragged firelight; the dreary land, with boxcars passing endlessly across it.

Light died in the amplifier valve. Ol' Black Rock's son pulled the ring from his fourth can of Schlitz.

Both Englishmen, somewhat belatedly, clapped their hands and exclaimed, "Yeah!"

The interviewer added a perfunctory "Whew!" then leaned forward again. "That was your first record for Okeh. Isn't that right?"

"Yeah – on Okeh," Ol' Black Rock repeated. "We done that on Okeh Records."

"In Chicago."

"Yeah, in Chicago. We made that one in Chicago."

"We done the jug, too," PT said. "Ol' guitar, we never did have but five strings on it. Man, when he starts goin' blind, I see this cat run outa a saloon – with some shootin' goin' on in there, you know – he's near blind, but he done got outa there somehow and went straight through a man's cornfield. This guy musta run clean through a six-strand wire fence. Them little guitar strings, you know, would hit a cornstalk, and with ever' 'ping', he'd run that much faster."

"What was the personnel?" the interviewer resumed doggedly. "On those early sessions for Okeh."

"We done the jug, too," Ol' Black Rock said.

"People on the street that heard us, they'd fill that jug up," PT said. "They'd put quarters and half dollars in there."

"Yeah, right," the interviewer said, in a tone that dismissed the jug and its contents. "I'd like to ask you, Black Rock . . ."

"They'd put quarters in," Ol' Black Rock said. "Sometimes they'd put half dollars in there."

'Mm – right!" the interviewer said, firmly. "But the personnel on those early Okeh sessions – . . ."

"Mel Williams, he was Okeh manager," PT said. "Workin' for them in Chicago. He walked up. The jug was full. People put quarters and half dollars in there. Mel Williams told us, 'You all come up to my office, 166 Lake Shore Drive, tomorrow – you too good to be messin' round here.' So we went up an' made a record. And from then on, New York City. But we never could give up that habit. All that money in our pockets, and we still rode the freight trains. Ever' time Okeh Records sent us the money to come over, we'd go buy ourselves a pair overalls and catch the freight."

"Those early sessions for Okeh," the interviewer said, leaping for his chance as if it were moving boxcars – "'Railroad Bull', 'Sometime Baby', 'Puttin' My House on Fire': they give you and PT as joint composers. Was there any set pattern to the way you got into writing songs?"

"I didn't catch you," Ol' Black Rock said.

"I said – maybe PT would like to come in here . . . how about 'Railroad Bull'? Did you write that to any set pattern?"

"'Railroad Bull'? That what they'd call the guy that rode the freight trains," PT said. "He was special agent for the railroad company."

"So – many of these songs were the result of direct personal ex – . . ."

"They had Winchester Slim," PT said. "He was the railroad bull, rode the train from Scarboro' to Efrin'ham, from Efrin'-ham down into Cairo. He had that bad Winchester rifle."

"Special agent," put in Ol' Black Rock suddenly.

"He made us git off the train at Cairo, but we was 'terminated to go anyway, 'cause we had those people's money, you know, at Okeh Records."

"Right," the interviewer nodded, having ceased to pay attention some moments earlier. "Can we break off a moment, fellas, while I turn the tape over?"

The photographer, who had grown steadily more fascinated, sat back on his cowboy heels and said, "I bet they never paid you all that much."

"A few bucks," PT agreed. "Jus' a few bucks and – boom. Gone. Drink and foolishness like that. At Okeh, man, they got rich off of us. They musta made a couple million dollars off that 'Railroad Bull', the one we just quit playin'. A couple million dollars."

Ol' Black Rock's fingers collapsed on a different chord. Opening his gums, he sang "I'll Be Glad When You Dead, You Rascal You" by way of a spectral grin. PT joined him on kazoo. The song, full of misplaced joy and buoyancy, faded before adjustments to the tape recorder were complete. PT looked at Ol' Black Rock, who remained gummily grinning after the last echoes.

"This here is the you-rascal-you, man," PT said fondly. "This cat ruin me. I cain't go to tell howsomany times he come along and say, 'I got me a trailer, PT, let's go.' I'd say, 'I just got married, man, I cain't leave. I done messed up so much.' I been married ten times – Ol' Black Rock take me 'way from all on 'em. And I'd do same for him when he got himself a good woman. We'd take off together down them dusty roads."

"Friends, eh?" the photographer said, holding up his light meter.

"I'd get mad ever' so often when we was paid off, and we'd git to cussin' each other. Once, while we was cussin' each other, this guy," PT said with admiration, "this guy fell plumb in one of them big vats they cooks whisky in! He was steppin' too high, I guess. 'Cause I saved this cat's life, you know, when he was like to git drowned one time. Some big Model A car run us right in the Mississippi River. This guy's floatin' in there like a drownded rat. I save his life, man. I bust the windshield an' bring him out. His eyes swelled up like that with water.

"We'd raise devil once in a while." PT guffawed under the ogling lens. "Buckin' 'gainst one another – I'd git mad at him, he cuss a while, we threaten each other. He done took away my best woman – Lord, I hated him back there for a while. Wanted to cut him an' see some of his blood.'

'Don't you have a family, PT?"

"Well . . . yeah." PT glanced round the cabin, at the children who were mothers, at the mothers almost children still. "Yeah – I'm gettin' me a family. A-all the time. I got Black Rock's oldest girl now. Maybe I stick with her – maybe. We both sick, tired ol' men now. 'f I take off, man, I know this cat be right behind me, tho' he so old and blind. I'd take off at night but he find me at mornin'. We always run into a good break, you know, 'soon as we get off on our feet. 'Soon as we start playin', why then we always hit. Only trouble's the freight trains they got today. Them ol' coal-burners, all you had to do was run along and git in there. These here diesel engines jerk one plumb off the track."

The photographer leaned forward, peering into the glutinous yellow eyes. "You still feel the Blues the same, Black Rock?"

His face turned, comprehending. "The same."

"Is it a sad or a happy feeling?"

"Happy feeling."

"When I gets to playin' this harmonica," PT said, "I'm like to feel pretty full o' the Blues at times. Then him an' me, we puts the Blues on each other. That makes both on us feel good."

The interviewer sat back at last from his tape recorder, both spools of which remained motionless.

"No joy," he said. "I'm afraid it's all gone phut somewhere inside." He began, quite cheerfully, to rewind the microphone lead. "Hey, well thanks anyway," the interviewer said, again cheerfully, for incompetence brings its own kind of relief. "It was really great meeting you, Black Rock . . . PT."

Ol' Black Rock sat with fingers stuck to the last chord, still studying a vista no one else had seen.

"Listen, I'd still like very much to have you on the programme. It just means we'll have to get by with archive material, PT – before I forget – you wouldn't happen to have any of your old Okeh recordings, would you, that I could take back?"

"We ain't got no phonograph," PT said.

"Okay – no sweat. Only, we may have to feature your stuff by other artists. B. B. King's done a lot, hasn't he?"

"B. B. King, sure. He done plenty our things."

"And Tina Turner even! She did a great version of 'Puttin' My House on Fire'. I'll have a good look around in Memphis at the Blue Light. It's a great record store, that. And anyway" – the interviewer laughed – "it's all on expenses. Well – goodbye, Black Rock . . . PT, thanks . . . and Black Rock's lady, is this?" He extended an almost regal hand. "Goodbye. This is a really nice place you've got."

The young woman, in her pink-ribboned ballgown, lifted up fierce and injured eyes.

"It's a no 'count place," she murmured.

"You all see that dress she's wearing?" PT said. "That dress was made a hun'ed years ago."

PT accompanied them outside, shook hands firmly with each, and inquired, "Where you all stayin' at Memphis?"

"The Rivermont."

"Oh." He came in closer, looking worried and sliding the chronometer along his wrist. He seemed about to warn them off The Rivermont. "Folks usually pay us, you know," he said. "After we done played a little set for 'em."

The interviewer was entirely taken aback by this. He had forgotten the warning that black people always try to rip you off. He glanced into his wallet, but saw only a ten-dollar bill. His colleague, meanwhile, handed over fifty dollars. The bill vanished, without undue thanks, into PT's plaid coat.

They drove in silence – for they were starting to hate each other – back down the ploughed hill, where wings of old newspaper still fluttered and gambolled in the wind. At the bottom, by a corrugated liquor store, they regained the Brownsville highway.

Two miles on, the interviewer gave a yelp: "I left the bloody mike back there!"

The cabin remained clinging to the hilltop, but PT's pick-up truck no longer stood outside.

Inside they were washing clothes. Ol' Black Rock's young wife, in her hundred-year-old ballgown, glanced up at the Englishman with surprise. The microphone lay where he had left it, on a chair.

Beyond the raised curtain, Ol' Black Rock had been arranged along the edge of a grey blanket. His skull's cheek rested pensively on joined fingertips. The Englishman drew near, as one brought to view a corpse.

"So long, Black Rock. I just came back for . . ."

An arm arose suddenly, like a cobra. A wrist, in its hospital identity tag, gripped the Englishman's white one with unusual strength. The blind yellow eyes glared into his, then, suspiciously, towards the door.

"How much?" Ol Black Rock whispered. "How much was it you give PT to gimme? I don't trust that sonofabitch."

# Susie Baby

When Colin started going out with Susie, his whole family felt a surge of thankfulness. At almost twenty-five he still lived at home, content to let his mother go on washing his shirts and making his bed, all for a studentish £6 per week. His crusty conservatism dismayed both his sisters, especially his view – acquired from colleagues in the building trade – that "all poofters ought to be put up against a wall and shot". Until Susie, no girl friend had been able to cope with his male chauvinism, selfishness and indifference. Jane, his younger sister, who first met them together, brought back an incredulous report of this girl whose society inspired Colin to unprecedented lovingness, attentiveness, pliancy and good manners. The family awaited her appearance with bated breath.

They were not disappointed. Susie came to lunch the next Sunday and did right by everyone: she talked horses with Rachel, stroked Jane's cat, helped Mrs Stowell with the washing up and talked louder, as directed, so that Mr Stowell would hear. She was no beauty – the sisters agreed – but thoroughly pleasant-looking with her shy little downcast face, somewhat like a Beatrix Potter rabbit, framed to its best by a gold-tinted "pageboy". The discovery that she lived on a Council estate and that her family was "very Hampshire" served only to brighten her aura. Susie had been to secretarial College and taken part in gymkhanas, in other words she had "made something" of herself. And the difference in Colin truly was remarkable.

It took a couple of Sundays for Rachel's more discriminating ear to notice that, in its effort to disown her Hampshire accent and preserve a uniform sweetness and compliancy of tone, Susie's voice could become a trifle insipid, and her manner the same. Rachel first became aware of this in the sitting-room after lunch, while chocolates were being handed round. Mr Stowell, at that stage, could still eat some solid food. The rustle of chocolate-box wrappings never failed to penetrate his deafness and bring him forward in his chair by the fire, tiny, gritty and tobaccoey, like some little Harris-tweed goblin living among the fire-tongs and the coal.

Everyone in turn studied the elaborate choice of centres on a pirate's treasure-map, selected their chocolate, then passed the box on. Rachel's first perception of something wearing about Susie occurred when, instead of accepting the chocolate-box, she collapsed sideways into Colin, made as if to hide her face in his sweater and, in a waif-like voice, said, "Col . . . pick one out for me." This gallantly and tenderly accomplished by Colin, Susie returned to her former occupation of looking through *Ideal Home* magazine and drawing Colin's attention to advertisements for French saucepans or duvet-covers in an inaudible murmur. It was then, too, that Rachel noticed the imperfections in Susie's skin, and her chubby little fingers as they turned the magazine-pages, and that, growing in clusters round nearly every finger-joint, there were warts on Susie's hands.

That Spring, when Mr Stowell returned to hospital for further chemotherapy, Colin and Susie went on holiday to Cornwall in Colin's latest rebuilt Morris Minor. They did not return until after Mr Stowell had been sent home again (as it would prove, for the last time). The next full family gathering combined Mr Stowell's first day out of bed with a review of Colin and Susie's holiday snaps. It seemed to Rachel, who loved Cornwall, that somewhat too many of these favoured Susie as a foreground and that, seated on the car-kerb, looking waifish round the half-open door, she was rather more prepossessing than this afternoon. For since their return, Susie had changed the way she did her hair. In place of the modest pageboy there was now a frizzy gold perm, which altered the whole proportion of Susie's face. Gone was the Beatrix Potter bunny look: in its place were fat little ears, a pronounced double chin and eyes that seemed permanently narrowed.

To celebrate Mr Stowell's homecoming, the holidaymakers

had brought back a small – in fact the smallest possible – carton of Cornish clotted cream. No one else had received so much as a postcard.

The improvement in Colin, however, continued to exceed all expectation. That summer, at long last, he announced he was leaving home, to live with Susie. His mother accepted the news with conscientious aplomb, privately taking comfort from the fact that one of Colin's old school friends had also been asked to figure in the arrangement. The friend was Iggy, a pleasant boy whose ill-treatment by his parents was famous in Colin's circle. Constantly thrown out of doors for no reason, he was a regular fixture at the Stowells' house, sleeping on the floor in Colin's room or out in the drive in his customised Morris Minor van.

The three found a cottage in Fox Lane, just off the main Salisbury road. Colin vacated his bedroom at home – all but for the posters of half-naked girls advertising engine-oil – and, in the following weeks, became totally involved in his new grown-up, independent life. His family were not invited to the new place since, as he explained, Susie wanted to get everything "straight" before they began entertaining. Helping Susie get everything straight also ruled out virtually all the jobs Colin had formerly been prevailed on to do at his family home and in the garden to save his father's strength. He visited his parents only for Sunday lunch when – as in former unindependent days – he and Susie would come straight from the pub, arriving an almost ritual half hour later than the time Mrs Stowell liked to dish up. Afterwards, they sat around for an hour or two, and Susie read *Ideal Home* with an absorption which deepened if Colin were ever asked to perform some small domestic or horticultural task. She accompanied him outside only towards the end of their visit, when they would pick spinach, carrots, runner beans and, in due season, tomatoes, redcurrants, raspberries and loganberries to take home.

At Easter, Iggy left the cottage after a row with Colin, ending the friendship which had lasted since their kindergarten days. The family received only incomplete details. There had been a row over money and a hi-fi deck, and Iggy had behaved badly. His guilt seemed the plainer if he was ready to give up his home with Colin and Susie, and return to the bosom of parents who made him ask permission before even pouring a glass of milk.

That summer, Rachel bought a horse. She did so against fierce opposition from Mr Stowell, despite his pride in her as a horsewoman and despite the two large fields he owned which were left empty by the farmer who rented them. Mr Stowell knew by now he had not many months left, and wished to do nothing to complicate the property he would bequeath to his wife. He visualised those two empty fields as his accomplices, rallying to her aid in Probate, surrounding her like the embrace he could no longer provide.

Rachel pleaded and reasoned with him in the shout necessary to pierce his deafness; it was mostly exhaustion which made her grow tearful at what seemed to her the obdurate reply, puffed into his pipe, that she would do far better to invest her money.

"It's my money and I want to do this more than anything. It could be an investment if I buy a mare and she foals at three. Those fields are just going to waste, and anyway, Mr Spencer gives you almost nothing for them." Here, at last, she made contact: Mr Stowell had long felt uneasy about the smallness of the rent he charged Mr Spencer.

"How are you going to exercise it while you're in London?" Mr Stowell persisted. "A horse needs a lot of exercising."

"I'll come down every weekend. You *know* if I start anything, I keep on with it." A sudden inspiration seized her, for it was Sunday afternoon: the sitting-room was crowded as usual.

"Susie – if I kept a horse here, would you be able to come over in the week and exercise it?"

Susie looked up from *Ideal Home*.

"Yes," she replied at once. This time, Rachel did not mind the drawing out of the vowel into "Ye-eth". Whatever qualms came later, she suppressed. You couldn't *catch* warts, could you? Not through reins or girth-straps, anyway.

Rachel did her riding in Yorkshire, from the stable of a dealer who imported cross-bred Connemaras for the Metropolitan Police. She went up as often as she could afford, travelling with a Police friend who was jailer at Great Marlborough

Street, and savoured, as much as Rachel did, the scruffy hunt across a breathtaking moor, and pub nights of ale and "mushy peas". Joe, the dealer, had been keeping an eye open for her. Last time, he had put her on a little grey mare, two years old, who kept up all day and jumped anything. She was 15.3, broken and the niece of a steeplechaser champion. She had been offered to Rachel for £800. No VAT was necessary if cash could be paid.

The next weekend, Rachel tentatively approached Colin.

"Do you think . . . if I hire the car and the horsebox and pay all the expenses . . . do you think you'd be able to drive up to Yorkshire with me and bring her back? I'd pay everything, like petrol and meals, and the hotel."

Colin seemed quite taken by the idea. "You'd need a fairly big engine. And a towing bar." He looked at Susie, who was sharing his armchair, leafing through *Ideal Home*. "Jeff Norris over at Whiteparish has got a little trailer; he might let us borrow that for a weekend."

Susie broke off from studying microwave ovens and nodded.

"And it's so *lovely* up there," Rachel said. "I'd like you both to see it. I can book us in at the Five Bells, where Brendon and I always stay. There's a lovely woman there called Mrs Brom-ige."

Nor was this all the family news. Despite a lodger (in Iggy's old room) Colin and Susie had decided the rent for their cottage was too expensive. In Salisbury they had seen a house, which Colin thought he could buy and do up. They had given notice to their landlord – though the lodger, as yet, knew nothing of this – and were secretly corresponding with several building societies. Meanwhile, they had already begun to collect things to decorate their new home, or help Colin with its restoration. These included an old iron plough they found at a farm shortly to be auctioned, a set of doorknobs from an empty house, and a heap of sand taken from a building site after dark. They did not regard this method of acquisition as anything but enterprising. The cache was left in the Stowells' boiler-house so that the lodger's suspicions would not be aroused.

The date for collecting Rachel's horse was now fixed. At

home, things had worked out better than she ever dared hope. Mr Spencer agreed – gladly – to provide grazing and stabling in return for an unrevised rent. Her father gave in (he was now very ill); her mother, secretly, promised her a bridle; she awoke each morning happy and grateful, to Colin and Susie as much as anyone. Amid intricate arrangements, for horse insurance and veterinary inspection, she took pains to construct a weekend that would repay their long journey on her behalf, booking them a double room, arranging mounts for them with Joe. Now, every plan was in its place. Colin and Susie would bring the car and horsebox to London on Friday night, sleeping at Rachel's. Early on Saturday morning, they would set off for Yorkshire.

On Wednesday night, her head aching with long-distance negotiation, she rang Colin to double check on the hire car and horsebox, and discovered he had made no move yet to obtain either. His voice in the receiver was slow and cantankerous, like their father's on a bad day, and he flatly denied ever giving any such undertaking. At one point, Rachel heard Susie's voice in the background corroborating how absurd was the claim. Curbing her passion, for the greater favour she wished from them, Rachel spent nearly all Thursday on her office phone to Portsmouth area car-hire firms, most of whose stocks were already cleared for the weekend. At the eleventh hour – literally – a single-size horsebox, an estate car and towing attachment achieved conjunction, though for a sum far exceeding Rachel's meticulous budget. Then she rang Colin again. She told him where to collect the car and horsebox. She warned him of the deposit-size, and promised to reimburse him that same weekend. She asked what time tomorrow night he and Susie would arrive with the horsebox in Islington. "About nine," Colin said.

Rachel prepared her only bedroom for Colin and Susie's use, putting the best cover on the duvet, and flowers and grapes and fresh dates on the cabin trunk by the bed. She had sped to Berwick Street for pork fillets at lunch-time: the casserole was timed to be ready at 9.30, allowing Colin and Susie to relax and start on the wine or, it could be, export lager. At 10.30, the casserole began to bubble ill-temperedly; Rachel turned off the oven and opened a tin of sweetcorn for herself. At 11.45, Colin rang: they had picked up the horsebox, he said, but had afterwards "got involved at this party": they would probably not reach Islington before 2 am. Rachel hung the front-door key inside the letterbox and retired to her small, hard sitting-room couch. When she woke at 6.30, the keys still hung inside; the bed had not been slept in. A perfume of dates and flowers mingled in the room.

They arrived shortly after 10. Colin explained that the clutch cable had broken outside Guildford; they had had to bed down in the car until a garage opened. He was freshly-shaved and Susie's jeans had the stiffness of recent drycleaning. Rachel, had she known nothing of clutch cables, would have smelled the untruth: she decided to let it pass. The horsebox, at least, was what had been promised.

They left London at a crawl in the midday traffic. The whole afternoon, and much of the evening, would be used up by the journey, but Rachel, in the back seat, consoled herself with the thought of Sunday, at least: a Sunday complete in Yorkshire, for she had Monday off, as did Colin and Susie, and they need not start back until late in the afternoon. She grew happy again, for such was her nature; she thought of the little grey mare with the spotted face, the mane she could comb and the tail she would plait, the hooves she would paint black, and those awkward long hairs to be trimmed behind each hoof.

"I thought," she said, leaning forward, "on Monday, if you don't want to ride again, we could always go and look at Scarborough. It isn't that far from where we're staying."

Colin looked at Susie, who sat close to him, toying with a curl on the nape of his neck.

"Well, actually . . ." Colin said, smiling mirthlessly. "We shall have to be getting back by Sunday lunch-time. We've made an appointment to see our bank manager first thing on Monday morning, about getting a loan for our house."

Rachel sat forward, between their two high, head-pillowed seat-backs.

"But – you knew you were coming to Yorkshire – you

knew I'd arranged for us to stay up until Monday. I've booked rides for us with Joe, tomorrow afternoon. It's not easy to get a horse there, Colin: I had to book the rides."

She looked at Susie, who remained looking at Colin and toying with the curl on his neck.

"I'm sorry," he said, pulling out to overtake a bulk transporter. "It's the house. It's important to us."

"But this is important to *me*! You knew it was. You could have fixed to see the bank manager on any other day."

"What we might do," Colin said, "is drive back overnight on Sunday. If we set off at two or three o'clock . . ."

"Colin, we're not staying *at* the stables. The Five Bells is half an hour's drive away. And a horse has to have a feed at least an hour before travelling. Do you mean, set off at one o'clock? And anyway – I wanted this weekend to be for you as well as me. I wanted you to see Yorkshire and –"

"We've made the appointment," Colin said.

There is no greater tyranny than that of the driver over the non-driver. Rachel pressed her hands to her face and began to cry.

"I've booked us in for two nights. I told Mrs Bromige – I even got you a double room. Oh, please stay up," she found herself sobbing. "Please. *Please*."

Susie turned and faced her between the high-backed seats, with an expression Rachel had not seen before – of anger seasoned already to middle-age, residing not in the eyes but in the forehead; the tight-pinched mouth; the plump little discontented chin.

"Oh, *don't* be so hysterical," Susie snapped – and no trace of a lisp was detectable in her voice. "We're coming back on Sunday, and that's *final*. Stop being so stupid about it. And another thing," she continued, as Colin grinned wanly and watched the traffic, and the tears froze on Rachel's cheeks:

"You owe us sixty-five pounds. Col had to give that bloke a cheque last night, *and* fill the tank up. When are you going to give us back our money?"

Mr Stowell faced what must be with his usual argumentativeness. He had been laid up only once in his life: in 1917, on the Messines Ridge, when a German sniper's bullet had struck him in the left foot. But for that interlude – painful enough at the hands of a Canadian MO – he could not remember a day's illness this century. Mr Stowell cared for two things, and these passionately: his business and his garden. The loss of one wife, the marriage to a second, thirty years his junior, and birth of three babies in rapid order, had caused little change in either preoccupation. He would nurse each baby, allowing it to try his pipe while his mind remained busy with kale or lobelias. For a bedtime story, he described to them Queen Victoria's Diamond Jubilee. Jane, the only one to be sent away to school, remembered his arrival on Speech Day, always an hour too early; how he would wander over the games field, digging up bits of turf with his penknife. His line was fertilisers, and they served his imagination as well as any symphony. He had retired, but only two years ago, on his eighty-first birthday: his shares and directorships were undiminished.

Old age, to Mr Stowell, had until now been a source of gradual irritation, like the sniffles. "I don't *like* being old," he would complain to his wife at night after he had lost the trick of sleep or done what was for him an unsatisfactory day's digging. He had the Edwardian's dislike of doctors and doses, and so it was not until far too late that he sat in the specialist's office, listening to an explanation of the 'funny feeling' in his throat. Outside there were lawns, some nice little rose bushes and wisteria. Mr Stowell had always liked wisteria. "Do you mind major surgery?" the specialist had said. "You're the expert," Mr Stowell had replied: the same as he said in 1917 to that Canadian MO.

He had weathered two operations, recovering with a promptness which made crueller the certainty that nothing could be done. His condition worsened more slowly than usual, because of his age; perhaps, because the disease is genuinely checked in those who do not fear it. He was already tiny; hairless, wizened like a filbert: the girls, when they saw him at weekends, noticed little outward change. He still roamed the shrubberies in his little crumpled hat; still brought the coal in – even drove them to the station if he could not be dissuaded. He refused all painkillers but aspirin. Only to his wife, late at night when the coughing came, would he confess: "This is very difficult, my dear. It's like trying to bring up string."

Chiefly he worried about his wife. Though he had married her for no better reason than the size of her bust, time had shown him her several virtues – her patience, good humour, her conviction that he always knew best. She was, he knew, a gullible woman, and must be provided for on a scale which would withstand her inevitable mismanagements. For some years before his illness, Mr Stowell had been converting his assets to an ironclad bequest, playing the Stock Market skilfully on his wife's behalf, then knotting it all up in trusts. His children figured in this strategy not at all. From each he had rejected a plea for capital, to fund a flat or a car, with a testiness that came harder with the knowledge that he paid surtax on unearned income. At other times his thrift caused the family amusement. A week ago, he had posted a cheque for a TV licence in an unstamped envelope with "On Her Majesty's Service" written on it defiantly in spidery blue-black longhand.

The other great worry on Mr Stowell's mind was the care of his garden. Who would look after it when he was gone? Already he felt his grip on it loosening; with the same will to work as ever, he often found himself sitting on the grass bank, next to the marrow bed, unable to prise his arms loose from his upraised knees. At such times he would review the half century he had spent out here, in strenuous tranquillity, ministering to an intricacy of seasons. The garden was his only contemporary at home, its asparagus beds forty years old, some of the rhubarb possibly older. And in the long greenhouses Mr Stowell breathed an aroma – of warm tomatoes, old rake-handles, green tank-water – which recalled to him the old days, and values now absent from the world.

He employed a gardener who lived in the next village; but the arrangement was unsatisfactory. Mr Stowell paid the going rate, and could not see any sense in raising it. He saw less of the gardener than of the gardener's little boy, a frequent visitor to announce that Dad would not be over today.

He worried about the lawns, back and front; about greenfly and blackspot; a loganberry bush that needed uprooting; all the unpicked broccoli; the baby marrow shoots which the crows drew out and laid on top of the earth. Most of all, he worried about the long hedge between his orchard and the lane. Privet and holly, yew, quickthorn and hazel, uncut for three summers, its cohorts stretched a shaggy half-mile in Mr Stowell's mind's eye. He longed to fetch the shears and short ladder, but knew he could not long control either; nor did he trust his children – except, perhaps Rachel – to do a level job.

Mr Stowell thought of the uncut hedge late at night when he could not sleep; and also, of gardeners who were no longer reliable, until worry drove him out of bed to sit on the edge with the sheet still covering his knees. Then, for some strange reason, he would think of the dug-out at Messines, and the label tied to his collar, and the face of that Canadian MO.

'Oh, can't you all make it up?'' thought Mrs Stowell on Sunday as she surveyed the faces around her in the cramped dining recess. She had begun to dish up – indeed, they had almost finished eating – by the time Colin and Susie arrived from the pub, and his mother, despite Rachel's stern exhortation beforehand, half rose from her chair and said: "Sorry, we started without you . . ." Something deep within Mrs Stowell rather liked men to spurn her efforts in the kitchen.

Mr Stowell was there also, though he could eat nothing but stewed apple, and his thoughts stayed mainly on their own track. His family spoke of him as if he were absent: occasionally, his voice would break in on a different wavelength, blurred but resonant, like signals from 2LO heard psychically on Radio One.

Mrs Stowell, with all her optimism, could not succeed in imagining harmony. A week before, Colin had asked permission to come home again to live until his new house became habitable – for the bills at his cottage had begun to oppress him. He had further proposed that Susie should live at home with him. It had not needed a vigorous action group, formed by Jane and Rachel in London, to elicit Mr Stowell's flat refusal. "Well . . .'

Colin had said grandly. "It's both of us or nothing." Mrs Stowell, deep down, regretted it was to be nothing: she had rather looked forward to picking up his soiled shirts again and loading them into the wash.

Then there was that upset over the horse. Mrs Stowell liked the horse and fed it secretly, apples and Polo mints; she would have ridden it but for her plastic hip joint. Jane had tried, even Colin – everyone, in fact, but Mr Stowell (who was game enough) and Susie. And yet, had not Susie been meant to exercise the horse for Rachel during the week? Since they all returned from Yorkshire, Mrs Stowell knew, Susie had not set foot near the horse's field. Colin had mentioned the matter to his mother; she, in turn, mentioned it to Rachel, who laughed harshly and said she must be joking. No warty little hands, Rachel answered, would come within ten billion miles of her horse's reins. It was all very mysterious and troubling.

"Couldn't you make it up?" thought Mrs Stowell again, and she said, indicating Mr Stowell:

"Have you seen the nice present we've given Father?"

"What present?" Colin asked. Susie continued eating with eyes demurely lowered, and quick, noisy jabs of her knife and fork.

"Rachel and Jane bought it really, but I fetched it. Smart clippers."

"We've given Daddy some electric hedge-clippers," Rachel said with a pointedness that her brother failed to notice. "I've seen those," he said. "They had some in Hill's in Salisbury. Like a blade, aren't they? You'd have to watch out for the teeth if you went near a wire fence." Rachel determined to speak to him after lunch, if she could get him alone for a minute.

"The grenades they issued us with weren't much good," Mr Stowell remarked suddenly. "The Jerries had much better ones. But they always were splendid toymakers. GHQ got me to write a handbook all about grenades and trench mortars. You didn't know I was an author, did you Suky?'

"*Susie!*" chorused the others automatically. "Susie I mean," Mr Stowell said. "You didn't know I was an author, did you?" Susie shook her head in an exaggerated way, then continued eating. At other times she ignored Mr Stowell's little jokes.

"Did I see jumps in the orchard?" asked Jane, who had just ridden down from London by motor scooter.

"I stood a few bits of wood up near the greengage tree," Rachel said.

"Did Nickel go over all right?"

"Yes – lovely. Not a murmur."

"They go just as well on a long wire as on an ordinary one," Mr Stowell observed.

Rachel laughed. "He means the clippers."

"No loss of power at all, it says in the instructions," Mr Stowell added.

"He needs an extra long flex to reach the orchard hedge," Rachel said to Colin. "We thought you could give that to Daddy as your share."

"Could do," Colin said slowly. He and Susie had both finished eating: she now leaned from her chair into his, studying him as he spoke and toying with a curl on his neck. Occasionally she murmured something, inaudible to the others, which caused her to topple sideways into his shoulder, gazing at him with consciously-shining eyes.

"Might take a bit of time to get one, though," Colin said.

"Why?" Rachel glanced up sharply.

"Until I find one lying around . . ."

"I didn't mean *steal* one," Rachel said. "Buy one, I meant, with that paper stuff: you know. It's called money . . ."

"Dear, oh dear," thought Mrs Stowell. "More fighting." She hoped there would not be still more over the washing up, which she was perfectly content to do alone.

After lunch they gathered in the sitting-room as usual. Mr Stowell sat close to the empty grate, reading a large-print library book by A. J. Cronin. Colin and Susie sat under the little window, sharing an armchair. The cat, which was black, with one white leg like a wading boot, stalked in and made its way to Jane. "Nice and peaceful," Mrs Stowell thought, reaching behind her for her knitting spectacles. Susie leaned forward and picked up a copy of *Ideal Home*.

Rachel, in her jodhpurs and socks, until such time as she

could escape to shampoo her horse's tail, used the *Sunday Express* for a screen between herself and the lovers. Since Yorkshire, she had been unable to look at Susie without feeling a genuine, clear-headed impulse to murder. She had hoped at first, the car incident might be a revelation to Colin: the next day, at Joe's stables, he had even apologised to her – or started to, for Susie had come up then and nestled against his shoulder, staring with a scowl into the middle distance. Rachel remembered that same scowl, bestowed on Yorkshire impartially, as if the very moors might conspire to check the descent of Susie's head upon Colin's shoulder. They had gone back on Sunday, as threatened, leaving Rachel behind to honour bookings she had made, though riven with despair to see her horse driven off, in its new bandages, without her. Mrs Bromige, at the Five Bells, understood the situation, and gave tactful solace: she, too, as it happened, felt an instant aversion to Susie. "Never mind, Rachel love," Mrs Bromige had said later. "There's justice in Heaven."

"Oh, look Col!" Susie's voice murmured. "I like those cushions. Aren't they ni-ice. Aren't they pret-ty."

"She'll get herself pregnant soon," Rachel suddenly thought.

Mr Stowell put down his library book and said: "Going over the top wasn't so bad once you were over. It was good fun. I only ever killed one German that I knew of: in a trench raid. He jumped down from a parapet in front of me, and I stuck the bayonet in. I remember thinking, 'head or stomach?' I chose stomach. And all the muddy water came up through him from the trench-floor. He stank of ether. Lots of Jerries did when they went into action."

Wheels scraped in the drive: a Morris Minor van drew up. "Here's Iggy," Mrs Stowell said. "Well I never!"

The criminal had come, at last to pay the debts he had left behind him. Suitably penitent, he declined to come in; Colin would not go out to him, and Susie read on fiercely through *Ideal Home*. It was Jane who spoke to Iggy and heard a somewhat different version of the quarrel. He had fled, he maintained, from excessive canoodling, and from Susie's despotism over housework and food. She counted the tomatoes, Iggy said: even measured the butter and milk; on several nights before decamping, he had fled outside to sleep in his van.

Their respective Morris Minors drew Iggy and Colin back to friendship. They did speak, at length, outside the kitchen window. Mrs Stowell, rinsing the teapot, saw Susie join them, then turn away almost at once with a heartfelt "Oh *God*!" Then it was that the same thought occurred to Mrs Stowell as had to Rachel and, quite independently, to Jane:

"She'll get herself pregnant soon."

Rachel did not return from the stable until after tea. With her bridle and riding hat she carried a wheel of black flex mounted on a frame.

"*Did* you shampoo Nickel's tail?' Jane asked.

"Yes. She didn't like it much. And," Rachel said to Colin, "I've borrowed Mr Spencer's extension flex. That ought to reach as far as the orchard."

He stared at her.

"Do you mean you want *us* to cut the hedge?"

'No, Colin," his sister replied with heavy sarcasm. "Of course I don't want *you* to cut the hedge."

They had gone into the kitchen, where Rachel cleaned her riding tack. Colin leaned on the Aga and Susie clung to him, staring at something on the wall. He held the Aga rail to support them both.

"Right *now*, I mean?"

"I'll help," Rachel said. "We must, otherwise, Daddy will try to do it himself. You know what he's like. And he's bound to fall through the hedge or something."

"I mean: has it got to be this afternoon?"

"Yes."

"Why has it? What's wrong with tomorrow?"

"Mr Spencer wants his extension back tonight. And it'll please Daddy so much. You know he's been worrying about the hedge. *Why* won't you?"

Colin glanced down at Susie. His voice silted with indecision, he replied: "It doesn't really fit in with our plans, that's all . . ." Seeing Rachel's face, he amended: "All right, we'll go and have a look – only don't nag so much." He and Susie set off across the lawn together, though now – Jane noticed – walking several feet apart.

The others were all outside, with the tea things. Only Rachel, hanging her bridle over the kitchen door, heard Colin and Susie come back from their inspection of the hedge, to hold a conference about it just outside the Playroom. Colin's voice said that, with the electric clippers, it would only take an hour or so. Susie's voice cut in repeatedly in a piteous note. "Oh, no-o, Co-ol, do-on't –"

"– just to help Dad."

"Oh, no-o, Co-ol, do-on't. Cut it another ti-ime. I want to go for a dri-ive."

Mr Stowell, under the nut tree, heard his son's voice hailing him. He lowered A. J. Cronin and looked up in hope. "Colin's a good boy,' he thought. "Colin will understand those instructions. They do the print so small these days . . ."

"Cheerio then, Dad."

"Oh – you're off, are you? And Suky?"

*"Susie!"*

"Susie, I mean."

"We're going for a drive up to Margham Tower."

"Are you?" said his father politely. There was little wrong with Mr Stowell's eyesight, and he, too, had perfectly evaluated Susie. But old men prefer to be popular with all, so Mr Stowell added playfully:

"Sukie's not going to walk through Margham Wood in *that* pretty dress!"

"Susie! No: she's going to change."

"Eh?"

"She's going to change!" Colin repeated, and Susie herself suddenly beamed, like a good little girl who has understood what the grown-ups say.

"Yeth," she agreed. "I'll put on my T-shirt an' my jeanth."

They drove off together up the lane, beside the long hedge. Privet and hazel hung high in wild plumes; gnarled holly, between, shut out the birds. Ivy climbed past the fence-wire to collar a yew tree, intent on its throttling work. A wide stretch lay dead, lashed down by brambles. In the hidden ditch, fat ferns lolled on a floor of dock leaves. The nettles grew straight-backed and silvery, safe in their untouched shade.

Susie nestled close to Colin, toying with the curl on his neck, and began to choose words for the news she had to give him.

# Words of Love

February 2, 1959

The last call she had from him came through just before noon. Outside the big studio window, ragged New York snowflakes drifted down, the way they had all morning. Fifth Avenue, below, was deep white, the traffic barely murmuring.

"Maria-Elena?"

"Buddy?"

"Hey, darlin'."

"Where are you?"

"Waylon," she heard him say. "Where we at?" Then: "Green Bay, Wisconsin. Waylon says Hi. Did I wake you?"

"Mm-mm. I was just doing my petit-point. Baby, it's so good to hear you. Te quiero."

"Te quiero, darlin'. Do you feel okay?"

She had told him she was pregnant only the day before he had to leave on tour.

"Remember now . . . you promised. When you go to that market, don't carry no packages home. Tell 'em they got to deliver it. Even a little package . . ."

"Buddy, I'm fine. Just fine."

"Do you have the new *Billboard*?"

"Oh . . . sure." She took it from the coffee table and turned to the Hot 100 page while he waited, somewhere out there in the Midwest.

"You went up to forty-three."

"Only forty-three!"

"I didn't get Cash Box yet."

"They don't like it, do they?" he said with an audible sigh.

"Sure they do, baby."

198

"It's hardly moved, though."

"You just got to give it a little more time."

"Is it still getting airplay?"

"Sure. Everyone."

"Who?"

"Alan Freed . . . The Wolfman. They're all crazy about it."

"I keep wonderin' if I made a mistake. Maybe I shouldn't have put those strings on there."

"Aw baby, it's just fine. Are you okay?"

"Cold."

"I miss you so."

"I miss you, Maria-Elena . . . goin' crazy. If I could, I'd quit this whole deal and come right on back, you know?"

"I know, baby."

"Did the lawyer call?"

"He called just to say he has a meeting with Norman scheduled for Thursday, and he feels confident they're gonna make some progress."

"Progress! They're my songs! I wrote 'em. I never asked anyone to come along and put their name on 'em."

"He said he's sure Norman will co-operate and release the money. It's just going to need a little more time."

"Shoot, why's he messin' round so dam' much? He knows we're strapped for cash. Why else he think I'd leave you with a baby comin' . . . go messin' round out here when I ought to be in New York, pushin' my record. Remember what we said? I'd stay in New York till I got another hit as big as 'Oh Boy'."

The snow was drifting faster past the big studio window.

"Any other calls?"

"Phil Everly."

"Phil?"

"He was in town just the one night. He'll call again when they come back from England.'

"Nothing from Jerry or Joe B?"

"Uh-uh."

"Remember what I said to say if either on 'em calls."

"I know."

"Tell 'em I could do with The Crickets where I'm at right now . . ."

She listened, saying nothing, while he talked of her only rivals for his heart.

". . . Tell 'em I miss 'em and I want to see 'em, here or down in Lubbock. I'll be back in two weeks."

He was laughing again now.

"Man, it's *cold* where we are! Dam' bus froze today. Whole dam' bus just clean froze out there on the freeway. We was lightin' papers in the aisle to keep warm."

"We have snow here, too. Just started a couple hours ago."

"One of the guys got frostbite. Can you believe it?"

"Which guy?"

"Charlie Bunch. He's in the hospital. So we got no drummer for tonight at Clear Lake. I guess I'll have to ask Ritchie to play drums behind Tommy, Waylon and me."

"Send Ritchie my love. And The Bopper."

"Maria-Elena, I got to go. I'll call you tomorrow from Fargo."

"Okay. Te quiero, baby."

"They're shoutin' for us . . . te quiero, Maria-Elena. 'Bye."

Five thousand miles away, others who loved him were just coming out of school. The afternoon was grey and blustery, and the sea below West Hill showed clouds of yacht-sails adrift on the white-capped waves. Even in February, the Isle of Wight seldom experiences snow.

As Ivor went for his bike, he fell under the disdainful eye of Gully, the prefect whose family kept the smart teashop in Union Street.

"Seaford-Warwick," Gully said in a tone of affected long-suffering. "What makes you such a wreck?"

He paused with his brown-skinned crony Truckle as Ivor hauled the bike backwards from the tin lean-to.

"You're a disgrace to the school, Seaford-Warwick. Look at your blazer — it's covered with dirt. Those shoes haven't been cleaned for months. And where's your house-badge?"

"I haven't got one, Gully."

"It's a school rule that everyone must have a house-badge, Seaford-Warwick. Make sure you get one by tomorrow."

The cyclists dispersed onto a blue tarmac road, opposite a parish church designed by Sir George Gilbert Scott. Phillips "Kingfishers" and Trent "Tourists" swooped off right and left, amid the anthem drummed all day on desk-tops, murmured downward into striped tie-knots:

"If you knew, Peggy Sue . . ."

Ivor sat stationary on his Raleigh "All Steel", pretending to check some fault in its three-speed. Exchanging the world of school for that of home each day required a conscious deep breath, like a high diver or a spaceman about to venture out of his craft.

Across the road at the bus-stop, a sympathetic boy named Sweetman caught his eye, smiled and sang "Peggy Sue, Peggy Sue."

"Pretty pretty pretty pretty Peggy Sue," Ivor sang back, mentally shaping that unexpected minor chord.

"Uh-oh Peg-gy!"

He rode down to the seafront by his usual elaborate system of back lanes and byways, to let as few people as possible see how shabby he was. Union Street at this hour was always full of beautiful Portsmouth Grammar girls, walking up from the ferry, their satchels clasped before them in both hands.

Freewheeling on his dusty green warhorse, he lapsed into an habitual dream. Instead of his faded blazer and shiny worsted flannels he wore a pale blue suit, buttoned high. The guitar in his hands was fish-shaped and white. He was looking severe and playing the heavenly intro to "That'll Be The Day", watched by a rapt circle of Portsmouth Grammar girls.

On the Esplanade, groups of his schoolfellows waited for buses to Sandown, Shanklin and Ventnor. Others passed him in bulbous family cars, bound for the respectable hamlets of Seaview and St Helens. He was the only one whose journey home lay half a mile out to sea.

Along the pier, the wind blew straight at him, making him stand on the pedals as he guided his front wheel clear of the long gaps in the planks. As always, a friend was there with an energising refrain, helping to push each reluctant pedal down:

"Well, rave *on* this crazy feeling and . . . *I* know you got me reeling I'm . . . *so* glad you're revealing your love . . . dummy-dimmy-dum . . ."

Winter-time life at the Pier Pavilion retreated to a small room known in summer as The Porpoise Bar. Its walls displayed pastel murals of the Walrus and Carpenter, the Whiting, the Snail and a porpoise standing on tip-tail, winking into a champagne-glass. Domesticity was provided by a roll-top desk, a Cossor television set, a one-bar electric fire, two meagre armchairs and Ivor's father's mistress's copious knitting.

She was there by herself, rinsing out something in the anteroom full of the backs of beer-barrels. She turned to Ivor with an indifference that three years of constant enforced contact had done nothing to diminish.

"Dad not here," he said hopefully.

"No . . . he's gone up into town to see about the supper licence for next season."

Tea, or what passed for it, would not be until at least half past five. That gave Ivor a good hour with his friend.

He went out of The Porpoise Bar, across the entrance hall littered with shrouded slot machines and cafeteria units, and mounted the dark, dusty staircase towards the promenade balcony. As he went, he felt in his trouser-pocket for the chip of tortoiseshell that was warm from being constantly fingered and turned.

Half-way up the stairs was a room, flimsily partitioned from the main kitchen for the benefit of summer staff. So deep in winter it contained nothing but a blistered grey table, some iron sun-roof chairs, a smell of mummified chip fat and the thing that made Ivor's life worth living.

Its shrouded shape was where he'd left it, propped against the ledge of the seaward windows. He slid it from its soft plastic case, sighing with joy to see the lustrous 'cello body and mother of pearl-dotted fingerboard. A faint, harp-like "plink" came from the strings coiled round the ivory tuning-pegs as he pulled the end of the case over them.

He took his guitar on his knee and brought the finger-warmed plectrum from his pocket. For the first time since awakening this morning, he was alive.

He shaped an E Major and stroked the pick down. From mellow sunburst deeps came the sound he'd been making under his breath all day, through Physics, Maths, Scripture, English Language and double Latin:

*Brr-angg.*

It was the sound that had discomposed the mind of many another English middle-class boy whose school blazer bore an inscription in Latin. The sound which to name, even in one's thoughts, brought a tremor of besotted guilt:

Rock 'n' Roll.

Everything gorgeous about it resounded in that simple three-finger chord. All the glamour, the drama, the brooding and becoming self-pity. Every shiny thread of insinuation that existence was not blandly straightforward, as one had always thought, but breathtakingly disordered, asymmetric and oblique.

He struck it again, further back near the bridge – the way to get an electric effect if you were only acoustic. The pick-point clippered down the metal strings almost at their root, then slid with his sleeve across the tortoiseshell guard.

*Brrr-annggg!*

It was the slightest hand-hold on a heaven whose deities were, for the most part, unreachably mysterious. Elvis Presley, Little Richard, the Everly Brothers, with their gold-scaly suits and wet liquorice bootlace curls, displayed no affinity with the human race. One loved them with unseated reason, having no idea what they were saying or how the sublime inferno around them was produced. One listened and listened vainly, gazing into the chrome and pink fonts of jukeboxes at forbidden coffee bars.

In all this brilliant, opaque Paradise, only one figure was utterly intelligible. Every record of his so far had instantly revealed itself to be played in basic three-finger E Major – then equally simple A and B7. To all learner guitarists in school blazers, he had become an example, encourager and friend.

Strange-shaped and lever-embellished as his guitar was, eerily as it travelled through stratospheres of quaver and echo. it always told you exactly what it was doing. As it played, you could join in on your fourteen-guinea Hofner "Congress". The music didn't mind.

What few pictures of him had been seen also gave hope and encouragement. Alone in the frowning, pouting pantheon, he was not specially good looking. He was skinny and long-necked, and wore outsize specs like a class swot. English boys, hitherto derided as "weeds", had looked at him and realised it didn't matter any more.

Likewise his voice, so ebony-dark and hicuppy-strange, was also somehow the voice of an English schoolboy, bashful about any public display. You could do it like a ventriloquist, murmuring down into your chin. You could become him, secretly, any time of day when it was intolerable to be you.

To this particular English boy, he was more than a friend, He was a best friend. Amid the drab bizarreness and flat-calm hopelessness of life, only his voice said, "It's so easy . . . Every day, it's getting closer . . . Look at me. You can do it. Listen to me."

Ivor turned on his chair to catch the dwindling light, and began to strum the Buddy Holly song that was most wonderful of all in its reined-back voice, its dark, rolling drumbeat, and total accessibility to him.

Strumming soft, then loud, he started to sing in the voice he knew, down to the slightest click of tongue against palate:

"I love you, Peggy Sue, with uh love so rare 'n' true, ah-oh Peggy . . ."

He forgot the staffroom with its smell of dead chip fat, the winter sea threshing under the pier's iron legs. He forgot what had happened today and what would happen tomorrow.

He became happy.


Around Clear Lake, the snow seemed to be thinning. The heat had come back on in the bus and you could see through the windows again. There was even a chill red sun, flickering through the pine forests that bordered the interstate.

In the back seat, Dion and Frankie Sardo reminisced about

Little Richard, before he saw the Russian Sputnik and thought it was a call from God.

"Remember that time we were stranded in New Jersey, and we asked Richard for a loan? He opened the trunk of his car and scooped out a handful of notes without even looking. The trunk was full of twenty- and fifty-dollar bills . . ."

". . . and that girl of his. What was her name – Echo?"

"No, Lee."

"Lee Angel. The stripper. Guess what size of a chest she had."

"Forty."

"Bigger."

"*Bigger?*"

"It was fifty inches. And an eighteen-inch waist."

"Nothing grows in the shade." The Bopper's voice rumbled from down the aisle.

"All the guys on the shows used to ball her. Richard used to dig that. He'd stand there and watch 'em."

"Didn't Buddy ball her one time?"

He turned round in his fur collar and grinned.

"Remember the New York Paramount? Irving Feld's Show of Stars?"

"God, everyone was on that one. Us . . . Larry Williams . . ."

"The Moonglows . . . The Del Vikings . . . Laverne Baker . . ."

"Six shows a day! Boy, that was a killer . . ."

"Go on, Buddy."

"I went into Richard's dressing-room one time. Remember those dressing-rooms of his? I'm wearin' my guitar, 'bout to go onstage. And here's Lee givin' him head . . . suckin' his titty. He just looks at me and says 'C'mon. There's room for you, too.'"

At the Swede House Inn, Tommy Allsup turned on the TV and lay back on his bed, not troubling to remove his stetson or cowboy boots. There were just two hours before the bus returned to take them to the Surf Ballroom. Then it was on through the night again, 450 miles to Moorfield, Minnesota.

Through the mustard yellow wall he could hear showers, toilet plugs, other TVs tuned to *The Untouchables*. And, somewhere down the hall, The Bopper's voice: "O my chickadees, it's a Swiss challay! So prett-ee!"

Tommy was a big, dark, gentle-eyed Texan who counted his blessings, like his mother always said. He was glad to be here, despite the cold, playing behind a big star, meeting girls every day, living on room service. He'd liked New York, too, staying with Buddy and Maria-Elena in the Village, going out to all those weird coffee houses and bars. And picking for Buddy on the demo' tapes he'd made before they started on tour. Everything all along real nice and friendly.

Patting his shirt pocket for a cigarette, he remembered the problem that had come up yesterday. He drew the letter on familiar violet paper from his pocket, unfolded it from the Post Office stub and re-read it. Then he picked up the phone and asked for Carroll, the tour-manager.

"Carroll – Tommy talkin'. What time we all get into Fargo tomorrow?"

"Oh – about six-thirty."

"Shoot. My mom's written me she sent a registered packet for me, care of Fargo Post Office. It's a silver money-clip my Uncle Blueatrice leff' me. This way we're gonna get in too late for me to pick it up."

He saw out *The Untouchables*, took a catnap under his stetson-brim, then rose, picked up his guitar-case and ambled along to Buddy's room, beyond the ice-machine. No one on the road can ever stand being alone for long.

He found Buddy looking at a huge pile of stage-suits and sweat-dried shirts, emptied from various cases onto the bed. In twelve days' travelling, they'd stopped nowhere long enough to get any laundry done.

"Hey, Buddy."

"Hey, hoss. You want to take a plane ride tonight?"

"A plane ride!"

"I can't go for another all-night deal in that bus, man. I figured, if we can charter a plane, we could get to Moorfield in a couple hours, maybe. Rest up, get our laundry done. Okay?"

"Okay. Neat."

Waylon came in in his buckskins, rubbing icy wet hands.

"You talk to the guy?" Buddy asked him.

"Yup. He'll do it for a hundred bucks and an autograph." Waylon took out a matchbook and peered at some notes jotted inside it. "My hand was so dam' cold ... he's called Jerry Dwyer. Dwyer's Flying Service. We'd have to drive to Mason City airport, 'bout three miles from here. We can go right on out after the show and he'll be waitin'. Says he can get us to Moorfield in around an hour, if the weather's okay."

"What type of a plane?" Buddy asked.

"Just a real small one ... single engine. Three of us can go along if we squeeze in real tight."

"Hey, that's rich!" Tommy exclaimed. "I can pick up my mom's registered letter in Fargo."

"Don't tell the other guys, though. They'll all want to be in on it."

"Any news on Charlie?" Buddy said.

"Carroll called the hospital and he's just fine. Now Ritchie says *he's* got frostbite, too, in his pecker, and he wants you to Western Union Julie London to come rub it for him."

They joshed around some more, then Waylon sauntered off to confirm arrangements with Dwyer's Flying Service. There being nothing else to do, Buddy and Tommy got their guitars and began picking, seated opposite each other on the yellow twin beds.

On guitar as in life, they had a good relationship. Up till meeting Tommy, Buddy had featured no lead on his records but his own strong downstroke "rhythm solos". It was why Niki Sullivan quit The Crickets, complaining he'd been hired as lead but all the guy let him do was stand there and strum E like a beginner.

Tommy had clicked right off, though, with a feel that was both bluesy and bluegrass. He'd played for Buddy since The Crickets folded, soloing on "Heartbeat", "It's So Easy", "Love's Made A Fool Of You"; all those good cuts that somehow never hit. Buddy dug him so much, he'd paid his fare up from Austin to be on this tour – him and Waylon Jennings on new-fangled bass guitar. GAC billed them as The New Crickets, but they knew better. They were just helping Buddy out, the way he'd help them if they needed it.

Across the room on the muted TV screen, a weatherman was saying something.

". . . Hey, that sounds good, man."

"What . . . this?"

"Do that in your second break in 'Maybe Baby', okay?"

Tommy knew that things with Buddy weren't going real good just now. There was still all that trouble with Norman Petty, down in Clovis, over who'd written which part of the early hits. The new single he set such store by still hadn't charted, so you'd notice. Though he gave good value every night and joshed with all the guys on the bus, you knew how much he wanted to be back in New York with that little Spanish doll.

"Let's do 'Learning The Game' on tape, okay?" Buddy said.

He leaned and switched on the big tape machine that went everywhere with him. Tommy hitched up his Martin and strummed the chords that were slow and solemn, almost like a hymn.

"Hearts that are broken and love that's untrue, these go with learning the game . . ."

His voice was quiet – somehow cold and lonely like the wastes of snow the bus was travelling through. Though the room was heated, a shiver suddenly ran up Tommy Allsup's back.

Ivor glanced at his watch under the table. It was past seven o'clock. The Portsmouth ferry had docked, bumping the pierhead so that it rocked perceptibly on its thousand legs. The few passengers could be heard scurrying past to queue on the windswept platform for their diesel tram down to shore.

Overhead strip-light shone harshly on The Porpoise Bar's mural of the Walrus and Carpenter. The table was still littered with restaurant china and remnants of sandwiches thinly darned with pinkish tinned pâté. Winter-time fare at the Pier Pavilion was mainly surplus summer kitchen stock: jam from seven-pound drums, pickled eggs and shellfish from outsize jars, baked beans and tomatoes from rusty tins bearing labels of the mid-1930s.

Ivor swallowed hard and said, "I'd like to be off now, please Dad."

His father glanced up from *Take Your Pick* on the television. His father's mistress stared into her purple knitting, pointedly distancing herself from all matters pertaining to his upbringing and character.

"Done your homework?"

"Yes, Dad."

A burst of applause came from *Take Your Pick*, mingled with dashes of Morse Code. TV reception at the pierhead was constantly interrupted by ships passing through The Solent to dock at Southampton.

"What did you have to do?"

"An essay about Wolfe at Quebec."

"And what nefarious plans have you got tonight?"

"I'm going up to practise with Andrew Harvey."

The hazel brown eyes looked keenly at him.

"You're sure that's where you're going, Ivor, are you?"

Sure as he was, he felt himself blush.

"Yes, Dad."

"So I could ring up Andrew Harvey now, could I, and confirm that?"

"Yes."

"All right, Ivor. I believe you."

"I really am, Dad . . ."

"I said 'I believe you', Ivor. Don't protest too much, old son, or I'll start to think you *are* hiding something."

The hazel eyes clouded with disappointment and disillusion and returned to *Take Your Pick*.

"Wherever you're going, just be sure and be back home at Grandma's by ten o'clock. Remember that rule we made."

"Okay, Dad."

Packing his school books into his duffle-bag, he wondered whether to ask for the five shillings a new house badge could cost. He decided not. Compared to the huge problems of the Pier Pavilion in winter, how could it possibly be important?

209

He slung his guitar-case over his shoulder and looked at his father, now totally engrossed in *Take Your Pick*'s "Yes-No Interlude".

*Gong!* came from the screen.

"Cheerio then, Dad."

As he opened the door, his father rapped:

"Haven't you forgotten something, Ivor?"

"Pardon?"

"You haven't said Goodnight to Miss Lott."

"Goodnight," Ivor said, not meeting her eye.

"Goodnight," she replied, not meeting his.

The wind was behind him this time, sweeping him away from the dark pierhead with all its complications, tensions and mysteries, down the lamp-lit planks to the terraced brightness and blessed simplicity of shore.

On the Esplanade he put his bike in the station-yard and boarded a waiting Southern Vectis bus. He sat on the long rear seat, his guitar-case between his knees. Other passengers looked curiously at it as they passed him. " 'Got your ukelele then," the conductor said, ringing the bell.

The bus roared him uphill, away from cafés, gift shops and arcades, into that enviable part of town unaffected by the strife of summer. Tranquil street light shone on yellowish Victorian villas, behind whose glowing curtains his classmates would now be, doing homework or watching television. Did they have any notion how lucky they were?

He got off the bus on Quarr Hill and walked down the unlit path to the Harveys' drive. The night smelled of earth and cold tea, from wet leaves underfoot. The sky was full of its usual quiet stars. Over the fields, beyond Quarr Abbey, the lights of Portsmouth, and the world beyond, winked and sparkled their promise across the uneventful sea.

Mrs Harvey opened the ironbound Gothic front door wearing a camel hair overcoat. In her distracted fashion, she waved Ivor down the stone corridor that was so very like a monastery's.

"Andrew's in the dining-room. And he's got what's his name's duberry."

"Amplifier?" Ivor asked hopefully.

"No. Another thing."

"Tape recorder?"

"That's it," Mrs Harvey agreed with relief.

"Is it Colin Pendleton's?"

"Yes . . . see they look after it, won't you Ivor? And don't let George record any burps on it. I don't want Mrs Pendleton to think he's been brought up a little street arab."

Andrew was waiting, guitar on his lap, his two sticks sloping beside him. He had been without both legs since early childhood but for all that was an expert yachtsman, winner of numerous trophies in the "Albacore" class. His tin legs had been specially designed not to rust and to give added buoyancy after capsizing.

He and Ivor practised two or three nights a week, not with any idea of forming a group or even performing; rather, as a commiseration between their acoustic guitars at the eternal mysteries of electric ones on records. Andrew owned a Dansette record-player and a pile of almost thirty singles. They would listen, then try to reconstruct what they'd heard. Now and again, the big, curly-haired, stiff-legged yachtsman would essay a vocal in his tiny, diffident voice.

"I got a new one today," Andrew said as Ivor slid his guitar from the case.

He put a 45 onto the red and beige Dansette. A stupendous growling chaos filled the stone-flagged room with its open fireplace and mantel of silver sailing trophies.

"What's it called?" Ivor asked.

"'Rumble'. By Link Wray."

"Who?"

"Link Wray . . . and The Wray Men."

"It's basically E, isn't it?"

"E to D. But there's that bit in the middle."

They listened to it four times more, plectrums poised, fingers wandering noiselessly and hopelessly up and down the strings where it came to the bit in the middle.

"Fabulous, isn't it?" Andrew mouthed.

"Fabulous."

He was putting it on for the fifth time when the door opened and his younger brother George strolled in, accompanied by their dog Snolly.

"Come on, Nip – come and do your chair trick," Andrew called out. When amenable, George furnished percussion to the still unformed, untitled group by beating with the flat of both hands on a wooden chair-seat.

"No, I don't think I will at this stage," George drawled airily. Snolly, meanwhile, lunged over Andrew's outstretched legs and gazed up in adoration at Ivor, wagging her apology for a tail.

'Snolly! You've had a bath!"

"Oh come on, Nip. We've only got Pendleton's tape recorder till the day after tomorrow."

"If I do, will you crew for me across to Stokes Bay this weekend?"

"All right – but you've got to do backing vocals."

"Oh no! You've got to crew for me again if I do that . . ."

As they argued, Ivor saw that Snolly had sat down on a 45 with the logo that meant only one artist: Vogue Coral. He rescued his friend from under the big woolly bottom, glanced at the label, and his heart leapt.

"Hey, Harvey, I've never heard this one."

"What one?"

"This one by Buddy. 'Mailman Bring Me No More Blues'."

Andrew pulled a face.

"It's not terribly good actually."

"Don't be crazy, Cassell."

"Honestly, it's not . . . Listen."

Mortifyingly, Andrew was right. For the first time in a year of constantly unfolding admiration and gratitude, Ivor found himself listening to a Buddy Holly record he didn't like. It was a tune of almost dirge-like slowness, lacking everything that made Buddy Holly wonderful as a rule. There was no throbbing drum, no jangly guitar, no background chorus going "Ooo" or "Doot-do-do". There was just his voice, somewhat strained and exposed, delivering its plea to the mailman to bring him no more blues. Because one blue letter was all he could use.

"What piss," George commented from the floor, where he lay with Snolly in a parodied embrace.

Andrew turned the 45 over in his big yachtsman's hands.

"Do you want the other side, Ivor?"

"What's it called?"

"'Words of Love'."

"Might as well."

It was a slow ballad with the same revolutionary idea as "Listen To Me" – using electric guitar not merely as a showpiece for intro and middle solo but as an element throughout the song, creating its mood, emphasising its sentiments. On "Listen To Me", though, the voice had been spectrally remote. Here it was close, confiding, twinned with a lighter ebony echo of itself. As voice and echo sang, they also gently hummed affirmation of what they said. The guitar was a third voice in descant, breaking through the soft-picked rhythm with downstrokes that somehow turned back on themselves, into icy, tangling single strings:

Words of love you
Whisper soft and true
Darling I love you.
Mm mm mm.

Ivor listened, hardly able to believe his ears. It was the best Buddy Holly song of all; better than "Maybe Baby", better even than "Well Alright". Why was it not in the forefront of Buddy Holly songs, instead of this B-side obscurity? He wouldn't have known of it but for this accidental moment in a stone-floored room, hung with yellow oilskins; looking into the face of a big, silly dog.

"Unusual, isn't it?" Andrew said as the arm of the Dansette clicked down to rest.

Ivor sat for a moment with eyes closed, struggling to understand the thing that had been whispered in his ear, along with comfort, reassurance and a tenderness he hoped he, too, might show someone someday.

He hummed and quietly stroked his guitar, then opened his eyes wide.

"It's E to A . . . we can do it. Put it on again! Quick! *Quick!*"

"All right, hold your horses," Andrew said good-naturedly. "George – will you stop making love to Snolly in that disgusting fashion!"

In Clear Lake, Iowa, the Winter Dance Party was over. All round the Surf Ballroom, shoals of red tail-light materialised over fuming, rose-coloured exhaust. The white dark roared with ignition, mixed with sudden squalls from radio-dials, and the voices of midnight weather forecasters, murmuring the need to get home quickly and stay there.

As Tommy Allsup went back inside for his guitar and sleeping-bag, he saw Ritchie trapped in a crowd of girls with Dion and the sax-player from The Belmonts.

"You gonna let me fly, guy?" Ritchie called to him.

"Nope," Tommy grinned.

Ritchie broke away from the group and came after him, over the big spartan ballroom that was more like a high school gym.

"C'mon, man. What you want for that seat? Ten dollars. Here . . . take it."

"I don't want it."

"Fifteen? Here . . ."

"You don't hear good. I said I don't want your money."

"What you want? Clothes? Any shirt of mine you want, take."

"You want to fly so bad, go hire a plane yourself."

"We tried . . . The Bopper and me. You guys got the only one."

" 'Reckon we was real sneaky there."

"Aw c'mon Tomaso, do this little thing. Didn't I play drums for you guys tonight?"

"Sure. We're 'bliged."

"And I got you that girl in Indianapolis."

"Which one?"

"Scooter Joe."

"Ritchie, I'll tell you . . . that just about guarantees I won't."

"Tell you what. We'll flip a coin."

His pleas were hardly serious any more. But as he dug a yellow silk sleeve into his vaquero pants and brought out a half-dollar piece, Tommy – for reasons inexplicable ever afterwards – suddenly decided to yield.

"Okay?" Ritchie said. "Heads you go, tails I do."

"Aw, shoot . . . if you want to, go. I don't care."

"Hey! You mean it?"

"Sure."

"Hey, Tomaso! Te quiero."

"It's thirty-five dollars apiece. You pay the pilot upfront . . . cash. And don't forget you got to take all the other guys' laundry."

As Tommy packed up his stuff in the dressing-room, Waylon appeared, eating a Krystalburger.

"I'm off that plane, man."

"Me, too," Waylon said.

"Who's been workin' on you?"

"The Bopper."

"Ritchie wouldn't let me be all night. So I fin'lly said, if you want to go so bad, go. How'd The Bopper work it with you?"

"Said he's got the flu real bad . . . wants to get to Fargo early so's he can get him a shot before the show."

"These guys sure do know how to flimflam a person."

"I got The Bopper's sleepin' bag, though."

"Where's Buddy at?"

"Last I see, he was callin' Maria-Elena . . . not gettin' through, though. Some lines must be down on account of the snow."

"How 'bout his Fender. He want that with him on the plane?"

"He said no, keep it with our stuff."

Tommy picked up the red Fender Stratocaster, and shook his head.

"Shoot!"

"What?"

"Jus' thinkin' where those guys'll be tonight while we're settin' and freezin' on that bus."

It was past 1 am when the three lucky ones came down the front steps of the Surf Ballroom and loaded their bags into the station wagon taxi, called from Mason City. The Bopper and Ritchie got right in, but Buddy lingered to sign autographs for two girls who had materialised from the bushes, squealing in clouds of frozen breath.

"Who do I make this one to?"

"Trish."

"Where you from, Trish?"

"Appleton, North Dakota."

"'Hope you can read the writin' there . . . Sure is a cold one . . ."

A few more minutes passed. The Bopper wound down his window and, in a woeful voice, said "Buddy, what's happenin'? We ain't got this kinda time."

"What's he doin'? Ritchie asked as The Bopper wound the window up again.

"Writin' notes to each of their folks so they won't get roasted for stayin' out late."

As Buddy finally made to get in, Tommy Allsup ran down the front steps, holding a slip of paper.

"Hey Buddy . . . I forgot. There's a registered letter from my mom waitin' for me in Fargo. Could you all pick it up when you get in?"

"Sure will."

"Ah, thanks man. Otherwise I believe I never will get to it. Here's the stub she sent. It's Fargo Post Office . . . Union and Third."

"I'll need some identification, though. Gimme your driver's licence."

". . . Buddy! Let's *go*!"

"Here, take my wallet," Tommy said.

"Okay. See you t'morrow."

"See you t'morrow. Have a good sleep for me, too."

The station wagon drew away with slithers of the chains round its wheels. Tommy went back inside with the others to wait for the bus. In the sky over the Surf Ballroom, no star shone, anywhere.


In New York, as snow buried the avenues and stilled the noises and alarms of night, Maria-Elena had a dream she would eventually remember.

She was alone on a wide stretch of desert or prairie, staring up into a hard blue sky. Suddenly voices behind her shouted "Watch out! Here it comes!" She turned and saw a ball of fire

216

spinning through the air – spinning and also sparkling, like some wild chandelier, flinging off shiny drops that might be crystal or flame. It passed over her and vanished noiselessly into the sun-baked ground.

At the same moment she heard his voice, close to her and very gentle, like when he'd told her, the very first day they met, that he was going to marry her.

"Don't worry," she heard him say. "Just stay here. I'll be back to get you."

"When?" she heard her own voice say.

"Soon. Just wait for me. Te quiero, Maria-Elena . . ."

She would not remember this until a long time afterwards.

She stirred restlessly on her side of the divan, her arm flung out across his empty place.

Outside the studio window, ragged snowflakes fell and fell, blotting out the building with red and blue light over on Union Square.

"Te quiero," she murmured in her sleep. "Te quiero, Buddy. I miss you."

Five thousand miles away, someone else who loved him was just waking up.

Ivor opened his eyes and looked round his room with automatic heart-sunken despair. He looked at the knobless chest-of-drawers, the dirty rattan chair, the table balanced on antelope-horns, the tangle of clothes, that mostly weren't his, on wire hangers behind the door. His cousin Spot also slept here when home from sea, sometimes bringing three or four fellow-stewards to doss on the green linoleum.

He shut his eyes again and gave a fatalistic sigh, remembering the end of last night. Absorbed in his practice with Andrew, he'd missed the late bus from Quarr and had to walk the full three miles home. His father's van had – of course – been waiting to monitor his return, its carnival loudspeakers looming retribution through the dark.

While his grandmother sat in bed upstairs, drinking gin and reading Jean Plaidy, there had been another of the castigations that regulated Ivor's days like traffic-lights.

"... you just can't be trusted, old son ... I let you go on the clear understanding you'd be back here by ten. You promised *faithfully*. And don't give me any cock and bull story about practising with Andrew Harvey. You've been with a girl, haven't you? Why not just admit it? Well, you're not going out again, Ivor. And I'm confiscating that guitar until you show me you can be a bit decent and honourable ..."

Taking down his blazer from among Spot's dirty shirts, he remembered Gully the prefect's warning about the house-badge. That meant three with the slipper in the prefects' room at break.

His Raleigh "All Steel" waited in the narrow front passage, leaning on the boxes of rock, sweet kippers and false teeth. He took his shabby school cap from the saddle-bag and put it on, tucking its torn lining under the rim at the back. Then – for no discernible reason – he paused and listened. His lips murmured something, and the fingers of his left hand curled into a triangular shape. A smile was on his face as he opened the blistered front door.

He pushed his bike slowly up Union Street – deserted at this hour but for the odd descending car. From windows above shut shops, toast and bacon smells mingled with the sound of a voice reading the BBC Home Service weather forecast:

"... Plymouth, Portland, Wight, Dover, Thames ... Tyne, Forth, Dogger ..."

This was the moment the plane took off from Mason City.